Cooking for YOU & ME

For Carlene....
 May this find a special
place on your cooking shelf, as
it has mine.
 A very happy + joyous Noel
 '92
 Warmest of love.

 Bill

Cooking for

YOU & ME

Jenny Ferguson

METHUEN HAYNES

First published in 1987 by
Methuen Haynes
(an imprint of Methuen Australia Pty Ltd)
44-50 Waterloo Road, North Ryde 2113
150 Burwood Highway, Hawthorn 3122
Cnr Allenby and Leichhardt Streets, Spring Hill 4000
1/19 York Street, Subiaco 6008

Copyright © Jenny Ferguson 1987
Photographs by Rodney Weidland

This book is copyright. Apart from any fair dealing
for the purposes of private study, research,
criticism or review, as permitted under the Copyright Act,
no part may be reproduced by any process without
written permission. Inquiries should be addressed to
the publishers.

National Library of Australia
Cataloguing-in-Publication data

    Ferguson, Jenny, 1947-
      Cooking for you and me.

      Bibliography.
      Includes index.
      ISBN 0 454 01155 5

        1. Cookery. 2. Cookery, French. I. Title.

    641.5

Typeset by Midland Typesetters, Maryborough 3465
Printed in Hong Kong by Dai Nippon Printing Co. Ltd.

Endpapers: detail of the painting
'You and Me' by Ross Davis,
106 x 121cm, oil on canvas.
Purchased by Jenny Ferguson in 1979.

CONTENTS

Introduction	1
Acknowledgements	2
The recipes	4
Of a time past	5
The beginning	9
The story of *You and Me*	11
When it comes to cooking	14
Being organised	17
My kitchen	18
Explanatory notes	19
Stocks and sauces	21
Hors-d'oeuvres	29
Soups	39
Salads	53
First courses	70
Fish and shellfish	94
Meat and offal	112
Poultry and game	134
Desserts	162
Petits-fours	198
Pastries, pasta and sweet sauces	209
Select bibliography	218
Index	219

For my mother and father

INTRODUCTION

I am self-taught. I learned all that I know from books, from watching other cooks at work, and from 'nutting things out' on the job.

One of the problems that I encountered when beginning the task of writing this book, was to pin things down to a rigid formula and call it a recipe. Time and again, no sooner did I begin to feel that one dish was *just right* than I discovered that it was not just right at all. There was always a better way of doing it just around the corner. This was, of course, why over the years I had been so negligent about recording much of what I was doing on a day-to-day basis—things were always changing in some small way. To record it is to say there, that's the end of it!

But of course I was wrong. This was not the end of it at all. It is a beginning. My recipes crystallise what was once done at a particular time, and no two people, not even myself, will ever do it precisely that way again. They are only the starting blocks and we are all off and running in slightly different directions according to our own quirks and fancies, which given time become our own style.

When I pour over the many volumes contained in my library, I find that there are some which speak in a language more akin to my own, and it is to these that I continue to gravitate time and again in the never-ending adventure of learning to cook. I hope that there will be those among my readers to whom this book will speak just as clearly, perhaps to some of those self-taught cooks like myself, who, given a little inspiration and encouragement, will cease to put limitations on themselves. May this result in many, many hours of enjoyment for them, their friends and families at the happiest place of all—the dining table.

Jenny Ferguson

ACKNOWLEDGEMENTS

When it was suggested that I might like to gather my recipes together and put them into book form, my first reaction was not another cookbook, for it seemed to me that there was very little that I could say that had not been said umpteen times already. There are volumes enough to tell you how to make pastry or poach an egg without adding yet another.

Of course, this is true, and this book is certainly not a text or teaching book. It is a collection of very personal recipes which reflect my prejudices, likes and dislikes, in the kitchen. It is the record of the work I did over a specific period of time, and it deals only with the dishes which interested me most, and with which I took the greatest pains to perfect. From a personal point of view I needed the discipline that an exercise such as this would impose. It would force me to put my recipes into some sort of order and to record those still carried around in my head before it was too late.

However, I soon found that there is more to the writing of a cookbook than the mere recording of recipes, just as I had learned that there is more to being a chef than simply putting food on plates. How many times had I said to those working in my kitchen—'If you want to do something badly enough, you can!'—and now when I needed the truth of those words so much, when a much-loved daily routine had come to an end, and the benches were scrubbed bare, and the plates washed and stacked for the last time and I *had to begin again*, my own courage was failing. This book would never have been started, much less concluded, without a great deal of advice and encouragement on all sides.

Things gathered momentum when *You and Me* closed. It was only then that I discovered fully how many people had truly enjoyed the food and loved the place. People I had not met before made themselves known and wanted to know what I was doing and when I would write my recipes for them, for they wanted to try for themselves some of the dishes they had remembered and enjoyed.

Then I was given some tangible advice. A more encouraging or warmhearted pair you couldn't hope to meet than Penny Smith and Diane Houligue. Both excellent cooks in their own right, been at it far longer than I, enthusiastic and dedicated teachers, and lovely friends. It all began with the *Between You and Me* column in *The Epicurean*. Penny and Di, and an equally encouraging editor, Tony Hitchin, pointed me in the right direction and my tentative first efforts got off the ground. Learning to write was even more difficult than learning to cook. In the beginning I would sit for long hours chewing pencils, tearing up paper, frustrated beyond belief at the difficulty of putting words together. 'Let me cook it,' I would say to myself. 'To write it is just too hard!' And then I met Susan Haynes my publisher.

Her patience and absolute faith in what I was doing buoyed up my teetering confidence. Thank you, Susan, for never getting tired of my excuses, my slowness or my moods. Thank you also, Rodney Weidland, for the most beautiful photographs.

Then there is brother Mark, who rang me constantly to see how I was getting on, whether in the kitchen or at the typewriter, to offer advice on matters of all kinds. He read all the recipes to be sure they made sense, and tested as many as needed a second opinion. This book is in many ways as much his as mine.

At home were my most loyal supporters. They always have been. All through the life of the restaurant, and now as well, my daughter Rachel, and husband Rob, have helped me in so many ways it is impossible to relate them all. Apart from getting up with me every morning, year after year, at an ungodly hour to go to the markets before attending to their own affairs, they have always been my best and fairest critics. Their part in this book has been to taste everything and to pass judgement. I know that they both felt great relief when things started coming to an end and we could get back to a normal diet. 'Three desserts in one night is a bit much, mum!' I recall someone saying, 'I'm getting awfully sick of these quails and pigeons and things. When can we have an ordinary old lamp chop.'

Finally, I say thank you to the countless numbers of diners who came time and again over the years and made *You and Me* the tremendous success that it was. It was a pleasure to cook for you. Your presence and gratitude made it all worthwhile.

THE RECIPES

This book contains as many of the best and favourite recipes used over the life of the restaurant *You and Me* as it is possible for me to remember or recreate. At times this work became one of piecing together the bits of a jigsaw puzzle, poring over bundles of old menus, piecing together little scraps of paper that had been filed away with scribbled notes as to why this worked and that didn't, telephoning ex-staff for the odd lost recipe, and resurrecting and deciphering the book from the very safe place to which it had been committed.

For the past ten years I have kept a little blue diary, now in a state of semi-decay, complete with loose sticky pages, blotches of blood and dollops of egg and dough, recording the passing of time through its many pages of recipes. It was a much-used book. Those who borrowed it were threatened with a fate worse than death should they lose it. The dog once chewed a hunk off the corner, and one day a wayward apprentice mislaid it in the coolroom under some bundles of beetroot. It was rediscovered at the end-of-week sort-out-come-clean-up and thankfully survives, a haphazard, personally priceless collection of recipes that work for me.

There's not much that's original under the sun or under the kitchen roof, and so it is true of my little blue diary and the recipes it contains. These are often adaptions of someone else's who got it from someone else, and so on and so forth. Some have been used in my family for three generations or more. Some I can put not only a name to—like Simon's scallop mousse—but almost the exact time and date, as I remember that day he arrived at work with the recipe. Here was the result of his persistence in getting something *just right*. It had taken him two years. Others somehow emerged as I wandered around the kitchen picking things up, talking to the other cooks, about all that we had to use that day—bunches of fresh sage, ripe purple figs, tiny homegrown (by my father) sugar cabbages still covered in dew, a pair of young hare, a bin of live prawns. Such a treat. If we liked what we did, it was recorded in the blue book. They were recipes we could trust. They had passed the repetition, mass production and first day apprentice test!

Some have changed so many times that it makes for very interesting reading to go back through the numerous crisscrossings to the original version. For example, the bavarois—did I really use that much gelatine or, heaven forbid *cornflour*, not to mention *egg whites*? And so it goes on. It must have taken all of those years for me to be perfectly happy with the gelatine content of that elusive dessert. The number of disasters doesn't bear thinking about, either too firm or too soft, nor those that ended up down the sink! Most of the recipes have a similar history.

OF A TIME PAST

FROM MY MOTHER'S MEMOIRS

Sometimes when we are able, my mother Joan, her mother Ethel, and I, get together, and cook up a wonderful meal. We talk without drawing breath for a whole afternoon and well into the night, eating and drinking with remarkable appetites, indulging in culinary chitchat, swapping advice on this and that, each one from the perspective of her own generation and experience.

There is much that I have learned from this pair. They are home cooks, who lived in the country in desperate times, but who always used and made the most of all the fresh ingredients that they could get their hands on: big 'horse' mushrooms found 'up the paddock', wild blackberries at the foot of Mt Canobolas, yabbies from the dam, and even bush-fresh morels. The fundamental rule that Ethel instilled in Joan, and she in turn in me, was that good food was the cornerstone of all health and happiness. It was their philosophy and number one priority.

We ate like kings, fed numerous neighbourhood kids as well, and grew up in kitchens which took first place over any other room in the house.

While I look back with great affection to the puddings and pies, roasted joints, bottled cherries and peaches, homemade icecreams and toffees that my mum churned out of her bare kitchen, with its ancient black fuel stove, and the old wooden table with the green linoleum nailed on top, around which our family feasts were held, she too looks back with just as much affection to her days as a young girl, when mother Ethel fed with style, and a determination worthy of ten chefs, not only a growing family of five children, a husband and the property owner but also from time to time numerous station hands and shearers, under conditions far more primitive yet again. They sometimes laugh at me with all my gadgets and machines and tell me the stories I love to hear over and over again.

The last time we girls got together, Joan gave me a little book to read. It was something of a diary. In her own precise handwriting were the recollections of a young girl growing up on a country property near Molong in central New South Wales in the 1930s. On reading this I understood how my own love of cooking was not something which just suddenly happened one day while holidaying in France, but was here firmly rooted in the past with these two wonderful cooks, Australian country women.

These excerpts taken from my mother's memoirs tell not only of the struggles of a time long past, but reveal something of the love of good food, which all three of us share.

'The barn, which was our home, was a unique construction, stark and ugly, squatting defiantly on the hill, as though daring anyone to find a single aspect of comfort or convenience within its walls. It was roughly built, rather like a lopsided box, of galvanised corrugated iron, with its few rooms divided by the bare iron sheets which stopped short at about 8 feet, leaving an uninterrupted view of the rafters. A huge post stood fast in the middle of the kitchen ensuring its durability. No freak windstorm would ever shift this monstrosity.

'There were two rooms for the owner, and two for us, one of ours being the kitchen which served as well as living room, dining room as well as kitchen for everyone.

'The laundry was simply a set of cement tubs, and a scrubbing board at the back wall, with a copper in the back yard. The bathroom was nonexistent.

'The kitchen boasted a fuel stove, an enormous whitewashed fireplace, a table, chairs, a big dresser, a shotgun behind the door for snakes, one of the first refrigerators (an "icy ball") and a pressure light attached to the centre post. The light was an unexpected touch of class, an improvement on the kerosine lamp used in the bedroom, but nothing to get excited about once you were down to the nitty gritty of getting the wretched thing to work. Luckily we were to have a mechanically-minded dad, who understood the temperamental antics of pressure lights. This one had to be fuelled and pumped up, out in the garage. You needed a steady supply of mantles, tapers, matches and patience, to keep it going.

'The refrigerator was an entertainment also. The "icy ball" apparatus had to be lifted out of the chest every few days, and "cooked" up on a primus, to keep it working. It was heavy and bulky, and left about a square foot of refrigerated space for food, a bit undersized when you had a whole bullock or lamb to handle. So the traditional hessian safe, complete with drip tray and wet cloths, and a hanging meat safe, were standard equipment on the verandah where they waited in hopes that a summer breeze might lose its way and drift along.

'The kitchen and bedroom had flooring boards, but not the rest of the establishment. Simplicity was definitely the keynote. Mum must surely have felt like scrambling back into the sulky and bolting off down the track the first day she stepped across its threshhold. I wonder how today's modern young mum would react to shotguns at the ready and a garbage pit within throwing distance of the front door. As children we accepted it as normal and survived; without shooting ourselves (or each other) or succumbing to the plague. But the garbage pit, placed so strategically near the kitchen (a haven indeed for swarming bushflies), was filled in, as one of the first improvements to the place. And very slowly, our living quarters were upgraded.

'The ceiling, fashioned from sisalcraft (a material resembling tough cardboard) was a relief to us all. It not only stopped wintry draughts, but also cut off our view of the rats roaming the rafters at night. We could still hear them, along with the possums, thumping about on the outside. Traps were virtually useless, and when the rats were tired of tormenting us the mice moved in. We were never short of "creepy crawlies". There were redback spiders, black and gold hornets, flies by the thousand, mosquitoes, meat ants, and brown snakes.

'These were the days of the Great Depression. Mum washed and ironed and mended for the owner; she scrubbed his old moleskin pants and patched them until the original material had all but disappeared. She cooked and scrubbed and sewed, and preserved fruits and vegetables and eggs; she made butter and dressed fowls and served meals with military precision, as was expected by the owner who ate with us.

'Those meals were wonderful. Under primitive conditions mum produced food which would be a credit to any gourmet cook. She had a good supply of fresh ingredients, meat, vegetables, fruit, butter, eggs and milk were usually plentiful, but with groceries she was strictly limited to the bare essentials. Dinner was always served at midday. A joint would be carved at the table, and vegetable dishes and a gravy boat passed around. Wild duck, rabbit, and young hares were a pleasant change. Dessert was usually an old-fashioned pudding. We all loved the baked custards, junket, lemon sago, plum duff, golden syrup dumplings (and depending on the weather and the season) fresh fruit salads, melons, blackberry pies with cream and apple charlotte — the list seems endless. We were never short of food.

'She baked vast quantities of pastries, cakes and biscuits. A firm favourite with everyone were her "hard timers", a concoction born of the depression. They were rock cakes based simply on dripping, flour, sugar and currants, and she carried the recipe in her head and hands. They never turned out right for anyone else. She would often mix them before breakfast (at least 4 cups of flour to the batch) to be served at morning and afternoon tea.

'She was an inventive cook too. A meal put together with "left-overs" was always enjoyable. When the owner headed off to Sydney for a few days, he usually brought back a parcel of New Zealand smoked haddock. It was a real treat. (Fifty years ago they really knew how to smoke fish.) He encouraged mum with her cooking. He provided ample equipment for preserving the produce, and at times the kitchen resembled a canning factory. Tomato sauce, chutneys, salted beans, pickled onions, Worcestershire sauce, relish, plum sauce, marmalade, all types of jams, jellies, bottled beetroot, mushrooms, crayfish, were all cooked on that old fuel stove in our kitchen. We rarely tasted food from a tin, or baker's pastry, or sausages, or anything else that had to be bought from shops.

'The vegetable garden was on the bank of a creek, quite a good walk from the house. Bore water was pumped for irrigation, but a lot of the watering was done by hand. The orchard, an acre block, was closer to home. Here were apricots, figs, peaches, grapes, persimmons, mandarins, almonds, and a hedge of blue and white lilac. In spring we would carry it home by the armful, together with the Cootamundra wattles from a neighbour's creek flat. But even with all this floral beauty, the old barn still looked like an old barn.

'People frequently told us we were lucky to have such plentiful fresh food. They were right, of course, but they were inclined to forget that "luck" plays no part in all the ploughing, planting, pruning, spraying, watering, harvesting and preserving routines. It is all sheer hard slog seven days a week.

'Those who considered us lucky would not have dreamed of swapping their nine to five jobs, their electricity supply, or their comfortable homes for our rural life. I wondered if these people thought that the fruit popped itself into preserving jars and that cows delivered butter ready for spreading? Or did they know that hens have to be fed, and watered and pampered, and that those wretched eggs had to have the living daylights belted out of them with an old hand egg-beater before they turned into a sponge cake? And that chips and kindling, and an armful of good box wood, had to be chopped before the oven was ready to cook it?

'Certainly they would never have believed the effort that went into getting the berries for the blackberry pie that we enjoyed so much. We tackled the blackberrying in boots and overalls, using ladders, wire hooks, billycans and buckets, and spent the whole day at the foot of Mt Canobolas, where the bushes grew by the roadside with wonderful abandon. The shire workers left them in peace in those days, and people gathered the berries for pies and jams and jellies. We returned home covered in scratches, purple stains all over our faces, hands and clothes, sunburnt and exhausted. And then the work really began. The berries needed washing and preparing; the stove had to be stoked up ready for action, and mum would begin the preserving process and weighing up for jam. (The rest of us would be thinking more in terms of a good sleep.)

'Walking the paddocks picking mushrooms was a favourite pastime with us all. We knew all the best places to scout for them, hiding under the tall grasses, or showing themselves clearly on the green slopes. Sometimes we found the small buttons, and larger flatter types, and sometimes it was the big "horse" mushrooms, despised by most people. These were rich in flavour, ideal for soup, and I remember grilling them whole, on top of the stove for snacks. We ate morels too, but these grew on the outskirts of town, not at the farm. Morels are more like toadstools in shape, with a fleshy, honeycombed cap, rather similar to tripe. Poisonous white mushrooms, puff balls, and toadstools grew side by side with the edible mushrooms, so we quickly had to learn the difference as a matter of survival.

'In those days we even made our own honeycomb and toffees and marshmallow sweets, and grew our own corn for popping. Soap, too, was boiled up by the bucketful, and poured to set in our round bath tub.

'Whenever I recall the meals of my childhood, I remember Mrs Beaton's famous words: "First catch your hare!" This is precisely what we did!'

Joan Jarvis

THE BEGINNING

Life for me has not always been one of pots and pans. I did not begin cooking professionally until I was 31. Those pre-kitchen days were of another realm altogether, for cooking had not always been my first love. That was music.

Cooking, or home science as I knew it then, was, along with art and other things you did with your hands, a subject taken by girls who couldn't cope with Latin and music. It was a subject for homemakers, not highbrows, and certainly had nothing to do with being a chef, for chefs were men anyway. And it was certainly not for girls in the A class. So I took the Latin and music instead.

We didn't have a piano at home, but an old pedal organ on which I used to practice. We had an even older violin, which I never really got the hang of, apart from a mournful and imperfect rendition of *All Through the Night*, the sound of which would start the dog howling. I loved music, and to my great joy, on leaving school, I won a scholarship to Sydney's Conservatorium of Music.

I sang, I composed, spent long languid afternoons in the Botanical Gardens dreaming of the future. At length I was able to buy an old German piano. It cost ninety pounds and took me two years to pay off. At last I was able to practise my scales and arpeggios without running out of keyboard (the old organ was missing a couple of octaves). The four years passed and I emerged with cap and gown and a Diploma of Music Education under one arm, and at the age of twenty, newly married, naive and full of hope, I took over the embryonic music department of a brand new high school in Sydney's southern suburbs. I am always reminded of a movie called *Up the Down Staircase* when I think of that place. Being absent-minded rather than wilfully disobedient, my shame was intense the day I was caught actually walking *up* the *down* staircase and chided severely by the deputy headmaster in front of my students. I felt trapped between uninterested, rebellious adolescents (who were not much younger than myself) and a stifling, unreasonable authority that prevailed there at the time. There were some sunny moments to break the bleak routine of the next three years: the before-school violin group, the lunchtime choir and orchestra, the brass band and the madrigal group. It just seemed that what happened in between, in the regular teaching hours, was for the most part a sad waste of time. Crotchets and quavers, and 14 and 15 year olds, and Mozart and Brahms and me, did not seem to go together. To cheer myself I would buy a couple of plump ducks and invite some friends over for dinner. It was at this time that my husband was offered a posting to Hong Kong and I jumped at the chance to escape.

In Hong Kong our daughter was born, and during my enforced homestay I took to the stove in earnest. I read a lot, too, a curious mixture and mostly women writers (don't forget that these were the liberating seventies): Simone de Beauvoir and Simone Beck, Germaine Greer and Elizabeth David, Betty

Freidan and Julia Child. I guess if I wasn't being angry I was cooking.

Hong Kong taught me more about table etiquette than about food, but it was here that my first serious attempts at grand cooking were tried — crown roasts complete with paper frills, Beef Wellington, made with indifferent, bought *puff*. It was all very proper and very English.

The most extraordinary dessert I have ever seen was presented at a dinner party in Hong Kong. The chef was a Chinese household employee. From pink meringue he had wrought a lifelike representation of a donkey pulling a cart filled with fruit salad. It was held trembling on a silver platter for me (as the sole female guest) to cut the first portion. How to avoid tipping the whole monstrosity over posed such a problem that I have loathed meringue ever since.

In Hong Kong I came to love open markets and to be able to buy perfectly fresh fruit and vegetables daily. There was such colour and variety when one turned from the English ways to the Chinese. I learnt a great deal about respect for ingredients and the art of *undercooking* using a hot wok and brisk stirring from a dear Chinese lady who let me watch her as she prepared her own meals.

We returned to Sydney with a small baby and I channelled my energies into doing an Arts degree at night. A few years later, I went back to teaching music, but the results this time were even more disastrous than the first time.

The posting was to a boy's high school in Sydney's inner west. The chances of imparting an appreciation of my beloved music to boys, who, for the most part could not speak English, was negligible. I felt that the situation was hopeless, and having almost completed that 'long distance' degree in English language (it took nine years) I made a sharp right hand turn and spent the following four years teaching English as a second language to infant children. It was wonderful, but then something else happened.

It was at this time that we first went to France. It was like being hit over the head. I can still recall, blow by blow, each dish of each restaurant of that first trip. At the restaurant of Paul Bocuse I had my first truly grand meal. How nervous we felt when we found we were the first to arrive. How large the tables seemed, what a lot of waiters there were all seemingly looking at us, and when that famous truffle soup arrived, how cautiously we hammered at the pastry dome, not quite knowing where to begin and knowing that *they knew* we didn't know! I remember that the soup was so hot that we both scalded our tongues which somewhat spoilt the rest of the meal. Everything, no matter how simple, was to my eyes a revelation. A plate of cold braised leeks with vinaigrette and parsley followed by a dish of poached pears in heavy syrup was as much a miracle as the glorious foie gras and fresh salmon.

We came home and I went on teaching. One day I recall doing playground duty, pounding the asphalt in a dispirited fashion, sidestepping soccer balls and skipping ropes, wiping bloodied knees, mopping tear stains and runny noses, and dreaming all the while of quenelles and consomme, beurre blancs and demi-glace. Three months later I dusted the chalk dust off my sleeves once and for all, and another six months later, with the trembling foolhardy courage of one who learns to swim by jumping in the deep end, I opened a little restaurant. And so a new chapter began.

THE STORY OF
YOU AND ME

This is the story with a beginning and an end, for the restaurant was sold last year. I remember saying to a friend late in 1977 that what I would most like to do, if ever I got the chance, would be to open a little lunchtime restaurant, somewhere in the heart of the city. The idea was a simple one, in fact *too* simple.

The food was to be fresh and 'homemade', with me and just one other doing the cooking. I had visions of fresh fruit tarts laid out on tables, masses of fresh flowers, ripe cheeses and baskets of crusty loaves. I imagined stiffly starched white linen cloths and napkins, sparkling silver and glasses. I didn't think much about waiters, though in the back of my mind I knew I would need them, and things like shopping and washing up were the last things to worry about, along with the other minor problems of how to tackle the laundering of the linen and similarly mounting piles of paperwork.

It was fortunate that I did not know what was in store or this most fruitful and rewarding episode of my life would not have survived those perilous early days. What I did know was that I wanted to cook more than anything else, and so it was that the search for a suitable dining room began.

It was six months later, after much knocking on doors, of old pubs and office buildings alike, that a place in the Tatler hotel in George Street was discovered and settled upon. It was a small, dark, inner room, and *very old*, but it was there, and after three weeks of painting and cleaning, some simple decorating and a little replumbing, it became a restaurant.

To my mind it was a beautiful restaurant. Among the many posters and paintings that hung about the walls in an attempt to bring colour to what was once ugly and drab, was one called *You and Me* by the Australian artist Ross Davis. At the very last minute, almost in desperation as I recall, the restaurant was named *You and Me*.

The opening day was memorable if only because it was so painful. I don't think any of us slept the night before, and at 6 o'clock on the day my brother Mark and I went over the menu for the last time. Today Mark is a talented and thoroughly capable chef in his own right, but on the morning of 13 September 1978 he was a raw novice who hardly knew one end of a carrot from the other. He was my assistant in charge of vegetables, cold entrées and desserts. I had two waiters as well, a friend to arrange the flowers, and my mother supplying coffee, words of encouragement, making salads, washing up, and chasing the dockets on which the orders were written. These kept blowing about the kitchen floor whenever the oven door was opened. Some were temporarily lost until the poor hungry customer to whom it belonged made plaintive appeals to the waiter to find out what was happening.

The lack of an exhaust fan further aggravated the situation, for the billowing smoke and fumes meant that one could see only about a metre in front at a time. And the light fuses blew regularly, leaving us more in the dark than ever. Michel, one of the waiters who was gradually taking an assertive role amidst the chaos, was seen at one time waving his arms about, running with an order, and crying out, 'Where are you, Madame la chef (a nickname that stuck)? I can't see a thing.'

By 6 o'clock that evening, all was clean and tidy. The piles of dirty dishes and cutlery were washed, polished and put away, the linen was bundled into garbage bags ready to wash and iron, and the refrigerator was bare. My mother turned to me with a very weary look and said, 'Jen, you've got to do all this again tomorrow.' She shook her head and went home.

The next day Michel arrived early with hammer and nails to built a proper docket system. We fixed the old window and set up a fan so that we could both see and breathe, and Mark reorganised his bench and cupboards. Much had been learned in 24 hours.

The next six weeks went by pretty smoothly and quietly. Mark and I managed to do everything in the kitchen, all the cooking and washing up as well, and I was managing to wash the napkins and cloths at night and iron them at 4 o'clock the next morning before setting out for work. Michel, later to be known as 'Sarge', ran the dining room with precision and humour. Each day saw some improvement with the gaining of knowledge and just that little bit extra experience, so painfully lacking when we were first finding our restaurant legs. Then came our first review. The next week I advertised for a kitchenhand and an extra waiter and decided to send the tablecloths to the laundry.

Eighteen months later, *You and Me* at the Tatler moved around the corner and up the hill to King Street. There are still people who say to me that they preferred that first little place and that hurts a bit because I know what novices we truly were in those days, and how much my cooking improved as the years went by. It wasn't that I wanted a larger restaurant — far from it — just a place of my own with a larger, more workable kitchen, and above all, light and air. King Street had all that, and it was larger; my two waiters became four, and we two cooks five, and what had once been an idea to do something simple and well, became a fullscale business.

Mark stayed for three years before leaving to tour France and work in other restaurants. He had turned out to be a gifted and intelligent cook as well as a constant and devoted friend. His many duties included taking my daughter to and from school while en route to the fish markets. Will we ever forget the day she took a brown paper bag full of quails eggs in mistake for her lunch? I wonder what the teacher must have thought. Mark and I shared many misadventures and triumphs, and I missed him terribly at first. It was also at this time that Michel went back to France. But new people filled the gaps, and things went on much as before. A new period was beginning.

During these years I cooked the sort of food I liked to eat. There were no other limits. Anything from hearty fish soups and homely rabbit stews to elegant roasted pheasants, sparkling consommés and fine pastries. Our tray of tiny decorated petits-fours became a well-established, time-consuming, but appreciated fact. I liked things to look good, but never at the expense of taste. Partly for this reason, and also because I was not fond of excessive garnish, I did not like things on the plate that you could not eat, or were unlikely to eat, things like sprigs or leaves or bouquets of flowers (I've even been served poisonous ones). I liked food that was bare as well as elaborate, 'black and white' as well as colourful, restrained as well as flamboyant. Sometimes things are best left alone, and at other times it is as essential to garnish as wearing earrings or a colourful scarf or hat is to being well dressed. But whatever we cooked, it was done with a great deal of care and enthusiasm, and with much love.

We had a saying at *You and Me*: nothing stays the same! It grew partly out of the daily problem of getting good-quality fresh produce with which to work on a regular basis. Wild ducks are on? No, we couldn't get them today, something to do with the plucking machine breaking down, so today it's guinea fowl, but I could get only six nice ones, so after that it will be pheasant! Sometimes the menu changed with amazing speed, several times in the course of one lunch.

The other thing that kept on changing was the way we did things. This was all part of learning and developing. I will never forget the day that the sprig of mint disappeared from the face of the dessert forever. For years afterwards Michel would continue to ask like some old ghost 'Where's the mint?' The sprig of mint episode taught me how easy it is to get *stuck in a rut* with cooking as much as anything else, and how we constantly need to refine our ideas, to improve, and to discover *ourselves* in the face of changing fashion.

Many fine cooks worked over our stoves at *You and Me*: Layla and Fiona, Barbara and Simon, Jonathon and Stephen, to name just a few, and a pair of smarter apprentices you would never find than Coralie and Zita. Bob and Maurice displayed tenacity and endurance beyond the ordinary when it came to doing dishes, mopping floors and shopping for things forgotten. On our closing day, it would have been hard to find four more diligent, attentive and kindly waiters than Jean, Herbert, Colin and Michel (who had been back for several years). Even Mark was there, helping out in the last few months. He maintains that the last menu was the most deliberately complicated, most difficult thing he'd ever seen, and that I just wanted to make sure that none of us ever forgot it.

All our favourite people came on the last day to say goodbye. My mother was there again, but this time on the guest of honour table with father and grandmother, and I remembered as things moved swiftly and harmoniously all around that first frantic far-off day. This time, sipping champagne, my mother smiled and said, 'Well, you don't have to do that again tomorrow, Jen, *and I'm glad*!'

I knew exactly what she meant. Running *You and Me* was terribly, terribly hard, the hardest thing I've ever done, but it was also a wonderful time, rich in experiences, and if I had my time over I would certainly do it again. Well . . . almost certainly.

When it comes to cooking

I once had an apprentice who liked to put lots of gelatine into the whipped cream so that it would stand stiffly. He might have worked more durable monuments with bricks and cement, but no, he wanted to be a chef. One thing was for sure, I made no impression on his neat turn of mind. He would whip the piping bag from my grasp, to be helpful, of course, and pipe perfectly soldier-straight rows of biscuits in contrast to my more haphazard efforts. We despaired of each other and happily parted.

No two cooks are alike. Beneath those white aprons beat hearts of many different persuasion. The most important thing is to have a heart and to love what you are doing. Now while it may be a good thing to pipe your biscuits in nice straight rows, and to be able to whip the cream to perfectly indestructible peaks (though about this I have my doubts), it is more important that what we cook is *real food*, no matter how homely, or ordinary, or haphazard in production it may be, or how painstakingly slow and 'amateurish' we are. Where I and my apprentice differed most vehemently was on a matter of priorities. To me it mattered very much that the biscuits were crisp and golden, rich and buttery in flavour, and melted in the mouth. Anything else was of secondary merit.

Whenever I think about this I think of Aunt Alice. Some of the best sponge cakes ever made in our family were made by her. A spastic since childhood, twisted in body by cerebral palsy and afflicted with uncontrollable jerky movements, her hands could barely control the old-fashioned egg-beater she used to use and the flour sifter seemed to hang everywhere but over the bowl. She worked at that cake as if driven, and the results were perfect every time.

For me the kitchen is the centre of everything, a place where people, and in my case two cats and a dog as well, gravitate like moths to the light. Even in our mild climate, the warmth, the smell of coffee grinding or biscuits baking, the sound of kettles whistling and plates rattling, make it the place where we meet, talk, renew our strength and peace of mind amidst the clatter of pots and pans, and the daily celebration of good food and wine.

Over the years I've interviewed many aspiring young people wanting to work with food. All were determined that they had what it takes to be a good chef. Some I selected and 'gave a go' became just that. Others lasted sometimes a few months, a week, even a day, for what was a painful and misjudged experience on both sides.

After a while the qualities I was looking for became clearer and I spent more time reading faces and trying to get to know the sort of person I was talking to. I had quickly discovered that the caring sensitivity, quiet industry and genuine love of cooking that I needed were not always to be found in portfolios of achievements and references.

My priorities in cooking had been determined by my own background. A few early experiences at job hunting and being fobbed off by chefs and proprietors alike, without as much as a 'good morning', much less an interview (a bias in those days, I believe, as much against cooks in skirts, as those without papers), convinced me that if I was going to cook seriously it would have to be on my own territory, in my own way. I decided never again to be fazed by ambidextrous gentlemen in tall toques, whose expert and apparently effortless use of knife and whisk and equipment of immense weight and proportions had so impressed and cowed my own longings to cook. It took some time for me to accept my painstaking untrained ways as they were in those early days, particularly with young apprentices to guide and teach, some of whom were tremendously impressed with the 'show' of cooking. But I knew what I wanted to do, and how I wanted to do it, and while I cared very much that they learnt good techniques and tidy habits, I waged war daily on the side of care, feeling and results. Something as simple as chopping fine parsley was a common testing ground for care and patience. Having the fastest knife in the west means nothing if we end up with nothing better than a bowl of lawn clippings.

As it turned out some of my finest employees had had little cooking experience beyond their own kitchens, often being too 'old' to start an apprenticeship. They read avidly, ate out at good restaurants whenever they could, and bubbled over with enthusiasm. It shone in their faces as they begged for a chance to cook, even to wash up, just to be in the kitchen, absorb the atmosphere, and learn by observing. Enthusiasm, combined with stoic determination (to combat the aching legs as much as anything else) and a touch of humility was what I looked for in my people.

I thought about the question of good cooking long and hard while holidaying at some familiar old stamping grounds in France recently. Sadly by dint of many disappointing experiences in the dining rooms of some of the superchefs, and food no better than revolting at several 'charming' village restaurants (in stark contrast, I might add, to memorable experiences of the past), the question of well-prepared food became uppermost in my thoughts, because of its very absence.

At the lowest level canned asparagus and stodgy quenelles of uncooked flour in sticky brown flour sauces, vied for the heights of horror with tricked-up presentations, food so boned, stuffed, puréed and rolled, and hammered into new shapes and such homogenised bland consistencies, that the original ingredient — was it a chicken wing? — was lost forever. Is this thin watery brown liquid with blackened scum top, unpleasant to look at and bitter to taste, really a *crème brûlée*? If it is then I would rather have my mother's old-fashioned banana custard.

I am too aware of my own shortcomings ever to become pedantic. About cooking I have deeply held opinions which spring from a simply held belief in the enjoyment of eating, and I am saddened when confronted with a serious lack of enjoyment.

I am a firm believer in the big heart and generous approach to cooking.

The interior of You and Me, in King Street, Sydney.

Not by way of large servings, but loving, caring attention to all the details from beginning to end. Throw in a positive attitude to life, a nurturing attitude to others, and if you love life and love food, you're bound to have a good feeling for cooking. It begins with the spirit, the attitude and the determination of the individual. Good cooking can be elegant and refined, but it is never indifferent and mean. It is restrained, reflects a sound knowledge of the craft (however it was gained) and respect for taste. Above all, it is never dishonest.

Everyone needs encouragement and to have faith in their abilities. Good cooks come in all shapes and sizes. Outstanding cooks I've known are often so self-effacing, or shy, or both, that it hurts. And I've found that it's generally the ones who think they know everything who will burn the biscuits or curdle the *anglaise*.

Stories like these I used to relate time and again to my hardworking team. I guess what I was really telling them was that I didn't care if they were a bit slow at what they were doing, or if there were gaps in their expertise, as long as they were diligent and caring. If they weren't driven crazy by my nagging, and were still able to smile at the end of the day, there was always a place for them in my kitchen.

From *The Epicurean*, March-April 1986

BEING ORGANISED

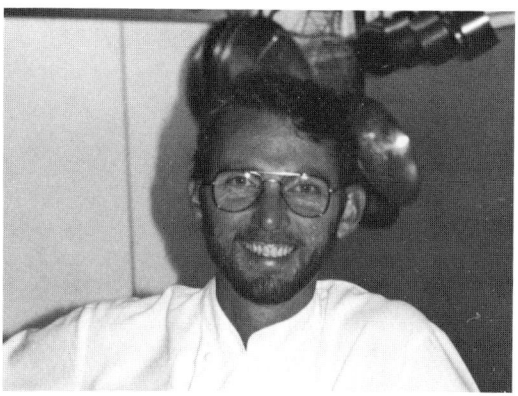

Mark Jarvis, Jenny's brother and second chef.

If being the chef of a busy lunchtime restaurant taught me anything, it was the necessity of being absolutely organised. Restaurant patrons are not forgiving people, and I can't imagine that they would be very impressed to arrive for a 12 o'clock luncheon appointment and be told, 'I'm sorry, but the chef isn't quite ready, would you like to come back in half an hour?' I sometimes felt like saying that, but somehow, every morning, we managed to get through the long lists of preparation, and we were usually whisking the last knob of butter into the beurre blanc, drying the salad, and mopping down the benches and floors, as the first diners arrived.

The clue to my organisation was to write everything down. Shopping lists were made every afternoon, orders rung through promptly, and the last thing to go into my basket at night was the list for the fish markets. At work, first thing in the morning, a list was pinned above my workbench, setting out in scrupulous detail the order of preparation, from the making of stocks, the deboning of fowls, right down to the smallest items of garnish, of fine chives or julienne of vegetable. Everything was ticked off as soon as it was done, and of course there was a great sense of achievement if you could get through your own list and help someone else with theirs.

Everything that could be prepared in advance was done. Trays of trimmed meats and fish, flasks of squeezed juices, bowls of blanched vegetables, small plastic buckets containing a variety of glazes and sauces, everything neatly in its place ready for that final moment during the service, when things combine in heat and steam.

I continue to work this way at home, and there is never a problem about 'desserting' one's guests if everything is *in its place* (the French call it *mise en place*). Scrambling eggs, last-minute pan frying, soufflées and sabayons are easy if all the bowls and whisks are at the ready, the egg whites are measured, the lemons squeezed and the cream whipped and there is nothing left to do except the final bringing together . . . and then the serving.

My Kitchen

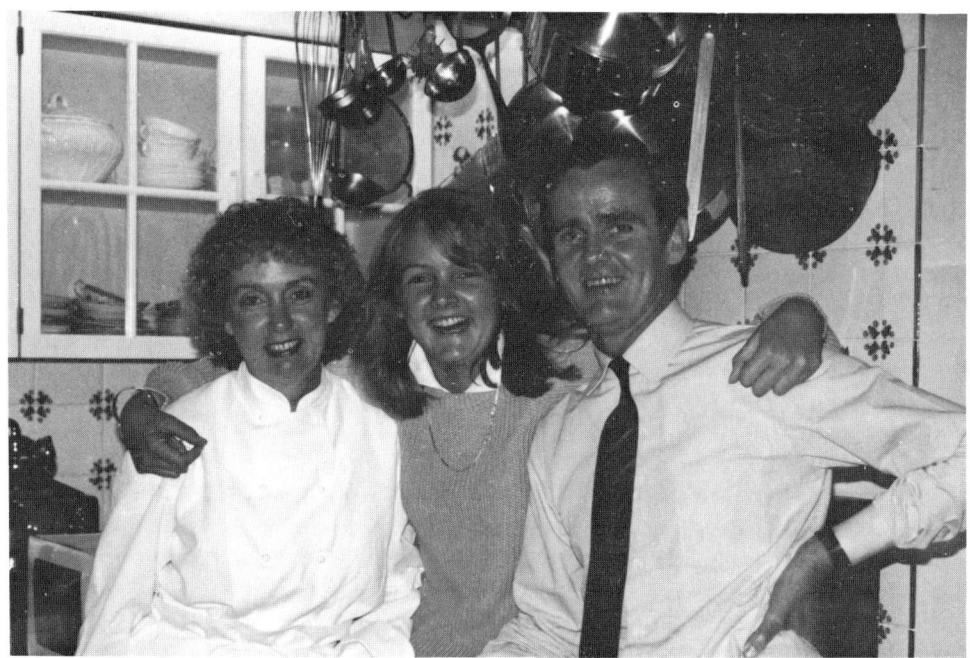

Jenny, Rob, and their daughter Rachel in the kitchen at home.

Once during a period of home renovations, I cooked for four months in my bedroom, using nothing but an electric frypan. Inventiveness can certainly make up for much, but it's far better, and it makes the work a lot easier, to have good equipment when you can.

The first thing I did when we moved to our new home was to gut the kitchen, put in a good gas commercial cooking range, some wide benches, and a long wooden table right down the centre, so that people could gather around and eat in the midst of where it was all happening.

It is a kitchen to live and work in, stocked with sturdy, practical, much-used equipment. The basics comprise an electric food processor and mixer, blender and juicer, and a wonderful icecream maker. I have a small pasta rolling machine, lots of chopping boards and small knives, a large Chinese chopper, several balloon whisks, a good set of scales, lots of bowls of various sizes, and stainless steel saucepans and pots ranging from tiny, to a 25 litre monster. There is an old wooden rolling pin, and a dented Willow measuring cup, an absolute treasure, and something I haven't seen in the shops for years.

Because of the peculiar bent that I would rather have a new saucepan than a new dress, my kitchen lacks for very little, that has not always been the case. There is nothing that I cook now, or that is contained in this book, that could not be achieved with a basic supply of cooking utensils.

Explanatory Notes

When I started work on this book I quickly discovered that there was more than one way to write a recipe. When it came to translating what were often no more than cryptic lists of ingredients into meaningful descriptions of procedure, I decided on ways to do this which require a few words of explanation.

1. All the recipes were tested using metric measurements. These were later converted to the nearest imperial equivalents.

2. At the end of some of the meat, fish and poultry recipes, mention is made of suitable vegetable accompaniments. In some cases a recipe is included, but not always.

3. After the list of ingredients, mention is also made of any special utensils that have been used. For example, I have pointed out such things as tart tins, soufflé moulds and gratin dishes, when special sizes are required, china pots for the little lime custards, a blow torch and water spray for the crème brûlées. Also in the icecream recipes I conclude with 'churn in your icecream maker'. Much cooking is the art of improvisation and the same applies here. I can only relate how I do it, and whether you make your icecream in the freezer, stirring regularly with a spoon, use a hand machine with lots of salt and ice, or whether you have a modern unit with its own built-in freezing system, is up to you.

4. Of all the labour-saving devices available to the modern cook, the food processor would have to be the most useful. Mincing, chopping, grating, and purées of all kinds, are easily done when you have one of these machines.

CONCERNING SOME INGREDIENTS

1. The eggs used are always the large — minimum weight 61g — size.

2. I have specified the use of *unsalted butter* only in the recipes where its use is of great importance. I always use unsalted butter in cooking because it allows me to have absolute control over the seasoning of each dish.

3. *Powdered gelatine* is used in the recipes for the various *bavarois* because I prefer the results. I like to use *leaf gelatine* when making aspics and terrines, but this is simply personal preference.

4. In several recipes I refer to *shallots* (sometimes called spring onions), *échalotes* (sometimes called shallots as well), and pickling onions. What I call shallots, are the narrow stemmed species of onion, with small white bulbs and long green tops. The échalote is the very small brown species of onion with papery skin, which divides into cloves, and the pickling onions I use are the tiny immature versions of the common brown and white onions.

SOME TECHNIQUES AND TERMS

1. Some recipes call for the peeling and de-seeding of capsicums and tomatoes.

For the capsicums: brush them with a little oil and place under a very hot grill or in the oven until the skin blisters or put them directly over a flame, turning them over and over, until the skin becomes completely blackened. Peel it off straight away under cold running water and cut the core and seeds out with a knife afterwards.

For the tomatoes: drop them into boiling water for one minute, then refresh in cold water. The skins will then peel off easily. Cut the core out and squeeze out the seeds.

2. To *blanch* something, in the context of these recipes, is to cook in boiling salted water for a brief time. The vegetable should be *only just cooked*, still with crunch, and then refreshed immediately in a bowl of iced water. This process stops further cooking and preserves the colour.

3. *Bake blind* means to bake the naked pastry, i.e. pastry which is without any protective covering such as aluminium foil, etc.

4. The *concentrated stock* is the result of the final stage in the reduction of a stock. It is rich in both flavour and colour. *Glaze* is another word I use to refer to this product.

5. To *deglaze* is to capture all the browned juices left in the bottom of a cooking pan. To do this we add a liquid such as water, wine or cream, bring it to a quick boil, while at the same time scraping up all the browned on bits and incorporating them into the liquid.

6. To *nap* something is to *coat* it.

7. To make a *julienne* is to cut into very fine strips.

8. A *bain-marie* is a pan half-filled with hot water in which various preparations, such as puddings, mousses and custards, which require gentle cooking, are placed.

I have endeavoured not to use an overabundance of foreign or technical terms when describing the food preparation except where I found such terms useful in serving the clarity of meaning. This was a natural thing for me to do, for I have written my recipes as I would speak to you if you were here in my kitchen, and as indeed I always speak to the cooks I work with — plainly.

Stock and sauces

Good stocks are the cornerstone of good cooking. I *never* use stock cubes or packet sauce mixes of any kind, and in this regard I am absolutely uncompromising. *Real food* must be made with *real ingredients*. As for those who say that stock making is not only time consuming but expensive — they are right on both counts. But good cooking is about making an effort and using the best ingredients that you can get your hands on. It is a matter of priorities, and if you are serious about cooking, you will organise kitchen life to accommodate this vital task.

In a restaurant, stock making is an everyday affair. There is hardly a moment when you will not find a simmering pot full of some fragrant brew of vegetables, meat, poultry or fish. At home, I like to make my stocks about once every three or four weeks, so that I always have plenty on hand. A bowl of rich veal or chicken jelly kept in the refrigerator is constantly delved into when a spoonful is needed to deglaze a pan for a simple gravy or for adding flavour to stews, or soups, or various poaching liquids. And as for accompanying sauces, these reduced stocks can be kept quite *plain*, with perhaps just the tiniest addition of cream or butter to thicken and add gloss. Alternatively they can be combined with any number of other flavours — wines, vinegars, mustards, fruit juices, puréed vegetables, mushrooms, peppercorns, or anything else that you can think of!

You don't always need a sauce — that's true — and you can often get by nicely deglazing roasting dishes and frying pans with just a little wine or cream. But when you have to make a sauce, please let it be the perfect drop and, even though we live in a time of much rushing about when there is absolutely no time to do anything, let it be *homemade*.

Many of my recipes call for a little stock (or its reduction) of one kind or another. That is why the bulk of my very limited freezer space is taken up with a multitude of small labelled and dated plastic containers, each filled with anything from the most common veal and chicken glazes, to concentrated crab, lobster and fish stocks, duck, lamb, rabbit, and even hare.

It is not necessary to go in for such variety. My trouble is that I just can't bear to throw away anything.

Veal stock

5kg (10 lb) sawn veal shanks (nice meaty pieces)
2 or 3 pigs trotters
3 leeks (the white part only)
3 large onions
3 large carrots
3 stalks celery
a small bunch parsley
some fresh thyme sprigs
a bay leaf
1 ripe tomato
mushroom trimmings
1 teaspoon black peppercorns

Chop the leeks, onions, carrots and celery into rough pieces. Wash well. Make a bed of these in the bottom of a large baking pan. Spread the pieces of meat over the top, and roast in a moderate oven until all is well browned, but *not black*.

Tip everything into a large stock pot. The bones with the vegetables well packed should fill it to about two-thirds. Deglaze the roasting pan very well with cold water, making sure that you scrape up all the stuck on bits and add all the residual brown juices to the pot. (You can do this with a little red or white wine if you like, but I usually use plain water.) Doing this will help enormously to give the stock its lovely rich colour. Add the herbs, bits of mushroom, tomato, and peppercorns, and cover with lots of cold water. Bring to the boil, then adjust to a gentle simmer for about 8 hours (or overnight). From time to time, skim the surface.

Now, strain the liquid through a conical sieve into another pot. Let it rest for a while, then ladle away any fat that settles on top. Boil rapidly to reduce by half. Cool, then refrigerate. Any remaining fat will rise to the surface and solidify, making the job of its removal very easy. You will now have a rich brown liquid ready for sauce making. You can freeze it at this stage, or as I do, reduce it to a syrupy *glaze*, almost sauce consistency. Doing this, you will end up with about 2 litres (4½ pints) of liquid from an original 15 litres (28 pints). I then freeze the glaze in 250ml (8 fl oz) batches until needed.

Brown or White Chicken Stock

1 boiling fowl
2kg (4 lb) chicken necks or other chicken pieces
2 medium leeks (the white part only)
2 medium carrots
2 medium onions
2 stalks celery
6 stalks parsley
a few fresh thyme branches
a bay leaf
3 or 4 black peppercorns

Chop and wash all the vegetables very well.

Section the fowl and chop the carcass into pieces. If your stock is to be *brown*, make a bed of all the vegetables in a roasting dish, put the chicken pieces on top and roast in a moderate oven until nicely browned. Deglaze the roasting pan very well, as you did for the veal stock, and add all the residual brown juices to the pot. If the stock is to be *white*, then skip the roasting bit, put everything straight into the pot — it should be about two-thirds filled — and cover with copious amounts of cold water. Bring to the boil, then adjust to simmer for 4 hours. Skim away the scum that settles on top as frequently as you can.

Strain the liquid into another pot and leave to rest for a while so that the fat can settle on top and be skimmed away before the final reduction.

If it is a white chicken stock to be used for soup making or poaching purposes, I store it at this stage, without any further reduction.

If it is a brown chicken stock to be used for jelly, I boil it to reduce by half, clarify, then store. If it is for sauce making I will reduce it to an even more intense, syrupy consistency before storing.

Duck stock and others

Make this the same way as a brown chicken stock, using 2 or 3 duck carcasses and a boiling fowl, or 2kg (4 lb) of chicken necks or other pieces. This stock will be a great deal fattier than many of the others, so make sure it is very well degreased. It results in a lovely golden glaze with a slightly stronger flavour than one made with all chicken.

You do not need enormous quantities of carcasses in order to make a fine stock. Use fewer herbs and vegetables and make stocks using only a few quail or pigeon bones, a couple of rabbit carcasses (including the front legs) and similarly a hare carcass. A wonderful *game stock* can be made from the trimmings and bones of venison, combined with some pheasant or pigeon carcasses and perhaps that of a hare. *Lamb stock* is not frequently made, lacking the flavour and colour of veal, but sometimes I have made one with good trimmings and some sawn shanks. It is nice, but not essential, for making lamb blanquette.

Vegetable stock

2 large carrots
1 large onion
1 leek (the white part only)
2 stalks celery
½ head fennel (optional)
1 small bunch parsley
a few sprigs of mixed fresh herbs, such as thyme, marjoram, tarragon
1 bay leaf
2 cloves
1 teaspoon black peppercorns
1 litre (35 fl oz) dry white wine
3 litres (105 fl oz) water
salt to taste

Chop the vegetables into fairly small pieces and wash very well. Chop and wash the herbs.

Put them into a pot and cover with the wine and water. Bring to the boil, then adjust to a gentle simmer for 2 hours. Skim away the impurities which settle on top regularly. Strain.

Note: This stock is so useful that I don't know how I ever did without it. Use as a flavoursome alternative to fish stock when poaching quenelles, scallops, or steaming fish. Add to soups and braises and use as a sauce base, particularly with fish and vegetable dishes. Clarify and add leaf gelatine to make jellies for salads, terrines and other vegetable moulds. This recipe will produce about 2 litres (70 fl oz).

Fish stock

2kg (4 lb) trimmings and bones of John Dory, whiting or sole (or any other white-fleshed and delicate flavoured fish that you prefer*)
1 large carrot
1 large onion
1 large leek (the white part only)
3 or 4 parsley stalks
1 celery stalk
6 black peppercorns
500ml (16 fl oz) dry white wine
1500ml (48 fl oz) cold water

Chop and wash the fish bones thoroughly so that they are free of blood and bits of gut.

Wash and chop all the vegetables and put, along with the fish bones, into a stockpot.

Cover everything with the cold water and wine, and bring to the boil. Skim away any scum that rises to the surface. When the stock has boiled, reduce heat to a gentle simmer for 20-25 minutes. Do not cook for any longer or the stock may become bitter.

Strain through a conical sieve, pushing everything well down to extract every bit of juice from the fish and vegetables. Rest for a few minutes and skim if necessary.

If the stock is to be used for poaching purposes, or soups, store at this point. If it is intended for sauce making, reduce by about half, until it is quite concentrated and golden in colour.

---

*Some cooks like to use rock fish or red fish to make their fish stocks. These are truly flavoursome, and so long as you steer clear of strong and oily varieties, it is worth experimenting for yourself.

The clarification of stock

3 litres (96 fl oz) cold stock (or thereabouts)
12 egg whites

Put the cold stock into a pot and pour in the egg whites. Commence whisking the whites through the liquid while you bring it to the boil. The stock is cold to begin with so that the whites do not cook immediately on contact. At this stage things will be very murky and cloudy, but do not worry.

When the liquid begins to boil, reduce the heat, stop whisking, and let it simmer *very gently* for 1 hour. A crust of the egg whites will form on top. To this will cling all the impurities in the stock.

When the hour is up, turn the heat right off and *do not disturb the pot by lifting it up*! Prepare a sieve lined with paper towels over a bowl. Now, disturbing the crust as little as possible, ladle the clear liquid out carefully through one of the vents which has formed in the surface of the crust during the clarification process. If there is not a hole large enough, very gently pull a little of the crust aside — just enough to fit your ladle through. Ladle the liquid into the paper-lined sieve and collect the now clarified stock in the bowl underneath.

Plain Mayonnaise

2 egg yolks
1 teaspoon salt
1 teaspoon pepper
1 teaspoon lemon juice
250ml (8 fl oz) peanut oil*

Using a balloon whisk, combine the egg yolks with the salt, pepper and lemon juice in the bottom of a bowl. Continue to whisk and add the oil, just a few drops at a time, to begin with. When the mixture begins to thicken, continue to add the oil in a slow steady stream right to the end. The mixture will become thick and creamy.

SAFFRON MAYONNAISE
1 recipe plain mayonnaise
1 teaspoon saffron threads
1 tablespoon boiling water

Infuse the saffron threads in the water for 10 minutes, then stir thoroughly into the mayonnaise.

TRUFFLE MAYONNAISE
1 recipe plain mayonnaise
1 tablespoon truffle juice
1 truffle, chopped

Combine all the above ingredients thoroughly.

---

*If you want the mayonnaise to have the distinct character of a particular oil, then use any good quality *olive* or *nut oil* instead, or you can use it 50/50 with the peanut oil.

Hollandaise sauce

Makes 1½ cups

4 egg yolks
2 tablespoons water
4 black peppercorns
½ bay leaf
350g (11 oz) unsalted butter, cold, and cut into pieces
2 tablespoons lemon juice
large pinch salt

Put the egg yolks, water, peppercorns and bay leaf together in the bottom of a double saucepan. Using a balloon whisk, mix everything together, then commence adding the butter, a bit at a time. Whisk continuously until all the butter is incorporated. Take the saucepan from the stove, strain out the bay leaf and peppercorns, then replace the sauce in a bowl over warm water or in a warm place until it is time to use.

Buerre blanc sauce

Serves 6 people

2 shallots, including green tops
⅔ cup good quality white vinegar
1 cup dry white wine
6 black peppercorns
⅓ cup cream
1 teaspoon salt
250g (8 oz) unsalted butter, cold and cut into pieces

Slice the shallots into small pieces and put into the bottom of a heavy based saucepan along with the vinegar, wine and peppercorns. Boil until all that remains is enough liquid to cover the bottom of the pan. Add the cream, and boil again until it thickens (the bubbles will be large). Add the salt and butter, bit by bit fairly quickly, whisking continuously until it is all incorporated. Strain and keep warm.

Hors-d'oeuvres

We were seated at last, napkin unfurled. Champagne poured, and menus handed around when the waiter arrived with what the French call the *amuse-gueule*. On each plate was a quail egg, hard boiled and sliced in two, resting on prettily piped rosettes of duck liver parfait in the centre of pale green pools of peppery leek purée. It looked wonderful, was *tasty*, and disappeared in a flash. This was the hors-d'oeuvre: what I call 'the art of taking a great deal of trouble over a very small matter'.

Hors-d'oeuvres can be many things: a dish of olives, tiny hot pastries filled with such things as ham or fish, cheese tartlets and various miniature quiches, little tarts of snails in creamy garlic, country tarts of tiny onions and cheese flavoured chou puffs; wee anchovy croissants, barbecued ducks, hearts with rosemary, chicken wings — boned, stuffed, rolled, marinated and barbecued — pizzas in miniature, melon balls wrapped in parma ham, crisp cheese wafers and crunchy fresh radishes. They can be also many other things, for the list is endless.

At *You and Me* we took a great deal of trouble over these very small matters for the sheer love of perfecting the small and seemingly unimportant, and for the ritual itself. This is the beginning, and the first chance we have as cooks to make our guests feel welcome.

Some of the following recipes are so simple that at first I hesitated to include them — little sandwiches, pastry turnovers? Who is there amongst us who has not grilled cheese and bacon on toast as a snack at some time? I offer these as ideas, because it is often the simplest, most common idea that is also the tastiest. That is what hors-d'oeuvres should be above all — small tasty mouthfuls to excite the tastebuds and get us in the mood for more good things to come. Small matters to be sure, but matters over which I think it is worth taking a great deal of trouble.

Fine tarts of smoked salmon, dill cream and caviar

For 16 x 5cm (16 x 2in) fine tarts

puff pastry, leftover pieces
4-6 good smoked salmon slices
23g (¾ oz) jar beluga caviar
egg wash (1 egg yolk mixed with 1 teaspoon water)

FOR THE DILL CREAM
1 cup whipped cream
2 tablespons dill, finely chopped
2 teaspoons lemon juice, or to taste
pinch salt
freshly ground black pepper

Roll out the pastry as thinly as you can. Drape over a baking tray and trim off the edges. Prick very well all over and paint with egg wash. Chill for 20 minutes, then bake at 200°C (400°F) until well browned and crisp (about 30 minutes). From time to time during the baking, use a kitchen cloth to press the pastry down firmly. This will help to prevent it rising, so that it will cook wafer thin. Before the pastry cools, use a biscuit cutter, or a wine glass, or anything you like, to cut out circles for the tart bases. Cool.

Prepare the dill cream by folding the listed ingredients together and tasting judiciously as you go.

Spread the cream evenly over the pastry circles, cover with the slices of salmon, very neatly trimmed at the edges, top with a little spoonful of the caviar, and arrange on a tray. Serve to your lucky guests with a glass of champagne.

Note: These tarts can be made any size you like. Larger, they happily turn into a small first course.

Tomato and Anchovy Croûtons

FOR THE CROÛTONS
white bread slices
butter, melted

FOR THE TOPPING
3 medium red tomatoes
1 red capsicum
3 sprigs basil
salt, to taste, freshly ground black pepper
1 tablespoon olive oil
6 anchovy fillets

To make the croûtons, choose a cutter that you like, or simply cut square shapes (minus the crusts, of course) from the bread. Brush a baking tray well with melted butter, put the bread shapes on top, and brush each of these with the butter as well. Bake at 160°C (320°F) until golden brown. These can be stored in an airtight container or even frozen until needed. They will only need to be popped into a warm oven for a couple of minutes to be ready for use.

To make the topping, peel and remove the seeds from the tomatoes and squeeze out any excess moisture. Blister and peel away the skin, and remove the seeds, from the capsicum.

Put the tomato, together with the capsicum, basil leaves, salt and pepper and olive oil into a food processor. Using an on/off movement, chop roughly but do not purée smooth. This can be done by hand. Store in the refrigerator overnight.

TO SERVE

Chop the anchovy fillets into small pieces and combine with tomato mixture. Spoon onto croûtons and serve at once.

FINE ONION AND PROSCIUTTO TART

300g (9½ oz) puff pastry leftovers
2 medium onions
1 tablespoon butter
6 slices prosciutto
½ cup parmesan, freshly grated
freshly ground black pepper
1 tablespoon chives, finely sliced

Roll out the pastry on a floured surface, as thinly as you can. Cut out the circles to whatever size you like. I sometimes use a wine glass held upside down to cut 7cm (2¾ in) circles. Other times I make one large one, using a dinner plate to trace around.

Put the pastry circle or circles onto a baking tray, prick very well all over with a fork, and chill for 20 minutes.

Slice the onions finely and fry in the butter until soft and golden. Drain well. Trim the fat from the prosciutto and slice into strips.

TO COOK

Do this just before your guests arrive so that they are fresh and golden. They do not reheat all that well, and if prepared too early get a dried-out appearance which is not very appetising.

Cover the pastry circles with the cooked onion, sprinkle the prosciutto strips around, then the cheese, pepper, and finally the chives. Bake at 220°C (430°F) until crisp and golden. This will take about 15 minutes.

PUFF PASTRY TURNOVERS

WITH SMOKED SALMON
puff pastry leftovers
smoked salmon (3 or 4 slices or any end bits or trimmings)
a little cream
black pepper
egg wash (1 egg mixed with 1 teaspoon water)

Roll out the pastry, *not too thinly.*

Cut out circles, approximately 6cm (2½ in) in diameter, put onto a baking tray, and chill.

Purée the salmon with enough cream to make a smooth paste (take care not to over-purée or it will separate and turn lumpy). Season with black pepper.

Pipe or spoon a little salmon cream onto the bottom half of the pastry circle.

Turn the top half over, press down and seal with egg wash and bake at 220°C (430°F) until golden.

WITH BLUE CHEESE

The ingredients remain the same as those listed for salmon, with the exception of the blue cheese (leftover broken bits will do) replacing the salmon. Also, omit the pepper.

CREAMY ONION TART

Serves 8 people

300g (9½ oz) puff pastry leftovers
2 large onions
50g (1¾ oz) butter
3 eggs
300ml (9 fl oz) cream
pinch salt
freshly ground black pepper

Roll out the pastry to line a 22cm (8¾ in) flan tin. Cover the pastry with aluminium foil pressed down well into the corners, and fill with dried beans or rice. Refrigerate for ½ hour.

Bake at 200°C (400°F) for 20 minutes — until the pastry is slightly done, and holding its shape. Remove the foil, brush with a little of one of the egg whites, and cook for a few more minutes, until golden. Put to one side ready for filling.

Slice the onions finely. Melt the butter in a pan, and when hot and foaming stir in the onions and cook until soft and transparent. Drain well.

Whisk the eggs lightly, add the cream, then salt and pepper.

Spread the cooked onion evenly over the pastry base. Pour on the filling and bake until a lovely golden brown. This will take about 20 minutes. Serve hot in wedges.

TOPPINGS FOR FRESH OR TOASTED ROUNDS OF BAGUETTE OR FICELLE LOAVES

CREAMY MUSHROOM, BASIL AND BACON
300g (9½ oz) mushrooms
200g (7 oz) bacon
1 tablespoon green shallot tops, finely sliced
knob butter
freshly ground black pepper
½ cup cream
2 tablespoons basil leaves, finely chopped
2 tablespoons parsley, finely chopped

Prepare the mushrooms, bacon and shallot tops. Wash the mushrooms, peel and trim if they are large (generally the little buttons will need only a wash). Slice them into small pieces. Remove the fat and rind from the bacon and slice into small pieces as well.

Melt the butter in a frying pan. Add the bacon and shallots and cook for 5 minutes before adding the mushrooms and pepper. Stir occasionally, and continue cooking until the mushroom juices run. Add the cream, basil and half the parsley, and boil until very thick. Taste and adjust the seasoning if necessary. (I have not included salt because usually the bacon is salty enough, but make up your own mind on this matter.)

Serve spoonfuls on fresh or toasted rounds of baguette or ficelle loaves. Top with a sprinkling of the remaining parsley.

CHICKEN LIVER PÂTÉ
500g (1 lb) chicken livers, well trimmed and washed
(buy 1kg (2 lb) livers)
2 spring onions, chopped
1 tablespoon butter
½ cup mixed fresh herbs, such as parsley, thyme, marjoram,
tarragon and oregano, roughly chopped
1 teaspoon juniper berries
1 teaspoon cracked black peppercorns
½ cup cream
1 tablespoon cognac
1 tablespoon butter
½ teaspoon salt

Gently fry the onions in the butter until soft and golden.
Add the herbs, berries, seasonings and finally the livers.
Cook, stirring all the while, for a couple of minutes only, leaving the livers pink inside.
Purée everything in a food processor, adding the cream right at the end.

(This is a rough textured pâté and will not require sieving.) Put into a bowl and refrigerate.

To serve, pipe the pâté onto fresh or toasted rounds of ficelle loaf. Use a decorative nozzle, and garnish with a sprig of fresh chervil or a wedge of lemon.

GRILLED TOMATO, CHEESE AND BACON
2 medium red tomatoes
3 bacon rashers
½ cup parmesan, freshly grated
1 tablespoon chives, very finely sliced
pepper

Peel and remove the seeds from the tomatoes. Chop up roughly.

Cut the fat and rind from the bacon and slice into 3cm (1½ in) squares. Cook partially by tossing in a hot frypan for a couple of minutes.

When you are ready to serve, top the rounds of loaf with a spoonful of tomato, a square of bacon and sprinkle the cheeses all over. Grill. When the cheese has melted golden brown, top with a few chives and serve.

Note: The loaves can be bought from any good delicatessen.

HAM ROLLS

300g (9½ oz) puff pastry
egg wash, 1 egg mixed with 1 teaspoon water

FOR THE HAM FILLING
250g (8 oz) ham
1 small onion, chopped
1 tablespoon parsley and sage, chopped and combined
knob butter
freshly ground black pepper
1 egg

Fry the onion in the butter until soft. Combine all the ingredients for the filling together in a food processor adding the egg at the end. Purée smoothly, but not to a 'paste'.

Roll out the pastry into a strip approximately 16 cm (6½ in) wide and 60cm (24 in) long. Roll the ham mixture by hand into a long 'sausage' and place right down the centre. Wrap the pastry over and seal with egg wash.

Chill very well. Cut the roll in half to make for ease of baking. Place onto a lightly floured baking tray seam side down. Brush with the remaining egg wash and bake at 220°C (430°F) until puffed and golden brown. This will take about 30 minutes.

Slice into bite-sized portions and serve hot.

Curried Lamb in Filo Pastry

1 packet filo pastry
butter, melted

FOR THE FILLING
500 (1 lb) cooked or uncooked lamb, minced (if using cooked lamb, anything like leftover leg of lamb will do)
1 medium onion, chopped roughly
1 clove garlic, chopped
knob butter
2 tablespoons curry powder (good quality or homemade — see recipe below)
1 teaspoon fresh ginger, chopped
1 teaspoon fresh chilli, chopped
1 teaspoon salt
2 tablespoons brown sugar
2 tablespoons concentrated tomato purée
150ml (5 fl oz) cream or coconut cream

Melt the knob of butter in a frying pan, and when foaming stir in the chopped onion and garlic and cook until soft.

Add the lamb, curry powder, ginger, chilli and salt, and cook for a couple of minutes before adding the sugar, tomato purée and cream. Simmer and stir for 5 minutes.

Purée everything so as to be a fine consistency but not to a paste.

Lay one sheet of pastry at a time on your workbench and keep the others well sealed in clear plastic food wrap. Cut each strip lengthwise into 4 strips. Put a teaspoon of filling 2cm (¾ in) inside the bottom edge of each strip. Flatten the filling a little and fold the pastry over squarely. Now, continue to fold the strip upwards in a triangular fashion all the way to the top. Trim off any overhanging bits of pastry. Put the filled triangles on a baking sheet, brush with melted butter, and bake at 180°C (360°F) until crisp and golden.

Note: I do not brush the filo strips with oil or butter before folding as is commonly done. I find this makes them unpleasantly greasy. Brushing the tops is ample, the filling provides all the necessary internal moisture.

What I like to do, whenever I have a quantity of leftover cooked lamb, is to make up a batch of these little triangles and freeze them. That way I always have some at hand when a tasty little appetiser is needed.

HOMEMADE CURRY
2 tablespoons onion, peeled and finely minced
2 tablespoons fresh ginger, peeled and finely minced
1 teaspoon brown sugar
½ teaspoon turmeric
½ teaspoon chilli powder
½ teaspoon salt

½ teaspoon ground black pepper
pinch cloves
knob butter

Fry everything in the butter until the onion and ginger is cooked.

MINIATURE CLUB SANDWICHES

*fresh white bread slices
soft butter
toothpicks
tiny lemon wedges and quartered cherry tomatoes*

FOR THE SMOKED SALMON SANDWICHES
*smoked salmon slices
tiny lemon wedges
quartered cherry tomatoes*

FOR LOBSTER OR PRAWN SANDWICHES
*1½ cups lobster or prawns, cooked and chopped
2 tablespoons saffron or truffle mayonnaise
(see recipe on page 27)
1 teaspoon chives, very finely sliced
pinch salt
freshly ground black pepper*

For the lobster or prawn filling, simply mix all the listed ingredients together in a bowl.

Cut the crusts from the bread and roll each slice out very thinly with a rolling pin. You will need 3 slices to assemble each lot of sandwiches. Butter the slices, and spread 2 with the chosen filling. Put them one on top of the other and place the third slice on top. Trim the sides square and cut into eighths (or quarters, if you prefer them a little larger). Spear a quarter cherry tomato and a tiny lemon wedge with a toothpick and then secure each tiny sandwich.

DEEP FRIED WHITEBAIT

For 6 people

500g (16 oz) whitebait
8 sprigs parsley
peanut oil
lemon wedges
flaky sea salt

Wash both the fish and parsley, then pat dry very well.

Heat the oil to 190°C (370°F). Test by dropping one of the little fish in. It should sizzle immediately it touches the oil, but it should not brown too rapidly. If it does, the oil is too hot and your fish will only shrivel and burn.

To cook, simply drop one handful at a time into the hot oil. They will only take 10-15 seconds to cook. Lift out with a slotted spoon, and drain on kitchen paper.

Serve in a starched napkin with lemon wedges, sprigs of parsley which have also been deep fried (stand well back when you drop them in the oil) and lots of flaky sea salt on the side.

Note: These fish are very tiny and should be eaten whole. Don't be like the lady who asked the waiter to fillet hers before she could start.

A word of caution when buying. There are two sizes of whitebait at the markets, so make sure that you do *not* buy the very tiny ones. These are so small as to appear mushy and stuck together, a veritable sea of eyes. These are generally cooked into fritters. The whitebait we use in this recipe are about 6cm (2½ in) long.

SOUPS

My daughter was seven years old when she joined us on her first French holiday. At that tender age she had her own very definite ideas about restaurants — and how to rate them — ideas not entirely formed by what went on at the dining table.

Concerning this ritual, it was most important that it was not too tediously long and drawn out. Slow waiters are anathema when you are only seven and sleepy. On the other hand, a large garden to romp in while parents sit over coffee is absolutely perfect, and if there is also a woolly dog to talk to (and feed when no one is looking) then things get even better, and being in France, there is generally a pampered pooch or two right under the neighbouring dinner table.

But even at the age of seven one has to eat as well as find amusement, and in those days a perfect little three-course meal was generally composed of soup, salad and sorbet. Of these, it was the soup which was most eagerly sought. Fortunately, so long as it was soup, it didn't matter greatly what it was made from, for her tastes were happily already of a diverse nature. A delicate asparagus cream at *Alain Chapel*, Mionnay, a heady fish brew, redolent of garlic, olive oil and tomatoes at *Moulin de Mougin*, a delicious potage of frogs legs perfumed with chervil at *L'Auberge de L'Ill*, or an unforgettable rich and creamy bisque d'écrevisses at the *Bristol Hotel*, Paris — all were consumed with the greatest delight and ease. It was her opinion then, and mine now, that a menu is not complete without it.

About twelve years ago, there was a restaurant in Sydney called *Le Chantilly*. The chef, Marc Fusilier, made one of the best lobster bisques in town. He eventually left and the restaurant closed, but I still remember his lovely bisque, an accomplishment of which any cook could be truly proud. The recipe I include here is not my own, but that of another Mark, my brother. It is a wonderful recipe, it *works*, and it is absolute proof of what a terrible waste it is to buy a lobster and eat only its tail.

I make soup out of almost anything that is meat, fish, fowl, or vegetable. Often these are so simple as to be nothing more than thinned-out purées enriched with butter and egg yolks, or basic broths in which boiling water is more interesting by the addition of some chopped edibles. Some of the soups I include here are not that simple, but they are the ones that I most enjoy making, and for that matter they are the ones I like best to eat.

> Beautiful soup so rich and green
> Waiting in a hot tureen
> Who for such dainties would not stoop?
> Soup of the evening, beautiful soup!
> Soup of the evening, beautiful soup!
> (The mock turtle in *Alice in Wonderland* by Lewis Carroll)

PIGEON AND LENTIL SOUP

Serves 4 people

2 plump fresh pigeons
600ml (18 fl oz) pigeon stock (using the pigeon legs and carcasses follow the method for the Game Stock on page 24)
1 cup dried brown lentils
¼ teaspoon each salt and pepper
2 nice pieces bone marrow
4 sprigs fresh chervil

Place the pigeons in a buttered roasting pan and roast in a pre-heated oven at 210°C (425°F) for 10 minutes. Remove the breasts and reserve. Chop the remainder of the bird into pieces, then place in a pot with assorted stock vegetables and herbs, already washed and chopped, as in the recipe on page 23. Cover with cold water. Simmer the stock for 2 hours before straining. Taste and season with the salt and pepper.

In the meantime soak the lentils for 30 minutes, then cook in boiling salted water until tender. Drain. Reserve 4 tablespoons of whole lentils, but purée and sieve the remainder to a smooth paste. Whisk the lentil paste and pigeon stock together until all is thoroughly combined. Taste and adjust the seasoning if necessary.

TO SERVE

Toss the breasts into a hot pan to warm through, then slice into fine julienne strips. Slice the marrow into rounds and poach in the hot soup until tender (but not completed melted). Warm the reserved whole lentils through by holding in a slotted spoon in the hot soup. Put a pile into the bottom of each large flat soup bowl. Place the pigeon meat on top, and pour the soup around. Pile the bone marrow on top of the pigeon and garnish with a sprig of chervil.

Note: The idea for combining pigeon with lentils in a soup was inspired by a dish once enjoyed at the *Chantecler* restaurant in the Negresco Hotel, Nice.

FISH SOUP

Serves 10 people

1 x 750g (1½ lb) snapper
1 kg (2 lb) uncooked blue swimmer crabs
6 red tomatoes
3 stalks celery
1 fresh chilli
2 medium onions
2 large carrots
1 medium head fennel (or 1 teaspoon fennel seeds)
½ head garlic
1 small bunch parsley
mixed fresh herbs, such as thyme, basil, tarragon, coriander
250g (7½ oz) butter
100g (3¼ oz) flour
75ml (2½ fl oz) cognac
500ml (16 fl oz) dry white wine
200g (6 fl oz) concentrated tomato purée
3 litres water
100ml (3 fl oz) cream
generous pinch saffron
1 teaspoon salt and freshly ground black pepper
garlic mayonnaise (see instructions at end of this recipe)

Melt the butter in a large pot, and put in all the vegetables and herbs, well washed and chopped. Add the salt and a good grinding of pepper, then stew for 8 minutes, stirring every so often, until everything is soft.

In the meantime, fillet the snapper. Skin the fillets, and put the boneless, clean fillets in a bowl to one side. Wash the head and the bones of the fish very well, and put to one side also.

Now clean the crabs. Lift up the little triangular flap on the under side and remove the upper shell. Discard this and also the soft feathery 'petals' underneath. Put what remains of the crabs into a large bowl and crush well with a mallet. Take care not to lose any of the juices. Put all of this in with the vegetables, scraping down the sides of the bowl with a spatula so that nothing is lost. Cook for a couple of minutes until the crabs turn red.

Add the cognac and boil for 1 minute. Stir in the flour and tomato, and cook for a couple of minutes before adding the wine. Boil rapidly until about half the liquid remains.

Add the 3 litres (105 fl oz) cold water, bring to the boil, and continue to simmer gently for 1 hour. During this time it is important to skim away any of the scum and oils which rise to the surface.

Strain the liquid through a conical sieve, pressing down hard on the shell and vegetable matter in order to extract all the juices. Discard this debris and boil the strained liquid for 5 minutes to reduce slightly. Skim thoroughly and add the fish head and bones. Simmer for 20 minutes.

Strain the liquid again, discard the head and bones, and add the chopped flesh of the fillets. Let this rest for a few minutes. Just being immersed in the hot liquid is all that is needed to cook the fish pieces, and this resting will also give any oils a chance to settle and be skimmed away.

Put the liquid and fish pieces through a blender or push through a fine sieve. Add the saffron, taste, use extra pepper and salt if necessary, then stir in the cream to finish.

Serve with toasted croûtons, and a light garlic-flavoured mayonnaise. This should be stirred into soup just before eating.

TO MAKE A GARLIC MAYONNAISE

Follow the recipe for plain mayonnaise on page 27 only this time use equal parts good-quality olive oil with peanut oil. Crush a small clove of garlic and stir in thoroughly.

Mark's saffron lobster bisque
Serves 8-10 people

A.

2 x 1 kg (4 x 2 lb) lobsters (the heads only — use some of the tail meat for garnish and the rest in another dish)
2 large carrots
2 large white onions
2 leeks
3 stalks celery
½ head fennel (or 1 teaspoon fennel seeds)
½ head garlic
1 teaspoon peppercorns
mixed fresh herbs, a handful of each of any of basil, thyme, oregano, tarragon

B.

250g (8 oz) butter
75ml (2½ fl oz) cognac
250g (8 oz) concentrated tomato paste
100g (3½ oz) flour
500ml (16 fl oz) dry white wine
2 teaspoons saffron threads (or thereabouts, but be generous)
250ml (8 fl oz) crème fraîche
1 litre (35 fl oz) cream
salt to taste and freshly ground pepper
water to cover

A pot large enough to hold at least 7 litres (235 fl oz) of liquid

Kill the lobsters and *as soon as they are dead* remove the tails. Some of the tail meat can be cooked later, chopped and added to the soup. The rest can be saved for another time, using any of the recipes that call for lobster tail.

Clean the heads by removing the gravel sac found behind the eyes. If you are lucky enough to have a female lobster, be sure that you do not throw away the orange coral. This is very tasty and will add flavour when crushed along with the shell. Do this crushing very well. Break the heads into small pieces with your hands, then put them into a large bowl and, using a steel mallet, pound away furiously for several minutes in order to pulverise every bit of shell and release all the lobstery juices.

Put all the ingredients listed under *A* together in your large pot, along with the butter, and cook until everything is soft. Pour in the cognac, and boil to evaporate the alcohol.

Stir in the tomato concentrate and flour and cook, stirring regularly, for another 5 minutes.

Add the wine gradually to prevent the mixture sticking to the bottom. Finally, add the crushed heads with all the juices, cover everything with water, and simmer for 1 hour.

While the soup is simmering, skim regularly to get rid of all the scum and globules of fat. When the hour is up, strain the liquid into another pot and boil until it becomes very thick — about 1½ litres (51 fl ozs) will remain. Strain this concentrated liquid through a very fine sieve (a conical sauce sieve is ideal).

Add the saffron.

This basic stock will keep very well in the refrigerator for a week or a little more, and develop its flavour further. It definitely gets better as it goes along, so it's something to prepare well in advance.

TO SERVE

On the day you wish to serve the soup, adjust the seasoning with salt and pepper, and stir in the crème fraîche and the cream.

NOTES

To kill live lobsters, I first put them in the freezer for an hour or two, until they are very quiet (but not dead), then plunge them headfirst and upside down into boiling water. For detailed advice on the subject you can do no better than to read the chapter on Lobsters in Julia Child's book *From Julia Child's Kitchen*.

The quantity of cream stated in the recipe is an approximate one. This final blending of the soup is very much one of individual taste.

If you don't have any crème fraîche, make up the difference with ordinary cream.

The stock can be made up any time you can lay your hands on some lobster heads. It can be frozen before you add any of the creams, and provides a fabulous emergency entrée for unexpected guests.

To make a lobster sauce, add less cream, and aim for a thick 'sauce' rather than 'soup' consistency.

The complex flavour of this soup depends on its wide array of ingredients, so don't think it won't matter if you leave out the herbs, or the garlic, or the saffron. It will.

If you don't have lobsters, try using 2kg (4 lb) of uncooked blue swimmer crabs or yabbies. The flavour will be different — slightly sweeter — but very good.

Rich mushroom soup

Serves 8 people

250g (8 oz) fresh mushrooms
100g (3½ oz) dried cèpes
25g (¾ oz) dried morels
1 medium onion
1 garlic clove
2 sprigs parsley
75g (2½ oz) butter
250ml (8 fl oz) light white chicken stock
salt and freshly ground black pepper to taste
2 egg yolks
1 tablespoon flour
600ml (13 fl oz) cream
1 tablespoon liqueur muscat
200ml (6 fl oz) crème fraîche
a little finely chopped parsley for garnish

Soak the dried cèpes and morels in a cup of water each and set to one side for 20 minutes.

Chop the onion, garlic and parsley, and fry gently in 50g (1¾ oz) of the butter until soft and golden. Stir in the washed and chopped fresh mushrooms and cook for several minutes until their juices run. Now add the soaked mushrooms along with 1½ cups of the water they were soaked in. (This water must first be filtered very carefully through a fine cloth.) Add the chicken stock as well, season with the salt and pepper, and simmer gently for 5 minutes.

Purée everything in a food processor or pass through a sieve by hand.

Whisk the egg yolks into 300ml (10 fl oz) of the cream and stir into the mushroom mixture.

Melt the remaining butter, and when it is foaming, stir in the flour to make a smooth roux. Add the remaining 300ml (10 fl oz) of cream gradually to the roux, stirring all the while until the mixture is smooth and thick. Pour this thickened cream into the mushroom mixture and return to the stove for the final seasoning.

Stir in the liqueur muscat and crème fraîche and extra salt and pepper, if necessary.

TO SERVE

Ladle into bowls and sprinkle fine parsley over. Accompany with a basket of tiny hot fresh brioche rolls. (With their characteristic fluted shape they look like little mushrooms.)

Mushroom and Muscat Soup

Serves 8 people

500g (16 oz) big dark cultivated or field mushrooms
1 large onion
1 medium potato
4 green shallot tops
4 sprigs parsley
75g (2½ oz) butter
50ml (1½ fl oz) liqueur muscat (and a little extra at serving time)
salt to taste and freshly ground black pepper
600ml (19 fl oz) cream
a little cream and parsley for garnish

Wash the mushrooms, peel and trim the stalks if necessary. (Quite often, if they are cultivated, this is not necessary.) Chop up roughly.

Peel, wash and chop the onion and potato. Slice the shallot tops and parsley and stew in the butter until soft.

Stir in the mushrooms, season with salt and pepper, and cook in their juices for about 10 minutes — until everything is tender.

Add the muscat and boil for a couple of minutes, than add half the cream.

Purée in a food processor or sieve by hand. Add the remaining 300ml (9 fl oz) cream at the end, and adjust the seasoning if necessary.

TO SERVE

Ladle the soup into hot bowls and top with a teaspoon of whipped cream. Accompany with a small glass of the muscat for your guests to drink as they enjoy the soup.

Mussel and Vegetable Soup

Serves 6 people

2 kg (4lb) black mussels (cultivated are best)
50ml (1½ fl oz) mussel liquid
1 small head fennel
2 spring onions
1 medium carrot
12 English spinach leaves
4 tablespoons fennel leaves, chopped
1 clove garlic
500ml (16 fl oz) cream
knob butter
freshly ground black pepper
6 slices white bread
butter/peanut oil for frying

Clean the mussels well. Scrub and remove the beard. Put them in a baking pan or fish kettle one-third filled with simmering water. Cover with the lid and cook until the mussels open. Discard broken ones or any that remain closed. Strain and reserve 50ml (1½ fl oz) of the liquid. Shell the mussels, wash and set aside.

Cut away the underside of the fennel and slice the bulb into fine slivers.

Slice finely both the green and white parts of the spring onions.

Cut the sides of the carrot square, and slice into fine ribbons. A potato peeler can be used for this.

Wash the spinach leaves.

Put the fennel leaves, the peeled and chopped garlic clove, and the cream together in a blender. When smooth, put into a saucepan and boil until thick. Melt the butter in a saucepan and stir in the fennel and onion first of all. Cook gently to soften, then add the carrot ribbons and last of all the spinach. Moisten with the mussel liquid. Cook for a further minute, then stir in the mussels and some black pepper.

Pour over the thickened cream mixture and bring to the boil. Adjust the seasoning if necessary.

Remove the crusts from the bread and cut into small dice. Fry golden brown in the hot butter/peanut oil.

TO SERVE

Ladle the soup into hot bowls and pass a dish of the golden croûtons around separately.

Note: This soup is almost a meal in itself, so take care not to make the portions too large if it is only part of your menu.

Mussel soup

Serves 6 people

2 kg (4 lb) mussels (small and locally cultivated if possible)
1 medium white onion
2 medium carrots
1 stalk celery
2 medium potatoes
1 clove garlic
mixed fresh herbs, such as basil, chervil, tarragon
2 sprigs parsley
½ head fennel or ⅓ teaspoon fennel seeds
100g (3½ oz) butter
1 tablespoon peanut oil

250ml (8 fl oz) dry white wine
500ml (16 fl oz) fish stock
500ml (16 fl oz) mussel liquid (the water the mussels are steamed in)
freshly ground black pepper
pure saffron threads, a generous pinch
200ml (6 fl oz) crème fraîche
800ml (25 fl oz) cream

Scrub the mussel shells and discard those that are open and you suspect dead. Sometimes a mussel with a slightly open shell is still alive, and will close again if knocked, so test the ones you are not sure about. Take a large pan with a lid and put the cleaned mussels inside. Fill with clean cold water so that it comes about one-third of the way up the sides of the mussels. Put on the lid, bring to the boil and, giving the mussels a good shake around every so often, steam them open.

As soon as they open, take them out of the pot and hold under cold running water so that you can remove the mussels easily. Make sure that they are free of all the beard and the tiny crabs that sometimes lurk inside. Put the cleaned mussels into a bowl and reserve. If the mussels are slightly undercooked at this stage it doesn't matter as they will be cooked further when the soup is reheated. It is far better to be underdone than overcooked, shrunken, and rubbery.

Filter the water in which the mussels were cooked through a fine sauce sieve lined with muslin or some other fine-weave suitable cloth. Reserve 500ml (16 fl oz).

Wash, chop and fry all the vegetables and herbs in the first list of ingredients in the combined butter/oil for 5 minutes. Stir every so often so that they don't catch on the bottom.

Add the white wine and reduce by half.

Add the fish stock and mussel liquid* and simmer until everything is soft. Purée everything in a food processor, then pass through a fine sieve. Add the pepper and saffron, then the crème fraîche and cream.

TO SERVE

Warm the mussels in the soup. Pile some in the centre of each bowl, and pour the hot soup over. Accompany with toasted rounds of *baguette*.

JERUSALEM ARTICHOKE SOUP

Serves 6-8 people

750g (24 oz) peeled Jerusalem artichokes
1 white of leek
1 medium carrot
1 spring onion
1 medium potato
3 sprigs parsley
1 clove garlic
1 cup dry white wine
50g (1¾ oz butter)
1 teaspoon salt and pepper
2½ cups cream
a little whipped cream and sprigs chervil to garnish

Peel, chop and wash all the vegetables. Melt the butter in the bottom of a large soup pot. Stir in the vegetables, with the parsley, salt and pepper, and cook for a couple of minutes, until everything is coated with the butter and golden.

Add the wine and boil until it is almost entirely evaporated. Cover everything with cold water, and bring back to the boil, then adjust to a gentle simmer and cover with a lid. Cook until the vegetables are very tender.

Purée the vegetables and cooking juices in a food processor, then pass through a sieve. Stir in the cream and adjust the seasoning if necessary. Bring back to the boil and serve with a teaspoon of whipped cream and some tiny sprigs of chervil.

---

*A word of warning about the mussel liquid. It is very important to *taste* it before adding to the soup. If it is *too salty* use only a little and make up the rest of the liquid with fish stock. Remember, you can always add a little more, until you have added the entire 500ml (16 fl oz), but you can't get rid of the taste of too much salt.

OX TAIL CONSOMMÉ, ACCOMPANIED BY A LITTLE OX TAIL PIE WITH A MUSTARD BEURRE BLANC

Serves 8 people

FOR THE CONSOMMÉ
3kg (6 lb) ox tail, sliced
1 large onion
1 large carrot
1 stalk celery
4 stalks parsley
1 teaspoon peppercorns
salt to taste
6 litres (192 fl oz) cold water
12 egg whites

TO GARNISH
some sliced bone marrow*
some fine strands of carrot and leek

FOR THE PIES
200g (7 oz) puff pastry (approximately)
egg wash (1 yolk beaten with 1 teaspoon water)
1 ox tail, chopped
1 medium white onion
150g (5 oz) mushrooms
2 teaspoons fresh thyme leaves
3 tablespoons good port
knob butter
salt and pepper
vegetable or light veal stock to cover
8 very small fluted brioche tins

FOR THE MUSTARD BEURRE BLANC
125ml (4 fl oz) beurre blanc (see recipe on page 28)
1 tablespoon Dijon mustard
1 tablespoon cream

Prepare the consommé. Chop and wash all the listed vegetables and put into the bottom of a roasting pan. Put the sliced ox tail all over and roast until the meat is well browned. Scrape it all into a large pot and cover with cold water. Deglaze the roasting pan with some of the water, making sure that you scrape up all the brown residue on the bottom of the pan. Add all this to the pot. Bring to the boil, then simmer gently for 8 hours, or overnight. Skim regularly to remove the scum which rises to the surface. Strain, rest and remove any surface fat carefully with a ladle. Boil to reduce until only *3 litres*

(9f fl oz) remains or until the liquid is as rich as you wish the final soup to be. After boiling, let the liquid cool completely. Remove the last globules of fat using paper tissues to blot the surface.

When the liquid is quite cold, clarify. The method of clarification is explained on page 26. You should end up with about 2½ litres (80 fl oz) of beautifully clear liquid which, if refrigerated, will set into a golden jelly.

For the ox tail pies, put the chopped ox tail into a small casserole with a little knob of butter and brown. Season with salt and pepper, cover with the stock, put the lid on and cook in a moderate 180°C (350°F) oven for 3-4 hours until the meat is very tender and falling away from the bone.

Take the meat out of the liquid, and when cool enough to handle pull the meat off the bones. Put the meat to one side and discard the bones. Reserve 150ml (5 fl oz) of the cooking liquid for the filling. Strain and keep the rest for another purpose.

Gently fry the chopped onion with the mushroom, thyme, salt and pepper. When soft, and the mushrooms have released their juices, stir in the ox tail meat, the reserved liquid and the port. Boil to thicken. Check that the seasoning is just right, then purée briefly, so that the mixture is still *roughish* in texture. Cool.

Roll out the pastry and cut circles to fit the tops of the brioche tins. Roll the pastry again, and line the base of the tins. With the remaining scraps, roll little balls the size of peas between the palms of the hands. Chill all these pastry bits and pieces on a tray for ½ an hour before proceeding.

Fill the pie bases with the meat mixture. Score the tops with decorative markings and place on top of each pie and press the edges together firmly all around. Brush the tops with the egg wash and stick the little balls on top. Chill again until it is almost time to serve. (The pies are best cooked and served straight away.)

To prepare the garnish, slice some very fine strands of leek and carrot. Blanch and set aside. Slice the bone marrow into rounds.

To prepare the sauce, whisk the beurre blanc, cream and mustard together in a pan and bring to the boil for about 1 minute.

TO COOK AND SERVE

Bake the pies for 10-15 minutes at 200°C (400°F) until golden brown. Take them out of the tins straight away. Ladle a little of the sauce into the centre of small-sized serving plates (the size of bread and butter plates) and place a pie in the centre of each one. In the meantime bring the consommé to the boil. Put the marrow in a slotted spoon and poach in the hot liquid until tender. Ladle the consommé into bowls, garnish with the poached marrow and vegetable strands, and accompany with the little pies on the separate side plates.

---

*Every so often I buy 2 or 3 kilos of good marrow bones from my butcher. I let them sit at room temperature just long enough for the marrow to soften (without melting), so that I can gently push it out of the bone with my finger. I then parcel up small quantities of the marrow in plastic bags and freeze them until needed.

SALADS

In my 1894 edition of Cassell's *New Universal Cookery Book* by Lizzie Heritage, Holder of First-Class Diplomas in Cookery and Domestic Economy, the chapter on 'Salads and Salad Dressings' begins with the thought that salad making was never considered an art in England. What a relief! I can now put down my own early lack of familiarity, even nervousness, with oils and salad making in general, to my Anglo-Saxon origins, clouded from the beginnings as it seems in ignorance of the art. As one other late nineteenth-century writer summed up the miserable state of the English salad, blaming it on 'careless drying, sousing with vinegar and lack of oil', it is obvious that neither we, nor our English ancestors, were brought up on the edge of olive groves.

My mother and grandmother both detest oils, and unlike my own daughter who happily consumed anything at age three, as long as it had a nice vinaigrette, my own experience has been a slow growing familiarity with something other than the established dreary combination of iceberg lettuce, canned beetroot, sliced cucumber, tomato and onion rings, topped with blobs of strangely white commercial mayonnaise — or nothing at all. Now, my old wooden salad bowl, blackened with oil and much use, is a regular sight on the evening dinner table.

Lizzie Heritage points out that it is harder to give 'cut and dried recipes' for salads than for anything else. As Larousse defines them, they can be made up of virtually anything, and as we *compose* them, using what is best, fresh and in season, the Larousse definition and Lizzie's observation seems to be most definitely the case. In putting together the 'recipes' which follow for salads I have aimed at a variety of oils and vinegars as much as anything else, with best quality *virgin olive oil* remaining the all important one. There is no end to what can be used in salad. It all relies very much on individual taste.

My husband is an optimist. He believes everything keeps on improving, and as regards the attitude to food and cooking in this country, he is right. Where once there was an iceberg lettuce and not much else in our fruit and vegetable shops, now we find boxes of exquisitely tender lambs lettuce (mâche), several varieties of radicchio (chicory), from the variegated to the deep reds and purples and the baby 'sugar loaf' seedlings, large leafed cos, soft leafed mignonette and butter lettuces, rocket (wild chicory), witloof, and curly endive (though it is only the pale undershoots of this plant that I find usable).

As to the washing and drying of the leaves, let us go back for a moment to our knowledgeable author of yesteryear. 'After washing, to avoid breaking the leaves, either put the lettuce in a clean cloth, and take it by the four corners, and swing it round and round until all traces of moisture are lost, or, what is better, but it in a wire basket (a frying basket will answer for want of better) and subject it to the same treatment; these are of wire, globe-shaped, with a narrow neck, so that the salad cannot with ordinary care fall out during swinging.' And I thought I was so modern with my new Zyliss salad drying basket. It just goes to show that there has never been an excuse for those sodden leaves that we sadly sometimes find floating in their own washing water.

Mussel soup, page 49.

Fine onion and prosciutto tart, page 32.

Duck liver and currant custard, page 86.

A salad of grilled goats cheese and sweetbreads, page 68; and a Warm salad of baby red mullet fillets with artichokes and eggplant, page 59.

Poached egg and asparagus salad, page 64.

Pan fried cubes of tuna with the cream of red capsicums, page 75.

Medallions of lobster with little vegetables in a lime sauce, page 79.

Scrambled eggs with grilled brioche and school prawns, page 89.

LOBSTER AND PEAR SALAD

Serves 4 people

1 × 1kg (1 × 2 lb) live lobster
2 small pears
¼ cup sugar
selected salad greens (choose 3 or 4 varieties of the best quality tender undershoots of curly endive, watercress, tiny red leaves of radicchio, lambs lettuce, slivers of witloof or broken pieces of butter lettuce)
1 large red tomato
1 tablespoon chives, finely sliced
50ml (1½ fl oz) concentrated lobster stock
200ml (6 fl oz) cream
pinch salt and freshly ground black pepper
1 teaspoon lemon juice

FOR THE PLAIN DRESSING
125ml (4 fl oz) peanut oil
25ml (¾ fl oz) cider vinegar
1 teaspoon Dijon mustard
¼ teaspoon each salt and pepper

Prepare the live lobster in the manner already described on page 45, only this time cook the tail for 15 minutes to ensure that the meat is cooked all the way through. The meat should just change from being transparent to translucent. Cool by plunging into cold water, and shell immediately. Slice in neat medallions onto a plate, cover with clear plastic and refrigerate.

Put the peeled pears with the sugar into a saucepan and add enough water to cover. Boil until just tender, cut in half, take out the core, and chop into dice.

Peel the tomato, remove the seeds, and using the outer part only, slice into fine dice.

Make the lobster cream by combining the lobster stock with 150ml (5 fl oz) of the cream. Boil for approximately 1 minute to a thickened sauce consistency. Cool. Into the remaining 50ml (1 fl oz) of cream add the pepper, salt and the lemon juice.

Wash and dry the salad leaves.

Put all the ingredients for the dressing into a bowl and whisk to combine thoroughly.

TO SERVE

At one end of the plate pile the selected well-dressed leaves. At the other, a pile of pear dice topped with the lobster medallions. At each side of the plate place a small pile of tomato dice mixed with the chives and a little of the dressing. Drizzle the lobster cream over some of the medallions, the salad leaves and across the plate. Follow with a scant drizzling of the seasoned cream. Serve at once.

SALAD OF MUD CRAB WITH LEMON AND CORIANDER DRESSING

Ingredients for 6 people

2 live mud crabs weighing around 1kg (2 lb) each
1 red capsicum
2 ripe tomatoes
salt and freshly ground black pepper
2 soft leaf lettuce, such as butter lettuce, Roman lettuce,
or mignonette (you can use one of each kind)
1 small radicchio (red chicory)
1 large ripe avocado
6 tablespoons chives, very finely sliced

LEMON AND CORIANDER DRESSING
200ml (6 fl oz) lemon juice
2 tablespoons fresh coriander, finely chopped
2 tablespoons peanut oil
1 teaspoon soy sauce
2 teaspoons sweet sherry
2 tablespoons fresh ginger, finely chopped
1 teaspoon cracked black peppercorns

Make the dressing the day before so that it can mascerate for 24 hours. Mix all the listed ingredients together. After 24 hours, strain and discard the debris.

Make sure your crabs are well and truly alive, as the meat of a dead mud crab deteriorates very quickly. Quieten them by putting them into the freezer for an hour, then plunge into boiling water. Bring back to the boil and continue cooking for 10 minutes. Put into a bowl of cold water and shell. This is a messy and in many ways tedious operation, but one that your guests will thank you for. I use a kitchen mallet to crack the large claws and my hands and a small knife to empty the smaller legs. Lift up the little triangular flap on the underbelly side, and pull back to take off the upper shell. Remove also the soft, feathery 'petals' inside, rinse and break the body open. Now carefully take the meat from all the little cavities, and when every bit of crab has been put into a bowl, pick it over thoroughly to make sure there are no small pieces of shell or other debris mixed in by mistake. This often happens, no matter how careful you might have been. Chill.

Blister the skin of the capsicum, peel, remove the core and all the seeds, then slice and chop into fine dice.

Make a spicy tomato mixture. Drop the tomatoes into boiling water for one minute, then hold under cold running water and peel the skins. Cut open to remove the seeds and the stem end, then discard. Chop the tomatoes into small pieces and season with lots of freshly ground black pepper and some salt. Squeeze out any excess water. Chill.

Wash and dry thoroughly all the lettuce leaves. Break into quarters and chill.

TO SERVE

Make a fine julienne of the radicchio. Toss the other salad leaves with some of the dressing. Make certain every leaf is dressed without being drenched. Arrange them in the centre of serving plates. Slice the avocado into thin strips and arrange in the centre of the leaves. Divide the crab meat into 6 equal portions, squeeze into 'balls' and place in the centre of each salad. Spoon more dressing over the crab, and arrange 3 teaspoons of the spicy tomato about the crab. Scatter the radicchio and sprinkle everything with the fine chives and red capsicum dice.

MUD CRAB AND MANGO SALAD

Serves 4 people

1×1 kg (2lb) live mud crab
1 ripe mango
1 ripe avocado
assortment of salad leaves, such as mignonette, lambs lettuce, watercress, sorrel
sprigs of fresh chervil

SWEET ORANGE DRESSING
¼ cup fresh orange juice
½ cup peanut oil
1 tablespoon lemon juice
1 teaspoon grain mustard
1 teaspoon sugar
salt and pepper to taste

Kill, cook and shell the mud crab as described on page 56. Pick over the crab meat thoroughly to make certain that there are no bits of shell remaining.

Prepare the dressing by whisking all the ingredients together until they are thoroughly combined.

Peel and slice both the mango and avocado into long thin strips.

Wash and dry the salad leaves.

TO SERVE

Arrange the salad leaves on serving plates along with some of the mango and avocado ribbons. Squeeze the crab meat into a ball and pile in the centre. Arrange some more avocado and mango around. Spoon the dressing over everything and scatter with sprigs of chervil.

SALAD OF FRESH TUNA WITH BRAISED VEGETABLES

Serves 8 people

1kg (2 lb) fresh tuna, in 1 piece
2 large carrots
1 large onion
6 button mushrooms
6 medium red tomatoes
1 clove garlic
3 sprigs parsley, leaves only
3 sprigs thyme, leaves only
3 sprigs marjoram, leaves only
assorted salad leaves (for example, lambs lettuce, baby radicchio, butter lettuce)
pinch salt and freshly ground black pepper
olive oil

FOR THE CHERVIL AND LEMON DRESSING
125ml (4 fl oz) virgin olive oil
50ml lemon juice (1 juicy lemon)
2 tablespoons chervil, finely chopped
¼ teaspoon each salt and pepper

Skin the tuna and cut away any little bones and white fibres.

Peel and slice the carrots and onion. Quarter the mushrooms. Blanch, peel, de-seed and chop the tomatoes. Chop the garlic and herbs into small pieces.

Put a little olive oil into the bottom of a heavy baking pan. Stir in all the vegetables and fry to soften and colour. Add the herbs, salt and pepper, and put the piece of tuna on top. Pour a little more oil over, cover with foil, and bake at 190°C (375°F) for 30-45 minutes. The timing will depend on the thickness of the slab of tuna. If it is cut from near the tail, it will not be as thick as a piece taken from near the head and should be ready in 30 minutes. Cut a slice to test if you are in doubt. When done, put to one side to cool.

Prepare the salad leaves: select, wash and dry, then chill.

Prepare the dressing: put all the ingredients in a bowl and whisk until thoroughly combined.

TO SERVE

Slice the tuna. Put one slice in the centre of each serving plate. Spoon the braised vegetables around the tuna, and the salad leaves around the vegetables. Spoon some dressing over everything.

WARM SALAD OF BABY RED MULLET FILLETS WITH ARTICHOKE AND EGG PLANT

Ingredients for 4 people

12 baby red mullet (otherwise known as rouget or barbounia)
6 globe artichokes
1 egg plant (enough for 4 slices per person)
1 medium carrot
1 tablespoon peanut oil
knob butter
a little olive oil for frying the fish fillets
2 anchovy fillets
4 toasted croûtons, made with 1 slice of white bread
4 sprigs chervil

FOR THE CHIVE AND LEMON DRESSING
125ml (4 fl oz) virgin olive oil
50ml (1½ fl oz) lemon juice (1 juicy lemon)
2 tablespoons fine chives
¼ teaspoon salt and freshly ground black pepper

Put all the ingredients for the dressing in a bowl and whisk until well combined. Store in a lidded glass jar.

Scale, fillet and de-bone the fish. This is the worst part of the entire operation. It is a bit like cleaning goldfish. After filleting, make sure any remaining bones are pulled out with tweezers or your fingertips. Wash very well.

Before throwing the bones away, open the gut, pull out the tiny livers, and reserve.

Cook the artichokes whole in boiling salted water until tender. Peel off the outer leaves, trim the heart, and remove the hairy choke.

Slice the egg plant into 1cm (½ in) rounds. Salt and leave to drain for ½ hour. Wash the salt off and pat dry. Peel and slice the carrot thinly on the slant. Put the butter and peanut oil together in a frypan, heat, and when sizzling, fry the egg plant slices golden brown on both sides. Drain well and cool. Fry the carrot slices briskly so that they are just beginning to soften but are still *crunchy*.

Fry the fish livers briskly and briefly, then mash them well with the anchovy fillets. Spread this mixture onto the croûtons and garnish with a chervil sprig.

TO SERVE

Slice 1½ artichoke hearts onto each serving plate. Place the egg plant and carrot slices on top and spoon over the dressing.

At the last minute, panfry the fish fillets. Put a little olive oil in the bottom of the frypan, and when it is sizzling fry the fillets, skin side down to start. Cook very briefly on both sides, allowing about 15 seconds per side. Remember that they are very tiny and if you overcook them they will fall to bits. Put 6 cooked fillets per person on top of the dressed vegetables, pop a croûton on top, and serve at once.

Note: This salad is a bit fiddly to make, but having once spent a morning at the restaurant filleting 5kg (10 lb) of the little monsters, 12 fish does not seem so bad. The hard part comes right at the end, when you have to cook and serve them and make sure everything gets to the table hot and in place. My advice is to do no more than 2 plates at a time and to do them well. It's worth the effort.

These red mullet are no relation to the grey-coloured mullet common to the Australian fish market and Sydney fish and chip shops. They are a superb, delicate, fine-tasting fish, very similar in fact to the excellent pig fish that I describe in another recipe.

Salad of Spring Vegetables with Sweet Currant and Green Peppercorn Dressing

Serves 4 people

12 spears fresh asparagus
4 globe artichokes
1 cup broad beans (podded and peeled)
4 small leeks, the white only
2 medium carrots
1 celery stalk
12 snake beans

FOR THE DRESSING
⅔ cup virgin olive oil
⅓ cup white wine vinegar
2 tablespoons Dijon mustard
2 tablespoons lemon juice
2 teaspoons castor sugar
2 teaspoons green peppercorns
2 tablespoons currants
¼ teaspoon each salt and pepper

Prepare the vegetables. Snap the ends off the asparagus spears and peel away some of the lower leaves with a knife. Blanch and drain. They should be tender, but still with *crunch*. Remember after cooking to refresh them in iced water so as to preserve their lovely fresh green colour.

Boil the artichokes — stems and all — in salted water until tender. This will take about 20 minutes. Peel off the outer leaves and scoop out the hairy choke. Peel the rough outer skin of the stems to a tapering point. You should be left with a neatly trimmed heart with just a few tender inner leaves still attached.

Wash the leeks thoroughly, so as to be absolutely free of all sand and grit. Boil in salted water until tender for about 10 minutes. Refresh in iced water.

Slice the carrot into 2 x 1cm (2 x ½in) batons roughly the length of the asparagus spears. Blanch and drain.

Trim the celery stalk by slicing away the stringy bits cleanly and cutting the stem into large, rough-shaped triangles. Blanch and drain.

The broad beans should be both podded and peeled. Pod them first of all as you would peas, then peel off the coarse pale green outer skin from each individual bean. This will expose the tender emerald green heart of the bean. Blanch and drain.

Prepare the dressing by putting all the listed ingredients together in a bowl and whisking thoroughly to combine.

TO SERVE

Put a little of the dressing at a time into the bottom of a bowl. Dress the vegetables in turn, shaking off excess dressing, and arranging them haphazardly onto serving plates. Make sure each salad has its share of currants and peppercorns.

SALAD OF LAMBS TONGUES AND ROASTED CAPSICUMS WITH CUCUMBER AND MUSTARD

Serves 4 people

FOR THE TONGUES
12 fresh lambs tongues
1 small onion, chopped
1 medium carrot, chopped
1 celery stalk, chopped
1 parsley stalk, chopped
½ cup white vinegar
1 teaspoon pickling spices
water to cover

FOR THE CAPSICUMS
2 large red capsicums
2 tablespoons olive oil
2 large pinches salt and freshly ground black pepper

SALAD LEAVES
2 witloof (Belgian Endive)
some plain dressing (see recipe p. 55)

FOR THE CUCUMBER AND MUSTARD SAUCE
2 tablespoons grated cucumber
1 teaspoon capers
1 teaspoon pickled gherkin, finely sliced
2 tablespoons thick cream
2 tablespoons Dijon mustard
1 teaspoon champagne vinegar
¼ teaspoon each salt and black pepper

Prepare the tongues well in advance, preferably the day before. Put all the listed ingredients into a pot with water to cover. Bring to the boil, then simmer for 1½ hours. When the tongues are tender, take them out of the hot liquid and peel under cold running water (they are much easier to peel while still hot) and trim away most of the lumpish underneath part. Put the cleaned tongues into a bowl, cover with the strained cooking liquid, and refrigerate.

Quarter the capsicums. Take out the seeds and core, and lay skin side up in a roasting pan. Trickle the olive oil all over, season with salt and pepper, and roast at 190°C (375°F) for 10-15 minutes, until the skin blisters and the flesh is tender. Now peel off the skin and spread out the strips on kitchen paper to drain, and cool.

Grate the cucumber and leave it to drain for ½ hour. Put it into a bowl with all the other listed ingredients and combine thoroughly.

Wash and dry the witloof leaves and slice into fine strips. Toss in a little plain dressing.

TO SERVE

Divide the capsicum strips 4 ways and arrange on serving plates. Slice the tongues lengthwise into thin strips and arrange over the capsicum. Spoon the creamy cucumber sauce liberally over the tongues and top with the well-dressed slivers of witloof.

POACHED EGG AND ASPARAGUS SALAD

Ingredients per person

*1 egg
6 spears fresh asparagus
1 slice white bread
½ rasher bacon
a mixture of any of the following leaves, mignonette,
Roman lettuce, butter lettuce or curly endive (only the pale tender undershoots)
½ tablespoon chives, finely sliced
a little olive oil for frying*

*FOR THE VIRGIN OLIVE OIL DRESSING
1¼ cups virgin olive oil
¼ cup champagne vinegar (or a good quality white vinegar)
2 tablespoons Dijon mustard
¼ teaspoon each salt and pepper*

Prepare the dressing by placing the listed ingredients in a bowl and whisking until well combined. Store in a glass jar. Pick only the very best salad leaves, then wash and dry them thoroughly. Chill to keep crisp.

Trim the asparagus spears by snapping off the ends, and peeling off some of the lower leaves with a knife. Cook in boiling salted water for 3 minutes. Test by snipping a bit off the end of one. They should be *just tender*, still with a bit of crunch. Drain and refresh in a bowl of iced water to preserve the lovely green colour.

Cut the crusts off the bread and slice into tiny cubes. Fry these until golden brown in a little olive oil. Drain thoroughly.

Remove the fat and rind from the bacon, and cut into small dice. Fry until crisp.

Poach the egg. This can be done well ahead of time, thereby not only ensuring perfect eggs, but also saving a lot of last minute panic. Bring the pan of water to the boil, then return to a gentle simmer. Break the egg in and cook for only a minute, so that the white has set and the yolk is still soft. Lift out with a slotted spoon and put straight into a bowl of iced water to stop it cooking further. When completely cold, drain and trim the white neatly. Keep on a tray lined with kitchen paper, and cover with clear plastic wrap until needed.

TO ASSEMBLE THE SALAD

Toss the leaves and the asparagus in a bowl with some of the dressing. Make sure every leaf is well dressed without being saturated.

At the same time warm the egg briefly in a pan of hot water.

Arrange the leaves and asparagus on a serving plate, put the well drained poached egg on top, and sprinkle everything with fried bread cubes, bacon and chives. Make sure there is a pepper mill containing fresh black peppercorns ready to pass around.

Warm Winter Vegetable Salad

Ingredients per person

the white part of 1 small leek
4 medium Jerusalem artichokes
¼ cup sliced green beans
¼ ripe avocado
a little butter
½ teaspoon salt
freshly ground black pepper

FOR THE SWEET GRAIN MUSTARD DRESSING
⅔ cup virgin olive oil
⅓ cup cider vinegar
2 tablespoons grain mustard
2 tablespoons lemon juice
¼ teaspoon each salt and pepper
2 teaspoons castor sugar

Prepare the leeks and artichokes ready for roasting. Wash the leeks thoroughly, then peel and wash the artichokes. Place them together in a buttered roasting pan, dust with pepper and salt, and roast until tender. (Remember that the leeks will cook more quickly than the artichokes and should be removed as soon as they are ready.)

Blanch the beans and drain well.

Peel and slice the avocado into strips. Slice the leek into pieces the same length as the beans. These vegetables will cool to room temperature.

Prepare the dressing. Put all the listed ingredients together in a bowl and whisk until they are thoroughly combined.

TO SERVE

As soon as the artichokes are cooked, slice them in half lengthwise, and arrange the salad. Put the avocado slices in the centre of each plate, pile the leeks on top, then the beans and finally the warm artichoke halves. Spoon the dressing all over and serve at once.

SALAD OF HARE SADDLE WITH HARE PÂTÉ, PICKLED VEGETABLES AND HAZELNUT TOAST

Serves 4 people

This recipe has a multitude of components. Don't let this deter you, but perhaps it's best to forge ahead only if you feel like spending several hours in the kitchen.

1 fresh hare
knob butter
salt and freshly ground black pepper

FOR THE PÂTÉ
the back legs of the hare, stewed
200ml (6 fl oz) of the stewing liquid, having been reduced and strained
150g (5 oz) butter
1 medium onion
200g (7 oz) lean bacon
1 teaspoon juniper berries
2 teaspoons each thyme, sage, fresh rosemary
250g (8 oz) chicken livers
150ml (5 fl oz) cream
1 teaspoon each salt and pepper
2 teaspoons cognac
2 teaspoons truffle juice (optional)

FOR THE PICKLED VEGETABLES
1 cup white vinegar
1 cup water
1 teaspoon rock salt
1 teaspoon brown sugar
1 bay leaf
pinch mace
1 teaspoon cloves
8 little cauliflower flowerettes
4 pickling onions
4 radishes
1 small carrot
1 teaspoon turmeric

FOR THE HAZELNUT LOAF
250g (8 oz) plain flour
10g (½ oz) fresh yeast
250ml (8 fl oz) milk, warmed to blood temperature
1 egg, beaten
150g (5 oz) hazelnuts, chopped
pinch salt

FOR THE HAZELNUT DRESSING
1 cup hazelnut oil
4 tablespoons lemon juice
2 teaspoons Dijon mustard
¼ teaspoon each salt and white pepper

FOR THE SALAD LEAVES
assorted leaves, such as the tender undershoots of curly endive with a little watercress

The hare is prepared exactly as described in the recipe on page 153. The legs are marinated for 24 hours then stewed ready for making the pâté. The saddle is trimmed, left on the bone and roasted rare, only this time when the cooked saddle rests, allow it to cool completely.

TO MAKE THE PÂTÉ

Melt the butter in a pan and add the chopped onion, bacon, herbs and junipers, then fry gently until the onion is soft and golden. Now add the trimmed chicken livers. Cook for a couple of minutes only so that they remain pink inside. Purée the hot mixture briefly with the cream so that the pieces are small, but not smooth. In a food processor, use an on/off movement. Transfer the mixture to a bowl.

Now pull the leg meat off the bone and put it into the food processor with the reduced liquid from the stew. Purée for only a couple of seconds so that the meat is shredded but not smooth. Alternatively, you can pull the meat into fine stringy bits using two forks.

Combine the two mixtures in the bowl, adjust the seasoning and add the cognac (and the truffle juice if you desire). Refrigerate.

FOR THE PICKLED VEGETABLES

Make up a pickling mixture of equal quantities white vinegar and water, with the rock salt, brown sugar, bay leaf, mace and cloves. Blanch the vegetables separately in this mixture. When done they should still have *crunch*. Refresh in iced water, then cover with the cold pickling mixture in separate bowls. Add the turmeric to the cauliflower mixture. The onions and radishes are cooked whole, but later to be sliced in half. The cauliflower is trimmed into little sprigs, and the carrot is cut into Chinese flowers. To do this, peel the carrot, make several grooves lengthwise down the carrot, using a canneleur tool, then slice into rounds.

TO PREPARE THE LOAF

Mix the yeast with the milk, then stir in the beaten egg and add the sugar, flour, hazelnuts and a pinch of salt. Butter a small loaf tin. Put the mixture in and leave to rise in a warm place for about 30 minutes. Bake at 190°C (375°F) for 40 minutes, until the loaf is done and a golden brown. This loaf is usually prepared a day or two in advance. When a few days old, it slices thinly and has a particularly good flavour. You can substitute walnuts or pecan nuts for the hazelnuts if you prefer.

Put all the ingredients for the dressing together in a bowl and whisk to combine them smoothly.

Wash and dry the carefully selected salad greens.

TO SERVE

Slice the meat from the saddle into long thin strips and arrange on serving plates. Spoon a generous dollop of the pâté alongside, a selection of the pickled vegetables, and the well-dressed salad greens. Dress the strips of meat sparingly with some of the hazelnut dressing as well. Accompany the salad with thin slices of toasted hazelnut loaf.

Note: If you are particularly enterprising, you might like to add a spoonful of game or brown chicken jelly to this salad — but after all this, I hardly dare to mention it.

SALAD OF GRILLED GOATS CHEESE AND SWEETBREADS

Ingredients per person

2 × 1cm (2 × ½ in) slices goats cheese
2 tablespoons veal sweetbreads, trimmed and diced
assorted salad leaves, such as butter lettuce, radicchio, watercress, baby sorrel
salt and freshly ground black pepper
2 tablespoons butter
2 tablespoons peanut oil
6 × 2cm (6 × ¾ in) square croûtons (made from stale baguette slices)
1 tablespoon bacon fat, chopped
1 clove garlic, crushed
4 small oyster mushrooms (or the equivalent in slices from larger mushrooms)
3 cherry tomatoes

WALNUT DRESSING
(enough for 8 salads)
1 cup walnut oil
4 tablespoons lemon juice
2 teaspoons Dijon mustard
¼ teaspoon each salt and white pepper
4 tablespoons walnut pieces

Prepare the salad leaves: wash and dry thoroughly.

Poach the sweetbreads in salted water for 15 minutes. Refresh in cold water, then trim away all the gristle and membranes. Slice into 2cm (¾ in) dice, season with a pinch of salt and pepper, and fry until crisp in a little of mixed butter and oil.

Prepare the croûtons. Remove the crusts from the stale loaf, then cut into chunky dice. Put the rest of the butter, bacon fat and garlic into a baking pan and cook gently on top of the stove for 5 minutes. Add the diced loaf and bake in a moderate 180°C (350°F) oven until crisp and golden. You will have to give the pan a good shake every so often.

Fry the oyster mushrooms, well seasoned with freshly ground salt and pepper, in the remaining hot oil until browned. Set to one side.

Put all the ingredients for the dressing in a bowl and whisk together until well combined.

TO COOK AND SERVE

Dress the salad leaves well—without saturating—and arrange on serving plates. Make sure a few walnut pieces are included. Put the slices of goats cheese onto a sheet of aluminium foil and place under a very hot pre-heated grill. Cook until the cheese softens and begins to form a golden, bubbling crust. Lift off the foil with a spatula and place on top of the leaves.

While the cheese is grilling, slice the cherry tomatoes in half and fry also—just for a minute—alongside the hot sweetbread dice. Sprinkle the tomato and sweetbread pieces over the salad, then the croûtons and the oyster mushrooms. Serve while the cheese is still nice and hot.

First courses

If you have ever had anything at all to do with the running of a restaurant, then you will know that most people have a liking, if not a yearning, for seafood. Of all the first courses served at *You and Me*, one of the most popular by far was the plate of fresh and marinated seafoods.

Sometimes we steamed mussels open, then grilled them with a creamy pale green mixture of breadcrumbs, parsley, chives and butter on top. Little squid were sliced into strips to be pan fried for seconds only in a garlic-flavoured olive oil and served with strips of roasted, marinated red and yellow capsicums. At other times we poached the squid in a bath of wine and vegetables until tender, then stuffed the tubes with a purée of spinach, mushrooms and pine nuts, and sliced and dressed them later on. The tiniest baby octopus were marinated in lemon juice and olive oil for 24 hours, then barbecued and dressed with a tangy lemon dressing. Fresh oysters were left on the half shell, green prawns roasted and salted, sardines pan fried and scallops thinly sliced and bathed in lime juice, pepper and parsley until they became 'cooked' and white.

These are the tastes of summer and the sea, but being a country girl at heart my tastes lie in another direction.

One of the loveliest and simplest first courses I ever served at *You and Me* was a plate of fresh cèpes and chanterelles, barbecued in strips, peppered and salted, and lying in their own buttery brown juices. It was autumn, and a Sunday expedition to the pine forests beyond the Blue Mountains (with another cook who knew just where to look) resulted in bag loads of these large orangey/brown coloured, spongy textured mushrooms, and surprised diners at the following Monday lunch. One of the loveliest first courses I have ever eaten was a dish of simply sautéed fresh bolet mushrooms. It was served at Girardet's restaurant at Crissier in Switzerland. I must not forget another, late last year, at Boyer's restaurant *Les Crayeres* at Reims in France, a fricassé of girolles with chives and butter.

When I was growing up, we used to make an entire meal of field mushrooms which we picked ourselves and brought home in billy cans complete with bits of grass, twigs and other clinging bits. We stewed them first in butter with lots of pepper and salt, then added a sprinkling of flour. Milk was poured on and boiled up. The thick white sauce was turned *grey* by the blackness of the strongly flavoured fungi, and we ate ladlefuls on bread and butter. Hence the medley of mushrooms came into being, a dish which can be transformed into a meal, if like me, you also like softly poached eggs and the combination of the hot broken yolks mingling with all the creamy mushroom juices.

RAVIOLI OF QUAIL, ROSEMARY AND GARLIC

Serves 6 people

1 basic pasta recipe (see recipe on page 214)
4 fresh quails
1 sprig rosemary, plus 1 teaspoon extra leaves
1 clove garlic
pinch salt
freshly ground black pepper
knob butter
cream, to soften

FOR THE SAUCE
1 cup cream
1 clove garlic
1 sprig rosemary
1 small chopped onion
salt, to taste
freshly ground black pepper

FOR THE QUAIL STOCK
1 small carrot
1 small white onion
½ stalk celery
a little red wine

Put the quails in a small buttered roasting pan with the broken sprig of rosemary, the peeled garlic clove chopped in half, the salt and pepper ground over the birds. Roast at 200°C (400°F) 10-15 minutes (depending on size). When the quails are done, remove from the pan, and when cool enough to handle, strip the flesh from the bones of the birds and reserve. Pour away all the excess fat and deglaze the pan with a little wine. Break up the bones and put into the pan along with all the chopped vegetables. Cover with cold water, bring to the boil, and simmer for 2 hours. When ready, strain and boil to reduce the liquid to 1 cup.

To complete the sauce, put the peeled, crushed garlic clove, the onion and the rosemary into the melted butter and cook until soft. Add the stock and cream, season with the salt and pepper, and boil until thick. Strain.

To prepare the filling, mince the quail meat with the teaspoonful of extra rosemary leaves, a little salt and pepper to season, add enough cream to make the mixture moist.

Prepare the pasta dough. Slice the ball of dough in half, and work with only half at a time. Roll out the dough into a long rectangular strip, as finely as possible. Cut the strip in half. Lay one strip on a lightly floured workbench and dot with heaped teaspoonfuls of filling at equal distances (I usually make two ravioli at a time by placing double rows of mixture close together, side by side). Flatten the mixture with the back of a spoon and place the other half strip of pasta over the top. Press down well, and cut out squares around each mound of filling, using a crinkly pie cutter. Repeat the procedure with the remaining piece of dough. Place the finished ravioli on a lightly floured tray—to prevent sticking—until you are ready to cook them. Cook by boiling in copius amounts of salted water for 10 minutes. Drain well.

Serve with the garlic cream sauce spooned over.

Note: I make these ravioli extra large, so that I obtain 12 in all, thus serving 2 per person.

HERE ARE SOME OTHER IDEAS

1. Ravioli filled with minced, left-over lobster meat mixed with chives, a little cream, salt and pepper to season, then served with a rich lobster sauce.
2. Ravioli filled with minced, cooked chicken livers and mushroom, mixed with some fresh herbs, a little cream, salt and pepper to season, and served with a cream sauce of morels.

SMOKED SALMON AND BASIL CREAM WITH FRESH PASTA NOODLES

Serves 4 people

1 recipe plain pasta noodles (see recipe on page 214)
8 slices smoked salmon
4 teaspoons beluga caviar for garnish

FOR THE BASIL CREAM
1 cup cream
2 teaspoons lemon juice
1 tablespoon basil leaves, finely shredded
1 tablespoon green shallot tops, finely sliced
pinch salt and pepper

Slice the salmon into strips.

Put all the ingredients for the sauce together in a saucepan and boil until it is thick. Cook the noodles in boiling salted water until just tender. This will only take a couple of minutes. Stir the salmon strips into the hot sauce, then toss the noodles in the sauce to coat them without saturating.

TO SERVE
Pile the noodles in the centre of hot serving plates and top with the caviar.

Rare Roasted Tuna with a Rosette of Potatoes and English Mustard

Ingredients for 6 people

1kg (2 lb) fresh tuna, in 1 piece
buttered roasting dish
1 teaspoon hot English mustard
2 tablespoons whipped cream

FOR THE ROSETTE OF POTATOES
6 small to medium potatoes
butter, softened
salt and freshly ground black pepper
1 tablespoon freshly grated parmesan cheese

Make the potato rosettes first. These can be cooked and kept on the baking tray until needed.

Slice the potato into fine rounds (almost transparent). Grease a baking tray well with some butter. Make a circle the size of a bread and butter plate with the overlapping potato slices, one on top of the other, in a circular manner, ending in the centre. Dot with little knobs of the softened butter, dust with salt and pepper, and sprinkle the parmesan all over.

Bake in a fairly hot oven at 200°C (400°F) until crisp and golden — about 30 minutes.

Trim the tuna by slicing away the leathery skin and any small bones and white fibrous threads. Cut the remaining piece into 6 even slices of about 100-125g (3½-4oz) each. Get your roasting dish nice and hot, with the butter sizzling, and put the tuna slices in. Roast for just 2 minutes on each side, so that the fish is still quite pink at the centre. (You can almost see the progress of the cooking with the red flesh turning white as it cooks.) The centre of the tuna will appear as a gradually narrowing red strip.

In the meantime, fold the mustard into the whipped cream.

TO SERVE

Tip the hot rosettes upside down onto the centre of each plate. Slice the tuna into thin strips and place across the potato. Garnish with the mustard cream and serve at once.

Note: Tuna is an exciting fish to work with. This recipe enhances its beef-like qualities. Remember, much of its beauty will be lost if it is *overcooked*.

PAN FRIED CUBES OF TUNA WITH THE CREAM OF RED CAPSICUMS

Ingredients for 6 people

enough fresh tuna for 6 people, about 1kg (2 lb)
butter
peanut oil
salt and freshly ground pepper

THE VEGETABLES
1 egg plant
1 medium white onion
4 small zucchini
1 fresh chilli
½ red capsicum
salt and pepper

THE SAUCE
2 cups fresh juice of red capsicums (about 6 medium capsicums)
1 medium white onion
1 cup fish stock
300ml (10 fl oz) cream
2 teaspoons lemon juice
knob butter
salt and pepper

Slice the capsicums into strips and scrape out the seeds. Force these through a juicing machine (or you can purée and sieve them).

Put the juice into a saucepan and boil until most of the water has evaporated.

Chop up the onion and fry in a little butter until soft. Add the fish stock and boil until all that remains is a golden film on the bottom of the pot. Add the cream to this and continue to boil until very thick.

Strain out the onions, pour through a very fine sauce sieve, and add the lemon juice. Finish with a knob of butter whisked in at the end (or a little *beurre blanc* if you happen to have some handy).

Cut all the vegetables into thin 'julienne' strips, using mainly the skin sections of the egg plant and zucchini, toss briskly in a scant mixture of oil and butter, season with salt and pepper, and set to one side.

Trim the tuna into neatly shaped cubes, 3-4cm (1¼-1½ in) across. Heat a little more butter and oil together in a frying pan, and when sizzling hot sauté the cubes of tuna on all sides very quickly, so as to be crispy brown on the outside and rare at the centre. This is a very short operation to be done at the very last minute, just as you are warming the sauce through ready to serve.

TO SERVE
Ladle and spread some of the sauce onto hot serving plates. Toss the

vegetables momentarily back into the hot oil, drain well, and put a little heap into the centre of each plate. Around this place the fried cubes of tuna, allowing 5 or 6 per person.

Mud crab omelette

Ingredients per person

2 heaped tablespoons mud crab meat (1 x 1kg (2 lb) live mud crab should be ample for 6 people)
pinch salt and freshly ground black pepper
cream to moisten (the amount will depend on how many omelettes you are making)
1 large egg
2 teaspoons cold water
1 heaped teaspoon butter
1 teaspoon green shallot tops, finely sliced

21cm (8½ in) omelette pan

Kill, cook and shell the crab (see page 77). Make sure that the meat has been thoroughly picked over, for there is nothing worse than biting onto an unseen bit of shell. Season the crab meat with the salt and pepper, and set aside until you are ready to cook the omelettes. This will barely take a minute.

TO COOK AND SERVE

Put the crab into a pan with just enough cream to moisten. Warm right through. Make the omelettes one at a time (or several at a time if you have enough pans). Whisk the egg with the water and salt and pepper. Melt the knob of butter in the bottom of the omelette pan, and when it is foaming, pour in the egg mixture. Swirl it around so that the entire bottom of the pan is coated. When it is almost cooked—leave the centre slightly runny—spoon the crab meat into the lower half. Sprinkle with the shallot tops, fold the top half of the omelette over, and serve at once.

This is a lovely, simple way to serve mud crab without in any way detracting from its very particular, delicate flavour.

INDIVIDUAL FINE CRAB TARTS WITH CRAB SAUCE

Ingredients for 6 people

1 x 1kg (2 lb) live mud crab (or any variety of crab you prefer that is NOT FROZEN OR IN A CAN), to yield
1 cup crab meat or thereabouts
puff pastry leftovers
1 small capsicum
3 medium mushrooms
3 tablespoons shallot tops, finely sliced
knob butter
pinch salt and pepper
3 tablespoons shredded basil leaves
½ cup concentrated crab stock (see recipe on page 44, substituting crab for lobster)
1 cup whipped cream
24 smallest size cherry tomatoes

The preparation of the tart base is the same as for all the other fine tarts included among these recipes. Roll the pastry very thinly and drape across a baking tray. Using the saucer of a teacup to trace around, cut out 6 circles. Prick all over with a fork and chill.

Kill and cook the crab the same way as you would a lobster. Put it in the freezer for about an hour before plunging into boiling water. Bring back to the boil and cook for 10-15 minutes (depending on the size). Cool the cooked crab under cold running water and, when cool enough to handle, shell. I have described how to do this on page 45. Reserve the meat in a bowl until needed. The rest of the tart can be prepared a few hours in advance.

Blister the skins of the capsicum and peel. Core and remove the seeds, then slice into fine strips.

Chop the mushrooms and put into a frypan with the shallots, butter and salt and pepper. Fry until soft. Drain, then spread over the pastry circles. Strew the red capsicum strips and the basil over, and bake at 180°C (360°F) until the pastry is crisp and golden — but not too well done. Remember that the tarts will be returned to the oven later.

Combine the crab stock with the cream, whisk together and bring to the boil. Taste, and adjust the seasoning if necessary.

TO COOK AND SERVE

Spread the crab meat over the tarts. Slice the cherry tomatoes in half and place 8 halves on each tart. Put the tarts back into the oven to warm the crab meat through. When ready, spoon the crab sauce *over the crab* (not the plate).
Note: The most time consuming part of all this is the crab sauce. That is why it is a good idea to make up batches of crab stock whenever you can and freeze it. By the way, lobster stock will do just as well.

LOBSTER AND MORELS IN PUFF PASTRY

Serves 6 people

1 x 750g (1 x 1½ lb) live lobster
½ cup dried morels
small knob butter
1 tablespoon shallot tops, finely sliced
2 teaspoons parsley, finely chopped, and a little extra for garnish
4 button mushrooms, sliced
pinch salt and freshly ground black pepper
¼ cup reserved 'morel water' (this is the water in which the morels are soaked)
1 tablespoon crème fraîche
½ cup cream
200g (6½ oz) puff pastry, approximately
egg wash (1 yolk beaten with 1 teaspoon water)

Cover the morels with clean cold water and soak until soft, approximately 30 minutes. Swirl around to rinse away any grit and sand.

Kill the lobster. Put it into the freezer for an hour, then plunge head first and upside down into boiling water. If you wish to save the head for stock making, remove the lobster from the boiling water once it has gone limp and it is dead. Sever the connecting tissues and pull away the head from the tail. Clean the head and reserve. Wrap the tail well in aluminium foil, and continue to boil for 5 minutes only. Cool under cold running water, and when it is cool enough to handle, shell, and refrigerate on a plate covered with clear plastic film. You will notice that it is neither raw nor cooked but at a stage in between.

To prepare the sauce, melt the butter in a pan and, when foaming, stir in the shallots, parsley, the sliced button mushrooms, and softened, drained morels all seasoned with salt and pepper. Cook until the mushrooms release their juices, and everything is nice and soft. Filter the ¼ cup water used for soaking the morels through muslin or kitchen paper towels. Add this to the pan and boil until all that remains is a film. Stir in the crème fraîche, then the cream, and boil until thick.

Roll out the pastry to 1 cm (½ in) thick and cut out desired shapes (I sometimes cut 7cm (2¾ in) circles). Brush the tops with egg wash, making sure that none runs down the sides of the pastry, then chill on a baking tray for ½ hour. Bake at 220°C (430°F) for 15-20 minutes, until they are nicely puffed and browned. If after this time they are still a bit moist in the centre, lower the oven temperature, and dry them out for a few more minutes. Cool, and set aside until needed. (These cooked shapes can be frozen as well, thawed briefly, and crisped in the oven when needed.)

TO SERVE

Slice the lobster tail into neat medallions. Put them into the hot sauce to complete the cooking — allow 2 minutes only on each side, otherwise the meat will shrivel and toughen. Put the bottom half of your pastry puffs on each hot serving plate, spoon lobster, mushrooms and sauce over, and top with the pastry lid. Sprinkle a little extra finely chopped parsley all over the sauce.
Note: Fresh asparagus tips can be added to this recipe, trimmed and blanched, and popped under the pastry lid with the lobster and mushrooms. Also, you may like to substitute yabbies, or fresh green prawns, for the lobster.

MEDALLIONS OF LOBSTER WITH LITTLE VEGETABLES IN A LIME SAUCE

Ingredients for 6 people

2 x 1kg (2 lb) live lobsters
2 medium carrots
3 small zucchini
½ cup fresh shelled peas
12 fresh asparagus tips
sprigs chervil to garnish

THE SAUCE
¼ cup green shallot tops, finely sliced
½ cup dry white wine
½ cup water
300ml (10 fl oz) cream
½ teaspoon each salt and white pepper
100g (3½ oz) unsalted butter
4 tablespoons fresh lime juice from approximately 2 juicy limes

Kill the lobsters. Put them in the freezer for an hour, then plunge headfirst down into boiling water, and leave to cook for 7-8 minutes. If you wish to keep the heads 'green' for making lobster stock (as I always do, for it's a shame to waste them), plunge the lobsters into the water for just a few minutes until they are dead (they will go limp) then remove and reserve the heads. Wrap the lobster in aluminium foil to protect the exposed delicate meat, and put back into the boiling water for the remaining minutes. Take out of the boiling water, plunge into iced water and shell immediately. The meat should be *half cooked* only, and still quite raw at the centre.

Refrigerate on a plate covered with clear plastic wrap until needed.

The little vegetables can also be prepared in advance. The carrots can be cut in several ways, 'turned' into tiny oval shapes, or sliced into 'flowers' using a canneleur tool to make grooves lengthwise down the carrot before slicing into rounds, or cut into tiny balls, the size of peas, using a Parisienne cutter.

The zucchini are 'turned', and all the vegetables, including the peas and asparagus tips, are boiled for 1-2 minutes in salted water until *just tender*, then refreshed in iced water.

TO MAKE THE SAUCE

Put the shallot tops, with the wine and water, into a pan and boil rapidly until all that remains is a golden film. Add the cream, salt and pepper and boil again until very thick. Now start adding the butter, whisking in a bit at a time until it is all incorporated. Strain out the shallot tops. Add the lime juice, and adjust the seasoning if necessary.

TO SERVE

Slice the tail across into rounds. Warm the sauce and drop the lobster in. Cook for *just one minute*, turning the medallions over in the sauce. (Just warming the lobster through is enough to complete the cooking.) When the lobster is almost ready, drop the little vegetables into the sauce as well and warm through. Arrange the lobster medallions on hot serving plates, spoon over some sauce, and scatter the vegetables around. Garnish with some sprigs of fresh chervil.

Yabbies with Curry Butter and Wild Rice

Serves 6 people

4 dozen live yabbies (8 tails per person)
½ small red capsicum
1 medium red tomato
2 tablespoons chives, finely sliced
6 tablespoons wild rice
pinch salt

FOR THE SAUCE
½ cup concentrated yabbie stock (made with yabbie instead of lobster heads. Refer to page 44 for other ingredients)
1 tablespoon good curry powder or paste
¾ cup cream
¼ cup crème fraîche (optional — make up the difference with cream)

Put the live yabbies in the freezer for ½ hour, then drop them into boiling salted water. Bring back to the boil and cook for 5 minutes. Remove from hot water immediately and cool under cold running water. Shell the tails and set aside, and put the heads and claws together in a bowl, ready to be crushed for the stock.

Prepare the stock in exactly the same manner described for the lobster bisque on page 44. Substitute the yabbie heads and claws for the lobster heads, and use exactly the same ingredients and the same method to produce a rich, highly concentrated yabbie stock to the point just before all the finishing creams are added. You need only ½ cup of the stock to make the sauce for this recipe, so freeze any leftover for future soups and sauces.

To finish the sauce, whisk the stock together with the curry powder and the creams. Bring to the boil for 2 minutes, and adjust the seasoning if necessary.

Peel, core and de-seed the tomato and red capsicum. Chop into dice, using only the outer section of the tomato.

Cook the wild rice by dropping into boiling salted water and continuing to boil for 20 minutes until tender. Drain.

TO SERVE
Ladle some of the sauce into the bottom of flat soup bowls. Put a spoonful of wild rice in the centre, the yabbie tails around the rice, and the fine dice of tomato and capsicum sprinkled over the sauce. Dot the tomato and capsicum pieces with the fine chives.

GRATIN OF YABBIES

Ingredients for 6 people

48 live yabbies (8 per person)
1 small carrot
½ cucumber, de-seeded
1 medium zucchini
puff pastry (enough to make 6 pastry *claws* as garnish)
egg wash (1 yolk mixed with 1 teaspoon water)
knob butter
pinch each salt and pepper

SAUCE
100ml (3 fl oz) concentrated yabbie stock (made with the yabbie heads. The recipe is the same as that using lobster heads on page 44)
100ml (3 fl oz) cream
100g (3½ oz) unsalted butter
1 truffle sliced (optional)

individual gratin dishes

Prepare the yabbies and make a yabbie stock from the heads and claws, as described in the previous recipe. Shell the tails and set aside. If refrigerating, allow them to sit at room temperature an hour before serving.

The puff pastry *claws* demand a little artistry and imagination. You can first make a cardboard design if you lack the confidence to work free-hand. The idea is to cut shapes out of your pastry, allowing 1 per person, which resemble the claw of a yabbie. They can be large or small, as you prefer, as long as you have enough pastry to mop up the rich sauce later on.

Put the cut-out pastry shapes on a baking tray. Brush the tops with some egg wash and chill for 20 minutes. Bake at 220°C (430°F) for 15 minutes. Once they have risen, reduce the oven temperature and leave for a further 15 minutes in order to dry out the pastry centres. Set to one side.

Slice the vegetables into fine julienne strips. Peel the carrot before slicing, peel and de-seed the cucumber, and use the outer part only of the zucchini (throw away the soft centre).

The sauce can be prepared a bit in advance and kept warm. Boil the yabbie stock and cream together for a couple of minutes until nicely thickened, then adjust to a simmer and whisk in the butter, a little at a time. Season with the salt and pepper and stir in the sliced truffle.

TO SERVE
Arrange the yabbie tails in the hot gratin dishes. Warm the vegetable julienne in the sauce, and spoon the hot sauce over the yabbies. Brown under a very hot pre-heated grill. Garnish with the warmed puff pastry, sticking out to one side, and serve at once.

PAN FRIED KING TIGER PRAWNS WRAPPED IN LEEK

Ingredients per person

3 green King Tiger prawns
3 or 4 layers of the white of leek
freshly ground black pepper
1 teaspoon butter
1 teaspoon peanut oil
flaky sea salt

Discard the tough upper green leaves of the leek, and also any of the tougher layers of the white part. Slice the white in half lengthwise and wash the leek strands thoroughly. Drop into boiling water for 2-3 minutes, until soft, and refresh immediately in iced water.

Peel and remove veins in the prawns. Wash them thoroughly and pat dry. Wrap each prawn, from end to end, with the leek leaves, over and under, as if you were bandaging a leg. Do this as neatly as possible so that there are not bits hanging off. Overlap the leaves and trim ragged bits away with a knife.

TO SERVE

Melt the butter with the oil until hot. Fry the prawns, seasoned with salt and pepper, on each side for about 1 minute (do not overcook). They should be just done — the slightest bit raw in the centre does not matter as they will continue to cook a little more on the plate with the 'built in heat'. Pat with a paper towel to remove any excess grease, and serve immediately along with some little piles of the flaky salt for dipping.

This is a quick, simple and tasty dish — leeks and prawns seem made for each other. The important thing is *not to overcook them*. Simplicity can sometimes be deceptively tricky, and here a delicate cooking touch is certainly called for.

CHICKEN MOUSSE WITH A TARTLET OF WILD MUSHROOMS

Ingredients for 4 people

FOR THE MOUSSES
250g (½ lb) raw chicken
500ml (16 fl oz) cream
white of 1 egg
½ teaspoon each salt and white pepper

FOR THE TARTLET CASES
puff pastry scraps, enough to make 4 thin tart cases, about 100g (3½ oz)
1 egg yolk, beaten with 1 teaspoon water

FOR THE MUSHROOMS
1 cup mixed dried wild mushrooms, such as morels, mousserons, cèpes)
1½ cups fresh white button mushrooms, sliced
50ml (1½ fl oz) concentrated chicken stock
50ml (1½ fl oz) mushroom water (the reserved, filtered water used for soaking the mushrooms)
250ml (8 fl oz) cream
knob butter
salt and freshly ground black pepper

fresh chervil sprigs or finely chopped parsley to garnish
6 x 125ml (6 x 4 fl oz) timbale moulds
6 x 8cm (6 x 3¼ in) tart tins

Chop up the raw chicken meat and purée in a food processor, adding 50ml (1½ fl oz) of the cream towards the end.

Pass the puréed chicken through a mouli.

Now put the chicken into a chilled bowl over ice and work in the egg white, then the remaining 450ml (15 fl oz) of cream, a little at a time. Make sure everything is evenly combined.

Pass the creamy mixture through a double layer of muslin or some other fine kitchen cloth.

Butter the timbale moulds thoroughly and fill with the chicken mixture. Bake them, covered with buttered aluminium foil, in a bain-marie at 160°C (320°F) until set (about 40 minutes).

Allow them to sit for one minute before turning out. If you are making them ahead of time (even the day before) cool, refrigerate, then re-warm in a bain-marie.

For the tartlet cases you will need to roll the pastry out very thinly. Line the little tart tins, leaving a bit overhanging the edges to allow for shrinkage, prick the base very well, glaze with egg yolk, and chill for ½ hour. When ready, bake blind at 190°C (375°F) until crisp and golden. Remove from the tins and put aside until needed.

Soak the dried mushrooms in lots of clean, cold water until they are soft (30 minutes is usually long enough). As the mousserons and morels can be particularly full of gritty sand, wash thoroughly, by swirling them round and round. (Some are worse than others, and if they are still sandy, you may have to use running water, but try not to wash everything away, including their flavour.) Reserve 50mls (1½ fl oz) of the water you have used for the soaking, carefully filtered through kitchen paper towels.

Slice the button mushrooms into small pieces and fry in a little butter until their juices run. Add the soft dried mushrooms, season with salt to taste, and a good grinding of fresh black pepper.

Now add the chicken stock and 50ml (1½ fl oz) of the filtered water that the mushrooms are soaking in. Boil rapidly and reduce the liquid by half before adding the cream. Let it continue to boil for a few minutes to thicken slightly.

TO SERVE

Tip out the warmed chicken mousses onto hot serving plates. Place the warmed tart case alongside each mousse, and spoon the rich mushroom mixture inside. Garnish with the chervil sprigs or finely chopped parsley.

DUCK LIVER AND CURRANT CUSTARD

1 custard serves 8-10 people

500g (1 lb) fresh duck livers — they need to be very well trimmed, so buy 750g (1½ lb)
2 eggs
300ml (9 fl oz) cream
2 teaspoons madeira
¼ teaspoon each salt and white pepper
125g (4 oz) butter, melted
½ cup currants
2 cups (approximately) clarified chicken stock

26cm (10 in) circular gratin dish

Trim the livers very well of all threads and bits of gall. Wash, drain and pat dry, and purée in a food processor. Add the eggs one at a time, then the cream, madeira, salt and pepper, and last of all the melted butter.

Pass this mixture through a very fine sieve and then through double layers of muslin (or other very fine kitchen cloth) to remove all the unwanted specks of liver. It doesn't take long to do this because the mixture is so liquid, and the extra creamy finish that will result is well worth it.

Butter the gratin dish. Sprinkle the currants around the bottom and pour the mixture over.

Bake at 180°C (350°F) for 12 minutes, until just firm, so that the inside stays pink.

Chill well and when absolutely cold pour the clarified stock over and chill again so that the stock sets to a jelly.

TO SERVE

Roll *quenelle* shapes of the jellied liver, using a spoon dipped in hot water. Serve 1 or 2 rolls per person, and accompany with thick slices of toasted brioche or country bread, wrapped in a napkin to keep warm.

Note: To give the custard a chance to set really firm, it is probably best to make this dish the day before you wish to serve it.

MEDLEY OF CREAMED MUSHROOMS

Ingredients per person

*1 large flat cultivated mushroom about 10cm (4 in) wide
6 cultivated button mushrooms
4-6 oyster mushrooms (depending on the size)
2 heaped tablespoons mixed dried mushrooms, such as morels, mousserons, cèpes
2 or 3 toasted croûtons made from a baguette or ficelle loaf
butter
2 tablespoons shallots, finely sliced
1 tablespoon parsley, finely chopped
salt and freshly ground black pepper
½ cup cream*

To make the croûtons, slice a baguette or ficelle loaf into rounds. Brush with melted butter and bake in a moderate to hot oven 190°C (375°F) until golden.

Cover the dried mushrooms with lots of cold water and soak for 20-30 minutes. Give them a good swirl around in the water to make sure they are free of all sand and grit, particularly the morels.

Melt the butter in a frypan. When it is foaming, stir in the buttons, the well drained shallot tops, half the quantity of parsley, salt and pepper to taste. Stir frequently and cook until the buttons are soft and golden. Stir in the cream and boil to thicken.

Grill or fry the large mushroom and the oyster mushrooms. Brush with a little melted butter, dust with a good grinding of salt and pepper, then cook on both sides until tender.

TO SERVE

Put the large mushroom in the centre of a hot serving plate. Pile the buttons and the mixed dried mushrooms on top and spoon over the sauce. Put a few oyster mushrooms on top, then the croûtons, and one final oyster mushroom right on top to complete the pyramid. Sprinkle the remaining fine parsley over the mushrooms.

Note: This recipe is open to endless variation. Just use the mushrooms that are available.

It is a somewhat hearty opening to a meal, perfect for late autumn or winter dinners.

POACHED EGGS WITH TOMATO BUTTER AND CAVIAR

Serves 4 people

8 large eggs (2 per person)
2 litres (64 fl oz) water in a large saucepan
1 tablespoon white vinegar
sprigs fresh chervil
2 teaspoons beluga caviar per person

FOR THE PANCAKES
1 egg, separated
50g (5 oz) S.R. flour
1 teaspoon sugar
1 teaspoon chives, finely sliced
50ml (1½ fl oz) milk
pinch salt
knob butter

FOR THE SAUCE
1 medium red capsicum
2 medium red tomatoes
1 small white onion
2 tablespoons dry white wine
75ml (2½ fl oz) cream
1 teaspoon salt
¼ teaspoon cayenne pepper
150g (5 oz) unsalted butter
knob butter

Prepare the sauce first. Blister, peel, and de-seed the capsicum. Quarter the tomatoes, purée together with the capsicum, then sieve. Put the sieved purée into a small saucepan and boil to evaporate most of the water content. In another pan, melt the knob of butter, stir in the chopped onion, and cook until soft. Add the wine and reduce until only 1 teaspoonful remains. Then add the cream, cayenne pepper, salt, and boil until thick. Strain out the onion, then combine the thickened cream with the vegetable purée in the first saucepan. Whisk in the butter, a little at a time, and keep warm.

Now to poaching the eggs. Surprisingly, this is a job that can be done well in advance. Put the water and vinegar into a saucepan and bring to a gentle simmer. Have a bowl of iced water close by. Break the eggs into the water, one after the other so that they all cook for the same length of time. (Do four at a time if that makes things easier.) When the eggs are all in, stir the water about — for as long as it takes to set the whites — so that they don't stick to the bottom of the pan. They will take approximately 3 minutes to cook. When done, the whites are firm and the yolks still soft to touch. Take them from the water with a slotted spoon and slide them into the iced water. This will stop them cooking further. When they are quite cold, lift them out of the water, trim the edges neatly, using scissors or a sharp knife, and store on a tray covered with plastic.

To make the little pancakes, break the egg into a bowl and beat with a fork. Add the sifted flour, sugar, chives, salt, and combine smoothly. Stir in the milk at the end, a little at a time, until you have a smooth, fairly runny batter. To cook them you will need a frypan or hotplate. Put the knob of butter in, and when sizzling hot, drop in the batter, at well spaced intervals, a teaspoonful at a time. It will take only about 20 seconds to cook and brown each side. Lift out when done and keep warm. The pancakes should not be much bigger than a 20 cent coin.

TO SERVE

Re-warm the eggs by dropping briefly back into simmering water. Drain well, and put two side by side, on hot serving plates or in shallow soup bowls. Spoon enough hot sauce over to coat the eggs generously. Top each egg with a little pancake, and on top of each pancake put a teaspoon of beluga caviar. Scatter a few small chervil sprigs about the sauce, and serve at once.

SCRAMBLED EGGS WITH GRILLED BRIOCHE AND SCHOOL PRAWNS

Serves 6 people

500g (1 lb) green school prawns (sweet small prawns)
1 tablespoon parsley, finely chopped

FOR THE EGGS
9 eggs
200g (6½ oz) unsalted butter, softened
300ml (10 fl oz) cream
pinch each salt and white pepper

FOR THE SAUCE
1 small onion
knob butter
250ml (8 fl oz) dry white wine
300ml (10 fl oz) cream
pinch each salt and pepper
juice ½ lemon

FOR THE BRIOCHE
Make 1 loaf, using recipe for soft and easy brioche (see recipe on page 213)

Prepare the brioche loaf early in the day, and cool. Cut 6 slices and trim away the crusts. Cut an extra slice from which to make 6 little square 4 x 4cm (1½ x 1½ in) lids. Keep these on a tray well sealed with clear plastic wrap.

Cook the prawns by dropping them into boiling salted water for one minute. Cool under running cold water, peel, remove veins, wash, and set aside.

To prepare the sauce, chop the onion into small pieces and stew in a pan with a knob of butter until it is quite soft. Pour the wine over, and boil to reduce, until only a golden teaspoonful remains. Add the cream, salt and pepper, and the lemon juice. Boil again until it is of a thickened sauce consistency. Strain out the onion.

Cook the eggs when you are ready to serve them. Crack the eggs into a large saucepan and give them a good whisking before placing them over a gentle heat with the cream, butter, salt and pepper. Continue to lightly whisk as they cook to a very soft creamy mixture. Once they are done—SERVE. If you let them sit, they will dry out, and you had better throw them out and start again.

While you are cooking the eggs, put the brioche slices under a hot grill to brown and gently warm the prawns in the sauce.

TO SERVE

Put a grilled slice of brioche in the centre of each plate, pile high with the eggs, and put a little lid on top. Surround with some of the sauce and prawns, and dust the prawns with a little fine parsley.

QUAIL TERRINE WITH ACCOMPANIMENTS

Serves 10 people

Inspired by an original recipe of Paul Haeberlin from his book Les Recettes de L'Auberge de L'Ill

The accompaniments are to be found at the end of the terrine recipe

3 quails
75g (2½ oz) chicken livers
500g (16 oz) chicken breasts (about 4 medium)
1 medium carrot
1 medium onion
1 celery stalk
2 garlic cloves, peeled
1 thyme branch
1 bay leaf
knob butter
150ml (5 fl oz) water
some extra thyme and bay leaves to top the terrine when assembled
1 kg (2 lb) bacon, without the rind, to line the terrine

FOR THE FORCEMEAT
250g (8 oz) pork fillet
250g (8 oz) veal steak
250g (8 oz) chicken breast
125g (4 oz) chicken livers
100g (3½ oz) fat and tail of bacon (use the leftover eyes of the bacon to help line the terrine)
2 tablespoons shallot tops
25g (¾ oz) butter
50ml (1½ fl oz) cognac
150ml (5 fl oz) cream
1 egg
pinch salt and freshly ground black pepper

terrine 27 x 10cm (10½ x 4 in)

To prepare the forcemeat. Melt the butter and gently cook the shallot tops until soft. Chop all the meats roughly, and together with the liver and bacon, put into a food processor and begin to purée. Add the egg, the cognac and the cream, and continue to purée until smooth. Stir in the shallots and butter. Season with the salt and pepper, taking care not to overdo the salt as the bacon bits will contribute a bit. Before going any further, test the seasoning by frying a little knob of the meat, and tasting. Add a little more salt and pepper if you need to. Set aside.

Chop a fine dice of the carrot, onion, celery and garlic. Fry with the thyme in the knob of butter to release the flavours, then add the water. Put the chicken breasts on top of the vegetables, season with salt and pepper, and cover with aluminium foil. Cook gently for 20 minutes, then remove the breasts and chop them into small 2cm (¾ in) pieces, and set aside. Discard the vegetables.

Next de-bone the quails. Cut out the wings completely. Make a slit down the inside of each leg and ease the flesh away from the bone. Continue cutting close to the bone, all the way around to the back, taking care not to break the skin. Work around to the front and ease the meat away from either side of the breastbone. Fold the skin and flesh back like a sock, and continue to carefully remove the flesh close to the bone, until the carcass is completely separated. Make a slit straight down the back and lay the quails out flat, skin side down. Put 25g (¾ oz) of liver in the centre and roll up like a sausage. Repeat this procedure for the other two quails.

Line the terrine with the rindless bacon. Make sure that the strips lie snugly together so that there are no gaps.

Mix the chopped chicken with the forcemeat and fill the terrine to almost the halfway mark. Put the rolled quails in the centre, lying end to end. Cover with the rest of the forcemeat and the overhanging bacon strips, as well as a couple of extra ones right on top. Lay thyme sprigs and bay leaves on top.

Using a double sheet of aluminium foil, cover the top of the terrine very tightly. Put the terrine in a bain-marie of hot water (so that the water comes halfway up the sides of the terrine) and bake at 180°C (350°F) for 1½ hours. Test with a skewer—the juices should run clear and the skewer (when left in the terrine for 5 seconds) should be hot to touch. Replace the foil after testing and, if ready, take out of the bain-marie. Let the terrine rest at room temperature to cool until you are able to pick it up with your bare hands. Refrigerate. Put a heavy weight on top and leave overnight or approximately for 8 hours.

ACCOMPANIMENTS

FIG JAM
750g (1½ lb) figs (weighed after peeling)
750g (1½ lb) sugar
the zest of 1 large lemon

Peel, weigh the figs and cut into quarters. Grate the lemon rind all over the figs. Add the sugar and stand overnight. Next day, bring to the boil slowly, and continue to simmer until thickened.

SNAKEBEANS VINAIGRETTE
1 bunch of snakebeans
virgin olive oil dressing

Tip and tail the beans and cut into pieces about 10cm (4 in) long. Blanch. When ready to serve the terrine, toss in enough of the dressing to coat well, without saturating.

TOMATO CHUTNEY
500g (1lb) peeled, cored and chopped Granny Smith apples
500g (1 lb) cored and chopped red tomatoes
500g (1 lb) peeled and chopped onions
100g (3½ oz) currants
100g (3½ oz) sultanas
1 cup brown sugar
2 cups red wine vinegar
1 teaspoon cayenne pepper
1 tablespoon salt
1 teaspoon allspice
¼ teaspoon nutmeg
¼ teaspoon ground cloves
2 tablespoons grain mustard

Put all the ingredients together in a large pot. Bring to the boil, then simmer for 1½ hours. Pour into hot sterilised glass jars.

TO SERVE
Give each person a slice of terrine garnished with the dressed beans. Serve the tomato chutney and fig jam, separately in little pots, and pass around thick hot toast, wrapped in a napkin.

Fish and Shellfish

The auctioning of the fisherman's catch begins in the early hours at the Sydney fish markets. Arriving as I did each morning at 6.30, it was already in full swing. The only times I can remember the whole thing grinding to a halt was once a year on picnic day, once when the Fish Market Authority decided to go on strike, and the morning Australia II won the America's Cup. That morning, instead of the familiar drone of the auctioneer, the radio blared over the loud speaker to the cheering of accents distinctly Greek and Italian.

The markets keep getting better, there's no doubt about it. The choice of fresh seafood is extraordinarily good. Just a few years ago, fresh tuna was a fairly rare sight, and very cheap. Now it is in great demand and can command high prices when the catch is poor. So, too, the situation regarding live lobsters has certainly improved since the days when I had to sort through boxes of half dead 'Tassies' trying to find the hardy few who had survived the flight, the packaging, and the long hours on dry land. Now that they are held in tanks, both they and the cooks are a lot happier. Our local lobsters are *rock lobsters* or *crayfish*. For ease of discussion, I will simply call them lobsters. They do not have the large claws characteristic of the Atlantic variety, but they too have excellent, sweet tender meat when cooked simply and briefly.

The same can be said for a great deal of seafood, and in particular the exquisite Sydney rock oyster. I can't bear to cook them. Freshly opened, with just a little black pepper and a squeeze of lemon is enough.

In the early days at *You and Me* we served mostly whole fish, steamed or poached with wine and herbs, or fish stock and other small crustaceans. At other times we used a little beurre blanc with fresh lime or lemon and perhaps a drop of cream or butters flavoured with various fresh herbs, drizzled or melted over. There were silver breams, baby pink snapper, red mullets and pig fish, and of course the excellent and abundant John Dory and sand whiting. I experimented with many strange and exotic species, including one particularly gruesome piece of elephant fish.

But I kept coming back to a few favourites.

These days I use even simpler methods of cooking the fish which are now mostly prepared as carefully de-boned fillets and quickly seared on a Japanese-style hotplate. Instead of making a sauce I like to substitute such things as braised leeks or tomatoes, or barely cooked sorrel leaves moist with their own buttery cooking juices. And I cannot live without a pot of flaky sea salt, particularly when it comes to a plate of freshly cooked and peeled Sydney Harbour prawns.

I don't like to fiddle too much. The longer I cook, the more I respect and love the natural flavour of the ingredients I use. The is true of most everything, but in particular it is true of seafood.

WHITING FILLET WITH A MOUSSE AND SAUCE OF PRAWNS

Ingredients for 8 people

4 medium-sized whiting (1 fillet per person)
½ teaspoon pepper
½ teaspon salt
knob butter

FOR THE MOUSSE
500g (1 lb) medium-sized, green prawns
1 egg
600ml (18 fl oz) cream
½ teaspoon pepper
¼ teaspoon salt
1 tablespoon mixed parsley and chives, finely sliced

FOR THE SAUCE
250g (½ lb) green school prawns (the smaller the better)
1 stick celery
1 medium white onion
1 medium carrot
2 stems thyme
1 teaspoon peppercorns
125g (4 oz) butter
2 heaped tablespoons concentrated tomato paste
2 heaped tablespoons flour
50ml (1½ fl oz) cognac
300ml (9 fl oz) dry white wine
cold water to cover
250ml (8 fl oz) cream

8 x 150ml (8 x 5 fl oz) timbale moulds, well buttered

Fillet the fish and remove the skin. Carefully pull out all the remaining bones.

To prepare the sauce, wash the prawns and pound them up very well, shell, flesh and all. Melt the butter in a large pan and stir in the vegetables, all washed and chopped, along with the herbs and peppercorns. Cook until they are soft, then stir in the mashed prawns. When the prawns have reddened, add the cognac and boil to evaporate. Stir in the concentrated tomato and flour and cook for a couple of minutes, then add the wine a bit at a time to stop the mixture sticking. Cover with water, and simmer gently for the best part of an hour, skimming away regularly all the oils and scum that rise to the surface. Strain, pushing down hard to extract all the juices from the shells and vegetables. Put the liquid back into the clean pan and boil until very thick — until only a cup of liquid remains. To finish the sauce, stir in the cream and cook for a few minutes more until it is a coating sauce consistency. Strain through a very fine sauce sieve and season with the salt and pepper.

To make the mousse, shell, devein and wash the prawns. Pat dry and purée in a food processor with the egg, salt and pepper and 100ml (3 fl oz) of the cream. Pass this mixture through a mouli or sieve and stir in the rest of the cream. Now pass this mixture through a fine piece of muslin. This is not difficult at all — it only takes a minute and makes such a difference to the final smooth texture of the mousse. I put a rounded sieve over a bowl, drape the piece of muslin over the sieve, and pour the mixture into the cloth, holding the sides up a little in one hand so that the mixture does not flow over the sides. Pull all the edges of the cloth together and squeeze the ball of mixture firmly, pushing down from the top with your free hand. Once it is strained, stir in the very fine parsley and chives and combine thoroughly. Ladle the mixture into the buttered moulds and place in a bain-marie. Bake in a 180°C (350°F) oven for 20 minutes until done (the mousse will feel firm).

The mousse can be made up well ahead of time, even the day before, and reheated in a bain-marie before for serving. Always rest the hot mousse for a minute before tipping out.

TO COOK AND SERVE

Put the knob of butter on a hot grid or into a large frypan. When foaming, put in the seasoned fish fillets. Cook on each side for a minute only (whiting fillets are thin and delicate and do not take very long to cook). Put one fillet on each plate. Tip out a mousse alongside each fillet and nap with the creamy prawn sauce.

Note: This recipe can be made just as well substituting yabbies or lobster for the prawns.

POACHED CUBES OF BAR COD WITH MUSTARD BUTTER AND CHIVES

Ingredients for 4 people

1½ kg (3 lb) bar cod (you will need approximately 200-300g (7-9½ oz) trimmed fish per person
fish stock for poaching (see recipe on page 25)

FOR THE SAUCE
¾ cup beurre blanc (see recipe on page 28)
¼ cup cream
2 teaspoons Dijon mustard (or to taste)

FOR THE GARNISH
4 tablespoons chives, finely sliced
paprika for dusting

Fish kettle or other lidded poaching pan

Prepare the sauce in advance and keep warm. Whisk the beurre blanc, cream and mustard together smoothly, and simmer until a good 'coating' consistency.

Cut the fish into even-sized cubes of about 3cm (1½ in) width. Fill the bottom of your fish kettle with the prepared stock. Lay the fish cubes on the removable rack, replace the lid, bring the stock to a gentle simmer, and poach the fish for about 5 minutes. Make sure that you shake the pan every so often, and *do not overcook*. When the fish is tender all the way through, drain and serve immediately.

TO SERVE

Spoon a pool of sauce onto each serving plate. Pile the cubes of fish on top of each other pyramid-style. Sprinkle lots and lots of chives over the sauce and dust a little paprika over the fish.

Note: Bar cod is an enormous fish with tasty chunky white flesh that works well with mustard. Don't be put off by its appearance when next you are at the fish markets.

FISH FILLETS FROM THE MARKET WITH CHAMPAGNE SAUCE AND JULIENNE VEGETABLES

Ingredients per person

1 small fillet (or neatly trimmed portion of a fillet) of each of the following: John Dory, sand whiting, red mullet (or pig fish) and sole
pinch salt and freshly ground black pepper
hot buttered hotplate or large frying pan

JULIENNE VEGETABLES
1 heaped tablespoon mixed julienne of carrot, celery and leek

CHAMPAGNE SAUCE
½ recipe hollandaise sauce, see recipe on page 28
25ml (⅝ fl oz) cream, whipped
25ml (⅝ fl oz) bubbling champagne

Prepare the vegetables first. The julienne should be fine and of uniform length — 5 or 6 cm (2-2½ in) long. Blanch and put to one side.

Prepare the hollandaise and keep warm.

Wash, trim, and skin the Dory, whiting and sole, and fillet (where necessary). Cut into neat portions so that you know exactly how much each person will receive.

TO COOK AND SERVE

Have the buttered hotplate *very hot* before you start (without burning the butter). Lay the fillets down quickly, one after the other, season with salt and pepper, and cook for 1-2 minutes (till done), on each side. Remember they will not take long. Arrange on hot serving plates.

Transfer the hollandaise from the bowl to a pan, and stir in the vegetable julienne. Whisk all the time it is warming. When warm to touch, whisk in the cream and champagne. Ladle AT ONCE over the fillets, strewing the julienne over them as you go.

Note: By way of variation, make scallop mousselines (in small sized timbale moulds) and serve in the centre with the fish fillets all around. If you do this you can also omit one of the fillets and substitute 4 or 5 scallops instead.

STEAMED WHOLE PIG FISH WITH BASIL BUTTER SAUCE

Ingredients for 2 people

2 x 300g (2 x 9½ oz) pig fish
1 large carrot
1 medium leek
1 medium onion
1 stalk celery
4 stalks parsley
4 basil stems with leaves
water
knob butter

FOR THE SAUCE
½ cup beurre blanc (see recipe on page 28)
½ cup cream
2 tablespoons shredded basil leaves

Clean the fish thoroughly, both inside and out. The people at the fish market are usually happy to do the scaling and gutting for you, but give the fish another good going over with a small sharp knife under cold running water.

Chop up the vegetables and herbs and put into a heavy bottomed baking pan with the melted butter and cook until soft. Cover with water.

Lay the fish on top of the vegetables and cover with a sheet of aluminium foil. Simmer and cook for 15 minutes (test the fish for 'doneness' with the tip of your knife).

Once the beurre blanc is made, the rest of the sauce-making is easy. Put the cream and basil leaves into the warm buerre blanc, bring to the boil, and simmer until the leaves are limp and the sauce is of a coating consistency.

TO SERVE
Make sure that the fish is well drained before plating. Spoon a little of the sauce over, and send the rest around separately in a sauce boat.

Note: If you prefer to eat *fillets* which have been more carefully boned, do so, cook the same way, but remember that the cooking time will be considerably shorter.

The pig fish, contrary to what its name might imply, is one of the finest eating fish to be found in our coastal waters. It is particularly prized by our local Chinese people and fetches a high price at the Sydney Fish Markets. A pretty striped fish with a distinctively pointed, slightly snub nose, its flesh is white and delicate. I remember having it about 10 years ago at a restaurant which was then called *Le Marseilles.* The chef in those days was the inimitable Claude Corne. He prepared it with basil, and I never forgot that wonderful combination. Years later, Monsieur Corne would come to lunch at *You and Me* and, in his gentlemanly way, give me advice on all sorts of matters. Early one morning he rushed into my kitchen bearing a paper bag full of real French échalotes, the first I'd ever seen in Australia. His kindness and his gift will never be forgotten.

JOHN DORY WITH FRESH TOMATO SAUCE

Serves 6 people

3 medium-sized John Dory, filleted (1 fillet per person)
500g (1 lb) red tomatoes
75g (2½ oz) butter
75ml (2½ fl oz) cream
150ml (5 fl oz) fish stock
2 teaspoons fresh thyme leaves
1 tablespoon shallots, finely sliced
salt to taste and freshly ground black pepper

Fillet, trim and skin the fish and refrigerate until needed.

Chop the tomatoes up roughly and put them into a saucepan with half the butter and the salt and pepper. Cook for 20 minutes until everything is very well softened. Purée in a food processor and pass through a sieve. Return this purée back to the pan and boil until it is very thick. Transfer to a bowl.

Put the shallots and the stock into the pan and boil until only a golden film of liquid remains on the bottom of the pan. Add the cream and boil until nicely thickened. Strain out the shallots, then return the cream to the pan with the tomato purée. Whisk the two together to combine thoroughly, then whisk in the remaining butter and the thyme leaves at the end. Taste, and adjust the seasoning if necessary.

The cooking of the fish will take only a few minutes and should be done just before serving. Fry the fillets on a lightly buttered hotplate or in a large frypan for about a minute on each side. They should be only just done.

TO SERVE

Spoon some sauce onto the centre of each serving plate, and place the fish on top.

JOHN DORY WITH BROADBEANS, ÉCHALOTES, CONFIT OF RED CABBAGE AND RED WINE SAUCE

Serves 6 people

3 medium-sized John Dory, filleted
1 tablespoon échalotes per person
8 broadbeans per person
knob butter

FOR THE CONFIT
1 cup red cabbage, finely shredded
1 tablespoon butter
1 tablespoon water
1 tablespoon sugar
2 teaspoon white vinegar
¼ teaspoon each salt and pepper

FOR THE SAUCE
2 cups red wine
2 cups fish stock
2 mashed anchovy fillets
1 tablespoon carrot dice
1 tablespoon celery dice
1 tablespoon onion dice
1 cup cream
1 tablespoon butter
pinch white pepper

Trim, wash and skin the fish fillets.

Melt a teaspoonful of butter in a saucepan and stir in the anchovies, celery, carrot and onion. Cook for a minute, then add the wine and the fish stock and boil until only 25ml (⅝ fl oz) of highly concentrated liquid remains. Whisk in the cream and boil to a thickened sauce consistency. Strain and set aside.

To make the cabbage confit, put all the listed ingredients together in a pot and cook gently for 20 minutes until very soft.

Pod the broadbeans and peel off the thick outer skin of each little bean. You will be left with the tender emerald green heart of the bean. Blanch these.

Peel the échalotes.

TO COOK AND SERVE
Fry the échalotes on a hot buttered grid or frypan. When almost done, push to one side and add the fish fillets. Fry on each side for about a minute. While doing this, complete the sauce. Re-warm, and whisk the butter in, a bit at a time to finish. Plunge the broadbeans back into boiling water for a few seconds only, to rewarm, and bring the confit back to a gentle simmer.

Ladle a pool of sauce into the centre of hot serving plates. Put the fish fillet on top, scatter the broadbeans and échalotes around, and put a couple of teaspoonfuls of the confit to one side.

JOHN DORY WITH BRAISED LEEKS AND TURNIPS

Ingredients for 4 people

2 medium-sized John Dory
2 leeks
2 small white turnips
salt and pepper
a couple of knobs butter

Discarding the tough green leaves, chop the whites of the leek to a dice, wash well, dust with a pinch each of salt and pepper, and cook with a little butter and 2 tablespoons water, until very soft.

Peel and wash the turnips. Slice into thin rounds and dust with pepper and salt. Place in a pan with a knob of butter and water to almost cover, and cook until tender but not mushy.

Remove the skin from the fillets by sliding your knife at an angle between the skin and the flesh, and taking hold of the tail lip, pulling the skin towards you. Fry on a lightly buttered grid or hotplate for about a minute on each side. Do not overcook. Serve immediately the fillets are done.

TO SERVE

Make a bed of the leeks and turnip slices in the centre of hot serving plates. Place the cooked fillet on top and serve at once.

TROUT SOUFFLE

Ingredients for 5 people

This dish springs straight from the famous salmon soufflé prepared at *L'Auberge de L'Ill* in Illhaeusern, Alsace, the restaurant of Paul and Jean-Pierre Haeberlin. Having enjoyed the original version on more than one occasion, I decided to substitute local fish for the unprocurable salmon, and work out my own way of doing it.

The *odd* number of serves comes about because 1 fillet of fish is required for each person plus 3 for the mousse. If you wish to serve only 4 people, simply divide the leftover fillet 4 ways and put on top of each serving of fish (see the detailed instructions at the end of the recipe). Likewise, if you wish to serve 6 people, buy 1 more fish and divide the leftover fillet again. I'm afraid the quantities need a little bit of juggling around.

FOR THE FISH AND SOUFFLE MIXTURE
4 x 300-400g (9½-12½ oz) rainbow trout
1 egg
150ml (5 fl oz) cream
125ml (4 fl oz) egg whites (25ml (⅝ fl oz) per person)
pinch each salt and white pepper

½ litre (16 fl oz) fish stock for poaching (make it from the trout bones)

FOR THE SAUCE
1 cup shallots, finely sliced
250ml (8 fl oz) fish stock (see recipe on page 25)
250ml (8 fl oz) dry white wine
250ml (8 fl oz) water
scant tablespoon lemon juice
50ml (1½ fl oz) crème fraîche (optional – or substitute cream)
300ml (9 fl oz) cream
100g (3½ oz) unsalted butter
pinch salt
freshly ground black pepper

FOR THE GARNISH
1 red tomato
1 tablespoon chives, finely sliced

Fillet the fish, de-bone and skin the fillets, and set aside all except 3. These 3 fillets should weigh around 150g (5 oz). Trim off a bit if you have too much, and if you are a bit short, pinch little bits from the other fillets. These fillets are for the mousse. Purée them in a food processor, adding the egg, then the cream, and a good pinch of salt and pepper. Pass this creamy mixture through a mouli, taste and adjust the seasoning if necessary.

Put into a bowl and chill well.

To make the sauce, put the shallots, fish stock, the wine and water together in a pan and boil until only a bare 50ml (1½ fl oz) remains. Strain out the shallots, put the liquid back into the pan, and add the lemon juice, the crème fraîche and cream. Boil again until it becomes a thickened sauce consistency. Add salt and pepper to taste, then whisk in the cold butter, a little at a time.

For the garnish, blanch, peel, and remove the tomato seeds, then chop very finely.

TO COOK AND SERVE

Choose a shallow baking tray and cover the bottom with the ½ litre (16 fl oz) of fish stock.

Take the trimmed fillets — 1 per person — and slice each in half diagonally. Now put the 2 pieces back together again, only this time overlapping the pieces slightly in the centre. The reason for doing this is that we want to make an oval shape of fish to act as a base for the soufflé mixture. The fillet itself is too long and narrow, so by slicing and rejoining in a more compact way the fillet becomes shorter, thicker, and hopefully something of an oval shape. If it is still a bit elongated, trim the little ends off and put to the centre. Place these shaped fish bases well apart on the baking tray. The fish stock should not cover the fillets or wash too close to the top surface, otherwise you may find your soufflé floating away.

Put 1 heaped tablespoon per person of the puréed fish mixture into a bowl. Measure 25ml (⅝ fl oz) of egg whites per person into another bowl (preferably copper) and whisk until stiff. Stir, rather than fold the stiffened whites into the mousse mixture. This ensures evenness of mixing as the mousse is too stiff to fold and you will only end up with lumps throughout the whites. Place a good dollop of soufflé mixture on top of each serving of the fish fillets, moulding high at the sides and rounded on top to make smooth oval-shaped domes.

Bake in a fairly hot 190°-200°C (375°-400°F) oven for 12-15 minutes, or until the soufflé is done. It should be nicely browned on top. If it is cooked but not brown, put under a fiercely hot grill for a few seconds. Do not overcook. Remember, when the soufflé is done, so are the tender fillets underneath.

TO SERVE

Ladle hot sauce onto serving plates. Lift each soufflé from the baking tray by means of a spatula, drain momentarily, and put onto the pool of sauce. Garnish with a teaspoon of the tomato sprinkled with the chives.

Trout, Boned and Stuffed with Fresh Herbs and Vegetables

Ingredients per person

1 x 300-400g (10-13 oz) rainbow trout (small–medium size)
1 tablespoon carrot, chopped to a fine dice
1 tablespoon celery, chopped to a fine dice
1 tablespoon chopped mixed herbs — parsley, chives, thyme, marjoram
small knob butter
pinch salt and freshly ground black pepper

FOR THE HERB BUTTER *(again per person)*
½ tablespoon unsalted butter, softened
½ tablespoon mixed fresh herbs (as before)
slice of garlic clove
pinch each salt and white pepper

Wash and scale the trout under cold running water.

Remove all the bones between the head and the tail. Tip the trout onto its back and slice from the end of the open abdominal cavity, past the little fin, right to the tail. At the other end, sever the backbone at the neck. Now start on the rib bones. Slicing just underneath them, and being careful not to cut into the flesh, work your way slowly down to the backbone. Gently pull this out without tearing the skin. The bones from the fin in the centre of the back can also be removed — levered out with the tip of a knife, then pulled away. Flatten the fish out, wash, and make sure that it is clean and absolutely *bone free*.

Mix the chopped carrot, celery and herbs together and cook gently in the butter to soften. Sprinkle salt and grind pepper over the fish, then fill with the vegetable and herb mixture. Close the fish and lay on a sheet of buttered aluminium foil. Enclose in a sealed parcel and put into a baking pan with just a little water in the bottom and bake at 200°C (400°F) for 12-15 minutes.

In the meantime, purée all the ingredients for the herb butter in the food processor (or mix by hand) to make a smooth paste.

TO SERVE

When the the fish is ready, take it out of its foil package, and carefully peel off the top layer of skin. Lift the fish onto a serving plate, put the herb butter in little knobs all over, and put everything under a hot preheated grill for half a minute to melt the butter. Serve at once.

LOBSTER TAIL WITH BASIL AND CRUSHED TOMATOES

Ingredients for 4 people

2 x 500g (2 x 1 lb) live lobsters (small ones)
4 large ripe red tomatoes
1 tablespoon Spanish onion, chopped
1 tablespoon chives, finely sliced
½ cup basil leaves, finely shredded and tightly packed
100g (3½ oz) butter
pinch salt and freshly ground black pepper
500ml (16 fl oz) dry white wine

Kill the lobsters in the way described on page 45 and split the tails in half lengthwise. Clean and reserve the heads for another purpose (such as making lobster stock or soup).

Blanch, peel, and remove the tomato seeds, then chop up the flesh roughly.

Put half the butter in small pieces all over the bottom of a baking pan. Put the tomato on top, then the onion, basil and chives. Cover with the wine, bring to the boil, and reduce by half.

Add the extra butter in pieces all over, then put the halved tails on top, flesh side up to start. Season with salt and pepper, cover with aluminium foil, and put into a hot 210°C (420°F) oven for 10 minutes. Turn the tails over and cook for a further 5 minutes. The 15 minutes total cooking time is ample for such small lobsters, but if your lobsters are larger, allow more time accordingly.

TO SERVE

Spoon the tomato mixture onto the centre of each serving plate, and pour some of the buttery juices over them. Take the lobster meat out of the shells straight away and place rounded side up on top of the tomatoes.

MEDALLIONS OF LOBSTER TAIL WITH CREAMY SORREL AND POTATOES

Ingredients for 4 people

1 x 1kg (2 lb) live lobster
assorted aromatic vegetables and herbs, e.g. carrot, onion, leek
and parsley, washed and chopped to a fine dice
knob butter
salt and freshly ground black pepper

FOR THE CREAMY SORREL
2 bunches sorrel
1 teaspoon lemon juice
125ml (4 fl oz) cream
knob butter
pinch salt and freshly ground black pepper

FOR THE CREAMY POTATOES
400g (13 oz) floury potatoes (approximately 2 medium potatoes)
1 tablespoon butter
50ml (1½ fl oz) cream
large pinch of salt and white pepper

First kill the lobster and reserve the head for making stock. (This procedure is discussed on page 45). Split the lobster in half and remove the intestinal cord. Now put it to one side while you prepare the potatoes.

Peel and wash the potatoes and put into a pot with cold salted water to cover. Bring to the boil and cook until the potatoes are tender — about 20 minutes — but don't overcook to the point where they will fall to pieces. Drain and mash with a wooden spoon or an old-fashioned mushroom masher. Whisk in the butter and cream so that the potatoes are smooth, fluffy and lump-free. Season to taste with salt and pepper.

While the potatoes are cooking attend to the lobster. Melt the butter in the bottom of a roasting dish and cook the chopped vegetables for a couple of minutes to release their flavours. Make a compact bed of the vegetables and place the two halves of the lobster tail on top, facing downwards. Roast at 190°C (375°F) for 10 minutes. Take out of the oven and rest for a moment while you attend to the sorrel.

To prepare the creamy sorrel, chop the stems off, wash the leaves and sauté briskly in the melted butter. When the leaves wilt and change colour (this will happen immediately) season with the salt and pepper, add the lemon juice and cream, and boil to thicken slightly.

TO SERVE
Remove the lobster meat from the shell and slice on the slant into medallions. Arrange on hot serving plates and spoon alongside some of the creamy potatoes and the sorrel.

SIMON'S SCALLOP MOUSSELINE WITH SHELLFISH IN A SAFFRON CREAM

Serves 6 people

THE SHELLFISH
250g (½ lb) school prawns
18 mussels
18 fresh scallops

THE MOUSSELINES
200g (½ lb) scallops, trimmed
330g (10½ oz) sole, whiting or redfish
1 whole egg
600ml (18 fl oz) cream
pinch each salt and white pepper

THE SAFFRON CREAM
250ml (8 fl oz) dry white wine
250ml (8 fl oz) fish stock (made from the fish bones and trimmings)
1 small white onion
a small knob butter
600ml (18 fl oz) cream
1 teaspoon pure saffron threads, infused in 1 tablespoon water
pinch each salt and white pepper

extra fish stock for steaming

6 x 150ml (6 x 5 fl oz) dariole moulds

Prepare the mousselines. These can be made up well in advance, even the day before, and reheated in a bain-marie.

Purée the fish and scallops together in a food processor. Put the purée into a bowl set over a larger bowl filled with ice. Using a wooden spoon or spatula, work in the egg first, then the cream, a little at a time. Pass the mixture through a sieve or mouli, then through muslin or some other fine kitchen cloth. This is not difficult to do because the mixture is so creamy, and it is worth taking the extra trouble as it makes the world of difference to the texture of the finished mousse. Season with salt and pepper. Poach a teaspoonful of the mixture in hot water, taste, and adjust the seasoning if necessary.

Butter the moulds thoroughly and fill with the mixture. Put them into a bain-marie of hot water. The water should come halfway up the sides of the moulds. Cover with a sheet of buttered aluminium foil and bake at 180°C (350°F) until set. This will take 30 minutes.

To make the sauce, chop the onion into small pieces and stew in the butter until soft. Add the fish stock and wine and boil rapidly to reduce to a mere teaspoonful. Pour in the cream, add a pinch of salt and pepper, and boil again to a thickened sauce consistency. Strain out the onions, taste, adjust the seasoning if necessary, and add the infused saffron threads. The beautiful colour and flavour will intensify the longer the sauce is allowed to stand.

Now prepare the shellfish. Peel and clean the prawns. Put the mussels into a pan half filled with water. Cover with the lid and cook until the shells open. Take them out of the shell as soon as they open and clean away any remaining hairy beard and little lurking crabs. Trim the scallops and leave uncooked until it is almost time to serve.

TO SERVE

Gently steam the scallops over a pot of fragrant fish stock until they are just done. This will take less than 1 minute. If you overcook them they become tough and rubbery. Put the mussels and prawns in to rewarm when the scallops are almost ready.

Unmould the hot mousselines in the centre of each plate. Put the selected shellfish all around, and spoon some sauce over and serve.

SALAD OF BALMAIN BUGS, OCTOPUS, AND PRAWNS WITH LITTLE VEGETABLES AND A WATERCRESS AND PINE NUT MAYONNAISE

This recipe easily translates from a small first course to a main course size. The ingredients given here — per person — are for the smaller size.

2 green (preferably live) Balmain bugs (sand lobsters)
1 baby octopus
1 large green King prawn
1 tablespoon sliced snake beans or green beans
1 tablespoon carrot flowers (cut using a canneleur tool)
1 tablespoon broad beans, podded and peeled
1 tablespoon small beetroot, cooked and diced
3 large 3cm (1 in) square cubes white bread

1 garlic clove
olive oil
butter
lemon juice
salt and freshly ground black pepper
plain dressing for tossing the vegetables (the recipe is on page 55)

FOR THE WATERCRESS AND PINE NUT MAYONNAISE
(enough for 4 people)

3 tablespoons plain mayonnaise
1 bunch watercress
1 cup parsley (leaves only), well packed
¼ cup cream
2 tablespoons pine nuts, toasted
¼ teaspoon salt
lots of freshly ground black pepper

Fry the bread in a mixture of butter and oil until golden brown and set aside. Prepare the plain dressing.

To prepare the mayonnaise: discard the watercress and parsley stems. Blanch, then purée with the cream. Pass through a sieve, then place in a saucepan and boil to evaporate the water content until approximately 3 tablespoons of smooth green paste is left. Purée the pine nuts. Stir this along with the green paste into the mayonnaise. Season well.

Blanch the uncooked vegetables, drain, pat dry, and set aside in separate bowls.

Now prepare the seafood. Cook both the prawns and bugs by boiling in salted water. Boil the prawns for just a minute or two (depending on the size). They should be *just cooked*. Cook the bugs for a good 8 minutes. Cool both under cold running water and shell immediately. For the bugs you will need strong kitchen shears to cut through the tough shell. Slice the prawn on the slant into 2 or 3 pieces. Wash and chill. Wash the octopus thoroughly under cold running water to remove all sand and grit. Cut off the 'heads' and remove the beak. You can use just the tentacles or you can clean out the 'heads', slice, and use these as well. Marinate in a bowl in equal parts olive oil and lemon juice with a pinch of salt and freshly ground black pepper so as to just cover for 2 or 3 hours. Cook on a hot grill or barbecue for about a minute until *just cooked*. With this light cooking it will remain very tender. Chop into small pieces and set aside.

TO SERVE

Put the fried croûtons into the centre of each plate. Toss the vegetables very lightly in the plain dressing. Pile the seafood mixed with the vegetables on top of the croûtons and swirl over a tablespoon or more of the mayonnaise.

MEAT AND OFFAL

If people have firmly held views on what they like to eat, you can be certain that in the main it will be to do with the cooking of meat and offal. While there are those who won't eat meat at all, there are those who will eat meat, but not *innards*. And there are those who cannot live without red meat at least once a day, but who turn pale at the sight of a drop of blood (a similar reaction to those who faint at the sight of a fish head on the plate).

As a chef I encountered them all, and usually tried to make them happy, I'm afraid that I often lost patience: not with the vegetarians, but with the *squeamish* who are quite happy to eat a beast's leg, but not its tail, ears, or brains, and the *dictatorial* who will happily leave all the matters of judgement to the cook until it comes time for the steak.

I could recount numerous tales of previously held prejudices (for that's what they are) being completely swept away at sudden astounding discoveries: are these delicious morsels in the salad really sweetbreads or can tripe possibly be cooked any way other than boiled like rubber matting in a laundry vat and coated with flour paste sauce? How can this liver be so delicate? Don't you remember Aunt so and so's lambs fry that curled at the edges? This beef is so tender and succulent, simply because it was not cooked the requested *well done* way.

Looking back over the recipes included in this section, I suddenly realised that there was a slight imbalance in favour of lamb. Perhaps it is because my generation was reared on lamb, rather hogget, particularly in the country. I like it, I'm used to it, and I never tasted finer lamb anywhere in the world than in this country. (The New Zealanders may beg to differ on this point.)

The recipe for suckling lamb baked in a parcel presents alternative methods of parcelling and baking. The method using aluminium foil is the simplest and the results are very good. The method using clay is visually very appealing and I like this method myself. I suppose the method is as old as time. For instance, this is one way the Aboriginals deal with goanna: coating it in clay, putting it into the hot coals to cook, and when done, breaking the clay, then peeling it and the skin off all in one go. The leg of suckling lamb is just right for this kind of treatment.

The idea was inspired by two dishes. One that I once enjoyed at the restaurant *Jamin* (now called *Robuchon*) in Paris in 1982 was a delectable young chicken baked inside a hardened salt and flour crust. The other was Alain Senderen's recipe for haunch of venison baked in clay. Use aluminium foil by all means, but if you are looking for a little more drama, try clay and serve at the table. The moment when the casing is broken, and the trapped aromas of meat and herbs fill the air, is one of great excitement to everyone.

PRIME RIB OF BEEF WITH CARROT AND ONION MARMALADE AND A PURÉE OF CAULIFLOWER AND DILL

For 4 people

a prime rib beef with 4 ribs, weighing around 1½ kg (3 lb)
salt and freshly ground black pepper
2 tablespoons butter in little knobs

FOR THE MARMALADE
4 large carrots
3 large white onions
2 tablespoons butter
⅓ cup honey
½ tablespoon salt
½ tablespoon cracked black peppercorns

FOR THE CAULIFLOWER AND DILL PURÉE
½ head cauliflower
3 sprigs dill, finely chopped
2 tablespoons butter, softened
large pinch salt and freshly ground black pepper

Trim the meat and the rib bones very well, removing all fat and gristle. Dust with the salt and pepper, and dot with the knobs of butter. Cover with a sheet of aluminium foil, put into a lightly buttered roasting pan and roast at 190°C (375°F) for 1½ hours, so as to be nicely *rare*. Rest for 8 minutes before carving. Collect and reserve any juices that escape.

To make the marmalade, peel and slice the carrots into even-sized matchsticks. Peel the onions and slice into even slivers. Put all the ingredients together in a saucepan and cook gently for 30 minutes, stirring every so often, until everything is soft and *jammy*.

To make the purée, break the cauliflower into flowerets and cook in boiling salted water until it is just soft. Purée for a few seconds only in a food processor with the butter. It will be creamy with tiny bits of cauliflower throughout, not smooth like baby food. Stir in the chopped dill, black pepper, and adjust the salt if necessary.

TO SERVE

Serve one rib per person. Spoon the blood and juices over, and a dollop of the marmalade alongside. Accompany with potatoes which have been roasted alongside the meat and the cauliflower and dill purée.

BEEF FILLET WITH PORT AND ÉCHALOTES

Serves 6 people

1 long beef fillet weighing around 2kg (4 lb)
200g (7 oz) échalotes
butter, in knobs
salt and freshly ground black pepper
375 ml (12 fl oz) good port
375ml (12 fl oz) concentrated veal stock (see recipe on page 22)

Peel the échalotes and fry gently in a little butter until soft and golden. Put to one side.

Trim the fillet scrupulously of all fat and membranes. Remove the side strap and, starting at the 'head' (the large end), begin the trimming. You should end up with a very clean piece of meat, free of *all* surrounding fat and gristle. Dust with salt and pepper all over.

Prepare a lightly buttered roasting pan and brown the outside of the meat all over, working on top of the stove over a fairly high heat. Then roast in a 200°C (400°F) oven for 15-20 minutes. Test for 'doneness' with a touch of the finger. When nicely rare, it will still 'give' a little, without being spongey. If in doubt, there's nothing wrong with slicing a little bit at the end and *having a look*. When ready, take out of the oven and rest for 5-10 minutes in a warm place while you prepare the sauce.

Deglaze the roasting pan and pour in the port. Scrape up all the browned-on meat sediments from the bottom of the pan and boil to reduce by half. Add the veal stock, and boil for a further 5 minutes. Strain the sauce through a fine sieve. Add the échalotes and check the seasoning.

TO SERVE

Slice the meat into medallions and arrange on hot serving plates. Pour all the blood and juices that escape into the sauce. Spoon a little sauce and the échalotes around the meat, and hand the rest around separately in a sauce boat. Accompany with vegetables of your choice.

RACK OF VEAL WITH TRUFFLE CREAM AND A GRATIN OF POTATOES

(Alternate sauce: Madeira cream)

Serves 4 people

1 veal rack (usually made up of 7 cutlets)
2 small knobs butter
salt and freshly ground black pepper

FOR THE SAUCE
1 shallot, both green and white parts
1 teaspoon butter
1 tablespoon madeira
3 tablespoons truffle juice
1 truffle chopped
1 teaspoon concentrated veal stock (see recipe on page 22)
400 ml (13 fl oz) cream
1 teaspoon black pepper
¼ teaspoon salt

FOR THE GRATIN
1 medium potato
milk
pinch each salt and pepper
pinch nutmeg
parmesan, freshly ground

Trim the rack so that it is free of all fat and membranes. Make sure that the bones are also very clean. Dust with pepper and salt, dot with the butter, and roast in one piece, at 200°C (400°F) for 30 minutes (35 minutes at the most as the meat should be rosy pink inside). Let it rest for a couple of minutes in a warm place before slicing. When the rack is about halfway done, bake the gratin.

To prepare the gratin, peel, wash and slice the potatoes thinly. Do not wash them once they are sliced. Put them into a pot, with just enough milk to cover, add the salt and pepper and nutmeg, and bring to the boil. Adjust to a gentle simmer for 5 minutes. Put the potato slices into an oven dish (or individual gratin dishes), sprinkle freshly grated parmesan over, and bake until golden brown — for about 15 minutes.

In the meantime, prepare the sauce. Melt the butter and stew the chopped shallot until soft. Add the madeira and boil to reduce by half. Stir in the cream, truffle juice, veal stock, salt and pepper, and boil until thick. Strain out the shallots and stir in the chopped truffle.

For the alternate sauce: omit the truffle and truffle juice and increase the quantity of madeira to 50ml (1½ fl oz). Boil this with the cream and veal stock before straining out the shallots.

TO SERVE

To portion the rack of seven cutlets for 4 people slice out three of the bones and cut four good thick chops, using the meat provided by the three extra cutlets. Spoon the sauce over. Serve the gratin separately.

VEAL FILLET IN A CRUST OF HERBS AND JUNIPER BERRIES

Ingredients per person

1 short veal fillet weighing approximately 200g (7 oz) when trimmed*
2 tablespoons brown sugar
2 teaspoons juniper berries
2 teaspoons cracked black peppercorns
3 tablespoons fresh mixed herbs, such as chives, thyme, tarragon and parsley
1 teaspoon salt
knob butter
¼ cup concentrated veal stock (see recipe on page 22)

Pound the juniper berries up very well with a mallet, or mortar and pestle, and mix them together with the herbs, sugar, salt and pepper, in a bowl.

Trim the meat so that absolutely no fat or tissues remain. Coat the fillet with the mixture, cover with clear plastic film and leave overnight if possible, or for several hours.

Put the meat in a buttered roasting pan and brown. Continue the cooking in a hot 200°C (400°F) oven for about 12 minutes. Test the meat by prodding with your finger. It should be neither soft and spongy nor firm, but just give a little to pressure. The meat should be rosy pink inside.

TO SERVE

Slice the fillet crossways into medallions. Arrange on a hot serving plate and drizzle a little hot concentrated veal stock over.

---

*Veal fillets are described by my butcher as either *short* and *long*. A long fillet will serve 2-3 people and a short fillet, 1-2.

LOIN OF LAMB STUFFED WITH CARROT AND CELERY BATONS WITH A HERB AND VEGETABLE SAUCE

Serves 4 people

2 loins of lamb, off the bone
1 stalk celery
1 medium carrot
caul fat (1 good piece will do)
salt and freshly ground black pepper

HERB AND VEGETABLE SAUCE
1 tightly packed cup fresh herbs, equal parts of parsley, dill and chives
1 clove garlic
1 medium cultivated mushroom
14cm (5½ in) piece carrot
¼ cup concentrated veal stock (see recipe on page 22)
¾ cup cream
pinch each salt and black pepper

The loin of lamb consists of two fine pieces of meat — the *eye* and the little *fillet*. Everything else, all the fat and covering tissues and membranes, is trimmed off. This means completely removing the flap which the butcher sometimes uses to roll the loin. There is some meat on this, but not much. Cut all this off and discard. Pull out the fillet and trim, and finally the *eye*. When you have two neatly trimmed pieces of meat in front of you, flatten them a little bit with a mallet. Repeat with the second loin.

Now prepare the stuffing. Cut the sides of the carrot off squarely, then slice 1cm (½ in) wide batons, as long as possible. Blanch. Trim the celery of all of its stringy bits, then slice batons of the same size, and blanch.

Spread the caul fat out on your work bench. A good piece is fine and lacy, without thickish lumps throughout (sometimes these can be trimmed back a bit, but be careful not to make any holes in the caul). Cut out a square of caul large enough to roll the meat in. It doesn't matter if it is too large because the edges can be trimmed later. Put the slightly flattened eye of the loin in the centre of the square. Dust with salt and pepper, and lay half the carrot and celery batons all the way along. Put the flattened fillet on top and pull the meat edges together as you roll the caul around tightly so that everything is encased like a sausage. Trim off any excess caul. Put the meat on a plate, cover with plastic film, and refrigerate until needed. Repeat this operation with the second loin.

To make the sauce, first chop the dill and parsley *very finely*, and slice the chives, *very finely*. Slice the garlic clove, the carrot and the mushroom into *very fine dice*. Melt a small knob of butter in a pan and stir in all the vegetables and herbs and a good pinch each of salt and pepper. Cook gently to soften, stirring all the while, then pour in the stock and cream. Boil for about 5 minutes until it thickens. Taste and adjust the seasoning if necessary.

Put the loins side by side in a buttered roasting pan and brown them on top of the stove to begin with. When they are brown on both sides, roast in a 200 °C (400 °F) oven for 12 minutes, turning every few minutes. When done, rest for 3 or 4 minutes in a warm place, before slicing into 2cm (1 inch) thick medallions.

TO SERVE

Ladle some sauce into the centre of hot serving plates. Spread the sauce out a little and put 3 or 4 medallions in the centre. Accompany with a dish of buttery fresh pasta.

LEG OF SUCKLING LAMB BAKED IN A PARCEL WITH GARLIC AND TARRAGON

(Accompanied by a layered potato cake and creamy fried eggplant)

SERVES 4 PEOPLE
1 x 1 kg (1 x 2lb) leg suckling lamb*
4 cloves garlic, peeled and sliced in two lengthwise
4 long leafy sprigs tarragon
1 tablespoon jellied veal stock(see recipe on page 22)
salt and freshly ground black pepper
4 sheets aluminium foil or 1kg (2 lb) (approx.) clay** with 3 sheets of greaseproof paper.

FOR THE LAYERED POTATO CAKE
6 medium large potatoes, approximately
2 tablespoons butter, in knobs
2 tablespoons parmesan cheese, freshly grated
1 tablespoon fresh tarragon leaves
salt and freshly ground black pepper

1 x 16xm (6 in) cake ring

FOR THE CREAMY FRIED EGGPLANT
1 medium sized eggplant
1 tablespoon concentrated tomato paste
salt and freshly ground black pepper
butter
400ml (12 fl oz) cream
1 small white onion, chopped
juice of 1 lemon

To cook the lamb, begin by melting a knob of butter in a roasting pan and browning the leg all over. If making a parcel using *aluminium foil*, put the 4 sheets, one on top of the other, and place the leg in the centre. Make slits all over the meat and stick the sliced garlic cloves inside. Dust generously with the salt and pepper, and put the tarragon and jellied stock on top. Fold the foil up around the meat, and secure at the top, to make a tightly sealed parcel (so that none of the cooking juices can escape).

Roast at 190°C (375°F) for 35 minutes. (When done, it should still be nicely pink inside.)

---

*The leg used in this recipe is that of a milk-fed three week old lamb. When buying the whole lamb, it is a good idea to use both legs, cook them in individual parcels, and serve 8 people. If you don't want to buy the whole lamb, buy a small 1½kg (3 lb) leg of baby lamb and observe the longer cooking times given.

**Clay can be purchased from any supplier of potters' goods.

If you are using clay, proceed as follows. Cover your workbench with a couple of overlapping sheets of clear plastic film. Roll the clay out on top of the plastic using a rolling pin, until the sheet is large enough to wrap around the meat easily. Prepare the meat as already described, by browning, seasoning and arranging the garlic, tarragon and stock on top. Wrap the lamb in the greaseproof paper so that it is well covered and *watertight* on the bottom. Use cellotape to seal any joins so that liquids cannot escape into the clay, then lift the parcel into the centre of the clay and *turn it upside down*. Wrap the clay around (the plastic will help you to lift it up) pressing the edges together and smoothing out any holes or cracks that appear. Put it into a baking pan, *with the joined side on the bottom* (the joins in the paper parcel will now face upwards). If you don't intend cooking it for a while, cover with a slightly damp cloth. Bake in a very hot 240°C (475°F) oven for 20 minutes, then at 190°C (375°F) for another 40 minutes. (If you are using a 1½ kg (3 lb) leg, cook at 240°C (475°F) for 30 minutes, and at 190°C (375°F) for 60 minutes).

To make the layered potato cake, peel, wash and slice the potatoes into thin rounds. Butter the inside of the ring, and place on a buttered baking tray. Begin filling the ring with the potato, layering in a circular fashion until it is half filled. Dust with salt and pepper, sprinkle the cheese and tarragon leaves all over, and continue filling right to the top. Make sure the potato is packed well down, and put a row of vertical slices all the way around the inside of the ring to make a neat and decorative edge to the cake. Also make the top layer as neat and attractive as you can. Dot all over with a few small knobs of butter and bake at 190°C (375°F) for 1 hour. Unmould by running a knife around the inside of the ring and lifting it off. Serve hot in wedges.

To make the creamy fried eggplant, first slice the eggplant lengthwise, so as to obtain 4 more or less equal slices. Slice a thin piece off the two outer slices so as to make them flat, and to remove some of the excess skin. Sprinkle with salt and leave to drain for ½ an hour.

In the meantime make the cream sauce. Sweat the onion in a teaspoonful of butter. When soft, add the lemon juice and boil for a few seconds. Add the cream, a pinch of salt, ground black pepper, and boil again to reduce until thick. Check the seasoning and strain out the onions.

Wash and pat the eggplant slices dry and dust with pepper. Fry on both sides in liberal amounts of butter until well cooked. Place the slices in a shallow ovenproof serving dish and smear the upper side of each slice with some of the concentrated tomato. Grind a little more pepper over, and pour the cream sauce around (not over). Bake at 180°C (350°F) for 15-20 minutes, so that the buttery eggplant juices have mingled with the cream, and all is bubbling hot. Serve one slice per guest on individual side plates.

TO SERVE

When the lamb is ready, take it from the oven and let it rest for 10 minutes. Carve slices and arrange on serving plates. Spoon the juices that have accumulated in the bottom of the parcel over the meat. Arrange a wedge of potato cake alongside the meat and accompany on a separate side plate with a slice of the eggplant.

Note: If you are serving the lamb baked in clay, crack the parcel open (a sharp knock with the back of the carving knife will suffice) and carve at the table.

MEDALLIONS OF LAMB WITH KIDNEY AND ROSEMARY

Serves 6 people

6 x 6 cutlet racks of lamb
6 lamb kidneys
1 bunch fresh rosemary (about 8 sprigs)
250ml (8 fl oz) concentrated veal stock (see recipe on page 22)
1 tablespoon cream
salt and freshly ground black pepper

Trim the meat. Lever away the thick outer layer of fat and pull off. Trim the meat carefully of all the remaining fat and membranes. The meat should be absolutely clean. The cutlet bones don't matter, as they will be discarded halfway through the cooking.

Soak the kidneys in cold water and remove the transparent skins.

Pull the rosemary leaves off the stems, and press half of them onto the meat. Dust all over with salt and pepper and put to one side until about 15 minutes before you wish to serve them.

Prepare a lightly buttered roasting pan. Brown the lamb and the kidneys on top of the stove before putting them into a 200°C (400°F) oven. Roast for 5 minutes on each side, then take out the lamb and cut the whole piece carefully away from the bones. Discard these. Return the lamb to the oven briefly to complete the cooking (another couple of minutes will do). Remove both the lamb and kidneys and rest in a warm place while you make the sauce. The cooking time in all should be 10-12 minutes for both the lamb and the kidneys to be nicely pink.

Deglaze the pan very well. Throw in the remaining rosemary and add the veal stock. Boil for 3 or 4 minutes, and add the cream right at the end.

TO SERVE

Slice the lamb crossways into little medallions. Slice the kidneys longways into thin strips. Arrange both meats on hot serving plates, and spoon on a little sauce with rosemary around.

BLANQUETTE OF BABY LAMB SHOULDER

Serves 4 people

2 baby lamb shoulders
8 pickling onions (or small onions, halved or quartered)
½ teaspoon each salt and cracked black peppercorns
zest of one lemon
knob butter
light veal stock to cover (see recipe on page 22)
8 small new potatoes, peeled, quartered and turned
⅔ cup fresh peas
1 small yellow turnip
2 tablespoons parsley, finely chopped
1 cup cream
2 tablespoons lemon juice
2 slices white bread
1 tablespoon peanut oil

Trim the shoulders very well, so that the meat is completely free of fat and tissues, and cut the meat into even-sized chunks of about 3 x 3cm (1 x 1in).

Melt the butter in a saucepan, stir in the onions and then the meat along with the salt, cracked peppercorns and lemon zest. Cook for a minute to brown all the sides of the meat. Cover with the light veal stock, bring to the boil, then simmer with the lid on for 45 minutes.

Slice the crusts from the bread slices and cut the remaining bread to a small dice. Fry in the hot peanut oil until golden brown. Drain and reserve croûtons.

While the lamb is cooking, prepare the vegetables. Shell the peas, and 'turn' the carrot, turnip and peeled potatoes to neat oval shapes all the same size. When the meat is ready — it should be nicely tender — strain the cooking liquid into a bowl and reserve the meat in another. Put the liquid back into the saucepan along with the vegetables, bring to the boil, and cook for 8-10 minutes, until they are tender also. Now strain the liquid out again, into a bowl, and put the vegetables in with the meat while you finish the sauce.

Put the cooking liquid back into the pan and add the lemon juice and cream, and boil until it starts to thicken. Remove from the stove and whisk in the egg yolks. Stir the meat and vegetables back into the sauce along with the fine parsley.

TO SERVE

Ladle onto serving plates and sprinkle the tiny croûtons over.

Barbecued cubes of lamb with rosemary and vegetables

Serves 4 people

2 loins of lamb (including the little fillet) off the bone
peanut oil
2 sprigs rosemary
¼ teaspoon salt and freshly ground black pepper
1 medium red capsicum
½ small eggplant
4 medium zucchini
1 medium white onion
1 head fresh corn
4 tablespoons concentrated veal or lamb stock (see recipe on page 22)

4 long wooden skewers

Trim away every bit of fat and all the covering tissues from the eye of the loins and the little fillets. Cut this meat neatly into evenly shaped cubes, about 3 x 3cm (1 x 1 in). Thread these onto the skewers. Trickle a little peanut oil all over, sprinkle with the leaves of the rosemary, and season generously with salt and pepper. Put aside until serving time.

Blister, peel and remove the seeds from the capsicum. Cut into pieces of a similar size to the lamb.

Using mainly the outer sections of the eggplant and zucchini (the skin and about 3mm (⅛ in) of flesh) slice into squares of a similar size. Salt the eggplant and leave to drain for ½ hour. Wash then pat dry. Slice the onion into square shapes.

Boil the corn on the cob in salted water until it is tender.

Gently stir-fry the onion for a minute, then the vegetable squares in a little hot peanut oil, until they are cooked, but still crunchy. Lift out and keep warm.

Deglaze the pan, put in the stock and bring to the boil.

Barbecue the lamb so that it is crisped on the outside and juicy pink and tender inside.

TO SERVE

Slice the hot corn off the cob and spread across the serving plates. Scatter the other vegetables all over these. Push the lamb off the skewers and pile on top of the vegetables. Drizzle a little hot stock over and serve.

Roast Suckling Pig with Tarragon

Serves 10-12

1 x 8kg (1 x 16lb) suckling pig
6 stems fresh tarragon
500 ml (16 fl oz) concentrated veal stock (see recipe on page 22)
125ml (4 fl oz) tarragon vinegar (or to taste)
300g (9½ oz) butter
2 tablespoons peanut oil
salt and cracked black peppercorns

The first thing to do is to cut the pig into its various portions. The head, which is full of flavoursome meat, can be used to make brawn or it can be added to a stock. The rest of the pig is cut into the shoulders, legs and side pieces. The sides being thinner than the other pieces will cook more quickly and should be removed when done, and kept warm for the remainder of the roasting time. For a pig this size, this will be 2 hours. The meat will then be very well cooked, succulent and tender.

Place the portions, skin side up, in a large roasting pan. Score the skin with a sharp knife, rub with salt, scatter some cracked peppercorns over, and dot with butter. Roast in a 190°-200°C (375°-400°F) oven, basting frequently. After 1½ hours, take out the side pieces and keep warm. Continue the cooking for another half hour. Test for 'doneness' in the thickest part of the leg. The juices should run clear. Rest the meat in a warm place while you complete the sauce and crackling. Pull the skin off in strips and scrape off all the underlying fat. Heat the peanut oil in a frypan and fry the strips until very crisp taking care not to burn them. (Turn the heat right back if things get too hot.)

Prepare the sauce by boiling the veal stock with the tarragon leaves, the vinegar, salt and pepper to taste, until it thickens.

TO SERVE

Arrange slices of meat in the centre of hot serving plates, top with some of the crackling and ladle sauce over. Accompany with potatoes and baby parsnips which have been roasted alongside the pig after the side pieces have been removed. Pass around separately in a sauceboat a traditional purée of pears or apples.

SMOKED HAM HOCKS WITH MUSTARD VINAIGRETTE

1 smoked ham hock per person
1 carrot
1 stalk celery
1 medium white onion
2 parsley stems
2 sprigs thyme
2 bay leaves
teaspoon peppercorns
50g (1¾ oz) butter
cold water to cover

FOR THE VINAIGRETTE
1¼ cups good quality olive oil
⅓ cup good white vinegar (e.g. champagne vinegar)
2 tablespoons Dijon mustard
¼ teaspoon each salt and pepper

Melt the butter in a large lidded stewing pot. Stir in the chopped, washed vegetables and herbs, and the peppercorns, and cook for 2 minutes. Put in the hocks and cover with cold water. Bring to the boil, adjust to a gentle simmer, and cover with the lid. Cook for 2½ hours.

Prepare the dressing. Put all the ingredients together in a bowl and whisk until thoroughly combined (it will have quite a thick consistency rather like mayonnaise).

TO SERVE

When the hocks are done, take the meat from the bone and peel away all the skin and fat. You will end up with 2 or 3 knobs of tender rosy meat. Put these in the centre of serving plates in a pile and coat with the dressing. Accompany with a dish of salad greens and another of hot, crisp French fries. Delicious for a luncheon or informal dinner.

Note: The ham hocks can be prepared well in advance, even days ahead of when you wish to serve them. Leave on the bone and cover with the cooking liquid and simply reheat.

PAN FRIED LAMBS BRAINS WITH A ZUCCHINI FRITTER

Ingredients for 2 people

FOR THE BRAINS
2 sets of fresh lambs brains (1 set per person)
flour for dusting
knob butter
salt and freshly ground black pepper

THE CREAMED ZUCCHINI
2 small zucchini
2 teaspoons onion, finely minced
2 teaspoons lemon juice
50ml (1½ fl oz) cream
pinch salt and freshly ground black pepper
knob butter

FOR THE FRITTERS
2 small zucchini
2 teaspoons onion, finely minced
1 egg
4 teaspoons S.R. flour
pinch salt and freshly ground black pepper
knob butter

There are three parts to this dish, and *all* the cooking should be done very much at the last minute. I would prepare the fritter and the creamed zucchini before frying the brains.

Prepare the brains by separating the two lobes and soaking for 2 hours in clean cold water to remove the blood. Change the water regularly. Remove the covering membrane and pat dry. Roll lightly in some flour which has been seasoned with salt and pepper. Now they are ready for the final cooking.

For the creamed zucchini, grate the zucchini and mince the onion. Melt the butter in a frypan, and when foaming, stir in the zucchini and onion, dust with salt and pepper, and cook for a couple of minutes until soft. Stir in the cream and lemon juice and boil until thick.

To make the fritters, mix all the ingredients together. Melt the butter in a frypan, and put in half the mixture (to make one fritter at a time). Quickly flatten the mixture out into a thin circle the size of a bread and butter plate, and fry each side briefly until golden brown. Keep warm.

TO SERVE

Fry the brains in hot butter for 3 minutes on each side. Do this just before you serve them. Put a fritter in the centre of each hot serving plate and top with the creamed zucchini. Slice the crisp brains in half lengthwise and arrange on top. Serve immediately.

LAMB KIDNEYS WITH BRIOCHE AND BONE MARROW

Ingredients for 6 people

18 fresh lamb kidneys*
2 cups sliced bone marrow
1 small white onion
1 cup concentrated veal stock (see recipe on page 22)
1 cup red wine
½ cup chives, finely sliced
large pinch salt and freshly ground black pepper
small knob butter
6 individual soft brioche rolls (see recipe on page 213)

Make the brioche first using small individual tins.

To make the sauce, stew the chopped onion in the butter until soft. Add the red wine and boil to reduce by half. Add the veal stock and boil again until a thickened sauce consistency is reached. Strain out the onion, taste, season with salt and pepper and set aside.

Clean the kidneys. Soak in cold water and remove the transparent skins. Pat dry, and roll in the chives, the salt and pepper.

TO COOK AND SERVE

Cut lids in the tops of the brioche and re-warm the rolls. Gently poach the sliced marrow in the prepared sauce for a few seconds on each side (it does not take long) until softened right through but not melting.

While you do this, cook the kidneys. This can be done either on a charcoal grill or on a hot buttered grid. Cook the kidneys whole, to the point that the insides are still *pink* but not *raw*. On the other hand, don't overcook them or they will quickly become leathery. (Test during the cooking by prodding with a finger. Too soft and they are not cooked enough, but they should never reach the point of feeling really firm.)

Slice the kidneys in halves and arrange on hot serving plates alongside the warmed brioche. Put some slices of the poached marrow over the kidneys as well as inside the brioche. Spoon some sauce over, replace the lid, and serve.

---

*Note: To make smaller first course portions, allow 1 kidney per person.

CALVES LIVER WITH FRESH BLACK CURRANTS

Ingredients for 4 people

1 small fresh calves liver*
1 punnet fresh black currants (if unavailable, use red currants)
2 tablespoons cassis liqueur
125ml (4 fl oz) concentrated veal stock (see recipe on page 22)
1 tablespoon cream
pinch salt and freshly ground black pepper
knob butter

Clean the liver by peeling off the outer layer of thin transparent tissue. If you leave this on, the liver will curl and toughen during cooking.

Avoiding all the tubes and tough bits underneath, slice 4 long slices, or several shorter slices, about 1 cm (½ in) thick. Dust with the salt and pepper.

Take the currants off their stems, and wash.

Now, take a heavy frypan, make it very hot, and swirl some butter all around. Fry the liver slices briefly on both sides. This will take only 1 or 2 minutes. The liver should still feel a little soft to touch, without being spongy. Remove the liver from the pan and rest in a warm place for 1 minute while you attend to the sauce.

Pour any juice or blood that escapes back into the pan, add the liqueur and the stock and boil for ½ minute. Toss in the fresh currants and whirl in the cream.

TO SERVE

Slice the liver on the slant and arrange thin slices across each hot serving plate. Spoon currants and some sauce over all.

---

*Make sure that the butcher gives you a nice pale *fresh* liver. Liver that has been frozen turns mushy when cooked. As freezing is a fairly common practice, it is important to be vigilant when shopping.

PAN FRIED VEAL SWEETBREADS WITH ENGLISH SPINACH, CORIANDER, SHITAKE MUSHROOMS AND PEAS

Ingredients for 4 people

2 x 454g (1 lb) pkts veal sweetbreads
16 shitake mushrooms (4 per person)
½ cup fresh peas, shelled
2 teaspoons Spanish onion, minced
125ml (5 fl oz) concentrated veal stock (see recipe on page 22)
8 leaves English spinach
2 tablespoons coriander, finely chopped, and a few extra sprigs for garnish
75g (2½ oz) butter
50ml (1½ fl oz) cream
salt and freshly ground black pepper

POACHING LIQUOR
1 medium carrot, chopped
1 small onion, chopped
1 celery stalk, chopped
2 sprigs parsley
a few peppercorns
water to cover

Take the stalks out of the mushrooms and soak in just enough water to cover them for at least ½ hour.

Soak the sweetbreads in lots of cold water for 2 hours. Put all the listed ingredients for the poaching liquor together in a saucepan and bring to the boil. Put the sweetbreads in and poach gently for 10 minutes. Remove and refresh in cold water. Trim away all the fatty and gristly bits and peel off the covering transparent membrane. Slice the sweetbreads into evenly sized pieces. Pat dry with kitchen paper.

Cook the peas in salted boiling water, refresh in iced water and put to one side.

Melt 50g (1¾ oz) of the butter in a frypan, stir in the onion and stew until golden, then put in the slices of sweetbread. Fry crisply on all sides, then take out of the pan and keep warm. Deglaze the pan with the veal stock, swirl it around for 1 minute, then strain through a fine sieve into a bowl.

Starting again with a clean pan, add the remaining butter, and when foaming, put in the mushrooms (left whole), the coriander and spinach, dust with salt and pepper, and fry briskly for just a few seconds. Put back the sweetbreads, pour the sauce over, stir in the peas, and finish with the cream.

TO SERVE
Spoon onto hot serving plates and garnish with some coriander.

GLAZED TRIPE WITH FENNEL

Serves 4-6 people, depending on the size of the portions and whether they are for the first or main course

500g (19 oz) tripe
50ml (16 fl oz) white wine
500ml (16 fl oz) vegetable stock (see recipe on page 24)
1 small white onion
½ head fennel (or a small one)
1 tablespoon fennel leaves, chopped
1 medium carrot
25g (⅝ oz) butter
2 cups cream
salt, to taste, 1 teaspoon cracked black peppercorns
toasted croûtons to garnish

Slice the tripe into thin, short pieces — about 6cm (2½ in) long. Put into a saucepan with the wine and stock, and poach until tender, about 1½ hours. Remove the tripe with a slotted spoon. Set aside on a plate covered with plastic wrap, and reserve 1 cup of the cooking liquor.

Slice both the onion and the fennel in half lengthwise, then into fine pieces across. Cut the carrot into matchsticks, the same length as the tripe strips.

Melt the butter in a pan, and gently sauté the vegetables for 1 minute. Add the cream and 1 cup of the cooking liquid with a pinch of salt and the pepper. Boil until the cream is thick, then stir in the tripe.

TO SERVE

Ladle the tripe and vegetable mixture, along with some of the sauce, into individual gratin dishes and brown under a very hot pre-heated grill. Garnish with the toasted croûtons.

SWEETBREADS AND GOOSE LIVERS WITH BRAISED WITLOOF AND BALSAMIC VINEGAR

Serves 2 people

1 x 454g (1 lb) packet veal sweetbreads
6 fresh goose livers (weighing around 30g (1 oz) each)
2 small witloof (Belgian endive)
75g (2½ oz) sliced button mushrooms
2 tablespoons balsamic vinegar
125ml (4 fl oz) cream
salt and freshly ground black pepper
a couple of knobs butter

POACHING LIQUOR
1 small carrot
1 small onion
½ stalk celery
2 sprigs parsley
a few peppercorns
water to cover

Soak the livers in milk for a couple of hours, then trim. Remove all threads and traces of the green gall. Wash and pat dry. Season with salt and pepper and set aside until serving time.

Soak the sweetbreads in cold water for a couple of hours. Put all the ingredients for the poaching liquor into a pot, bring to the boil, add the sweetbreads, and cook for 10 minutes. Drain, refresh in cold water, then trim very well, so that they are completely free of gristle, fat and covering membranes. Pat dry and dust with salt and pepper. Melt a knob of butter in a small roasting pan, put in the sweetbreads, and roast, turning frequently, for 20 minutes at 190°C (375°F). When done, they will be nicely browned and quite firm.

Separate the witloof leaves, wash, then blanch and drain.

TO COOK AND SERVE

Melt the remaining knob of butter in a frypan. Put in the mushrooms, dust with salt and pepper, and cook until golden. When almost done, put in the blanched witloof and toss briskly to heat through. Now push these well to one side and put in the livers. These will take less than a minute to cook — just a few seconds on each side. When done, they should still be soft and rosy at the centre. Test by prodding with a finger while cooking. They should never feel firm. When ready, take everything out of the pan and rest in a warm place while you deglaze the pan with the cream. Scrape up all the livery bits into the cream, boil for a few seconds to thicken slightly, then pour through a sieve.

Slice the sweetbreads and livers in half lengthwise. (The sweetbread pieces should not be too large.) Arrange these on serving plates with the mushrooms and witloof leaves, and drizzle the cream and the balsamic vinegar over everything.

PICKLED OX TONGUE WITH MUSTARD SAUCE

Serves 3 people

1 pickled ox tongue

POACHING LIQUOR
*1 onion, chopped
1 medium carrot, chopped
1 celery stalk with its leaves, chopped
3 sprigs parsley
1 few peppercorns
1 bay leaf
⅓ cup white vinegar
1 tablespoon brown sugar
water to cover*

THE MUSTARD SAUCE
*1 cup concentrated veal stock (see recipe on page 22)
2 tablespoons Dijon mustard
¼ cup cream
2 tablespoons cooking liquor
1 tablespoon chives, finely sliced, to garnish*

Wash and chop all the vegetables. Put the tongue and all the ingredients listed for the poaching liquor into a deep soup pot. Cover with water, bring to the boil, then simmer for 1½-2 hours, until the tongue is tender.

Lift the tongue out of the liquid and put into a pan of cold water. Now peel off the skin and trim away the bony parts underneath. (The skin is easier to peel when the tongue is still hot.) Put the tongue into a bowl and cover with some of the strained cooking liquid, and store until needed.

Put the veal stock, cooking liquor and the mustard together in a pan, whisk to combine, and boil for 1-2 minutes to thicken slightly. Whisk in the cream and boil for a further minute.

TO SERVE

Warm the tongue through the cooking liquid in which it was stored, then slice the hot tongue crossways into rounds. Arrange the slices on serving plates, spoon a little of the mustard sauce over and finish with a sprinkling of the chives.

POULTRY AND GAME

In our house there is a difference of opinion as to whose fault it was the day we missed our connecting train at Avignon. Our train from Valence must have been running late, and I maintain that there is only a certain speed at which I can go when it comes to leaping off one train with heavy bags and a young daughter in tow, dashing down stairs and along tunnels swarming with passengers, and up more stairs to catch another. Anyhow, we missed it, and here we were in Avignon, about 400 kilometres from Eugenie- les-bains, where we were booked for an 8 o'clock dinner. It was now midday.

We spotted the nearby Avis office, and spent the remainder of the day driving through what my daughter Rachel dubbed 'goose country'.

A year later we returned to Gascony and explored it at a more leisurely pace. We fell in love with the lovely confits of goose and duck of the region, a preparation as old as the surrounding hills and as old as the remarkable *foie-gras*, for which the birds are primarily grown. It has become one of my favourite methods for dealing with such birds. The meat is made succulent and tender, rather ham-like to taste because of the salting, and is delicious with potatoes roasted in the same goose fat and a tart vinegar demi-glace to cut the grease. It is the only way I have served the leg of Aussie duck where the bones have come back licked clean.

In the late French spring of 1984, my husband and I travelled by a new route south through les Montagnes d'Albrac, quite a way north of Toulouse and the underlying Gascony region where we were heading yet again. We stayed in Laguiole, a ski resort village edged with green fields abounding in wild flowers. The air was crisp though the snow was long gone. We dined where we were staying, at the Restaurant-Hotel of Lou Mazuc, and being heartily tired of rich classical cooking and overly worked nouvelle cuisine, we ate dishes reflective of the land about: hams, pressed tongue, duck skins stuffed with potatoes and sliced like sausage, and a wonderful confit of duck leg with crisp skin and golden potatoes. It is the sort of food one remembers because it is satisfying and warming, and above all *tasty*. When you think about it, isn't that what really counts?

Roast saddle of hare with pepper sauce and parsnip purée and rich hare stew with damper, page 152.

Medley of creamed mushrooms, page 87.

Rack of veal with truffle cream and a gratin of potatoes, page 116.

Salad of Balmain bugs, octopus and prawns with little vegetables and a watercress and pine nut mayonnaise, page 110.

Poached cubes of bar cod with mustard butter and chives, page 98

Gratin of vabbies, page 81.

Grilled spatchcock with sage butter, fried zucchini dice and cherry tomatoes, page 147.

Blanquette of baby lamb shoulder, page 123

CHICKEN BREAST WITH SORREL AND A GRATIN OF THE LEG

Serves 4 people

2 fresh free-range chickens, 800-900g (1½-2 lb) each
1 leek
1 large carrot
1 large onion
1 stick celery
1 teaspoon peppercorns
4 stalks parsley
600ml (19 fl oz) cream
1 tablespoon truffle juice (optional)
2 truffles, sliced (optional)
pinch salt and freshly ground black pepper
butter
2 teaspoons peanut oil
4 small bunches sorrel (1 bunch per person)

Cut each chicken into serving portions — the 2 breasts and the 2 legs. Prepare the breast by cutting the wing off at the first joint from the body. Scrape all the flesh and skin away from the little bone to make it very clean, then lop the rounded end off.

Chop the leek, carrot, onion and celery and wash thoroughly. Melt a knob of butter in the bottom of a soup pot and brown the vegetables. Add the wing tips, the chopped carcass and the legs, brown, then cover everything with cold water. Add the peppercorns and parsley, bring to the boil, and simmer until the legs are tender (about 1 hour).

When the legs are done, take out of the cooking liquid, and when cool enough to handle remove the meat from the bone making sure that you do not include any skin or gristle.

Strain the stock, allow to rest for a few minutes, then skim away the fat with a ladle. Measure 2 cups of the stock (you can freeze the rest to use on another occasion) and boil to reduce to a scant ½ cup. Add the cream, truffle juice and sliced truffles. Reduce again to a thick sauce consistency, taste, then season with salt and pepper.

To cook the breast, melt a knob of butter with the peanut oil in a frypan. When foaming, put the breasts in, skin side down and brown. Put each breast onto a square of aluminium foil, season all over with salt and pepper, then place a small knob of butter on top. Fold the foil over and secure tightly. Put on a baking tray and bake at 200°C (400°F) for 20 minutes — until just done.

Cook the sorrel at the very last minute. Wash, and chop off the thick lower part of the stems. Toss in hot butter, seasoned with salt and pepper, till it has all gone limp and the green leaves have turned a dull grey/green.

TO SERVE

Put the leg meat into individual gratin dishes and cover with the cream sauce. Warm through in the oven until the sauce bubbles, then glaze under a hot grill.

Take the breasts out of the foil parcels and slice them across on the slant into 4 or 5 pieces. Arrange these on a bed of cooked sorrel.

Note: These two dishes can be served together or separately, depending on the occasion and also on how hungry your guests are. Served together they make a substantial meal. What I often like to do is to serve the breast part on its own as part of a dinner menu one day and make a family meal of the legs the next day.

PAN FRIED BREAST OF CHICKEN WITH VEGETABLE PURÉE

Ingredients for 4 people

4 chicken breasts
50g (1¾ oz) butter, divided into 3 knobs
1 medium white onion, chopped
½ cup dry white wine
¾ cup cream
the white part of 2 small leeks, chopped (about 1 cup)
salt and freshly ground black pepper
½ cup peas
2 medium carrots
2 tablespoons chives, finely sliced

Melt a knob of butter in a frypan, stir in the onion and fry until soft. Add the wine and boil until it is a golden glaze. Now add the cream, a pinch of salt, pepper and boil until it is thick. Strain, then discard the onion, and set the cream to one side.

Wash the leek very well, and fry in a little more butter until it is very soft. Boil the carrots and peas in salted water until tender. Purée the cooked leeks, peas and carrots together and when smooth add the reduced cream and purée for a few more seconds. Put the purée back into the saucepan ready to be reheated.

Season the chicken breasts with a little pepper and a pinch of salt. Melt the rest of the butter in a frypan, and when foaming place the chicken breasts in, skin side down first. Cook for about 5 minutes on each side. The skin should be crisped and the inside tender and just done.

TO SERVE

Ladle some of the warmed vegetable purée into the centre of hot serving plates. Lay the breasts, thinly sliced on the slant on top, and finish with some very fine chives scattered over the purée. Simple, tasty, and sauceless.

DUCK CONFIT

Serves 6 people

3 fresh ducks, approximately 1.5kg (3 lb) each
1 cup mixed herbs, such as dill, oregano, basil, thyme
1½ cups rock salt (1 packet)
4 × 325g (4 × 10 oz) tins goose fat

THE SAUCE
2 cups brown chicken glaze
good quality white vinegar (1 or 2 tablespoons or to taste)

Slice the duck away from the bone into two portions. Starting from the neck, work your way down either side of the breast bone so that the breast (minus the wing, which is left on the carcass) and the leg come away in one piece.

Mix the herbs and rock salt together in a bowl and coat the duck liberally on both sides. Leave in the refrigerator for *3 hours*, then wash *thoroughly*. Pat dry. Place the duck in a baking dish, or lidless casserole, which is deep, but not too large. The pieces can be packed tightly together. Pour over enough goose fat to cover all the meat.

Poach in a moderately slow oven of about 170°C (340°F) to begin with, for 1-2 hours, until the meat is tender and a skewer can pass through easily. If during the cooking the fat becomes too hot, turn the temperature right back. It is important that throughout the cooking the surface of the fat should barely move. No more than a gentle simmer.

Cool slightly, then put the duck pieces into a plastic container or china dish. Cover completely with the strained goose fat in which it was cooked. Store in the refrigerator until needed. If well covered with the fat, it will keep very well this way for 2 or 3 months — possibly longer.

When you wish to serve the duck, remove it from the fat by tipping the whole thing out of its container in one large block into a baking dish, and melting the fat away from the meat in a just warm oven. Place the meat in a shallow pan with some light chicken stock or water. The liquid should not completely cover the duck, but allow the top skin part to crisp and brown slightly. The meat underneath will retain its pink moistness and any clinging fat will melt away.

Boil the glaze with the vinegar for a minute or two. Remember not to add salt to this sauce as the duck is already sufficiently salty. Season with pepper.

TO SERVE
Arrange the duck on hot plates and pour a little of the sauce over. Accompany with braised cabbage or one of the many varieties of dried beans. Fresh borlotti beans are wonderful if in season. Pod and boil in salted water until tender. If using dried beans, soak for several hours first. Fresh beetroot and peas are also good, as are potatoes roasted in goose fat.

Notes: Substitute goose for duck and cook for 2-3 hours. One goose will serve 4 people. Other confits can be made from turkey, pork, or even rabbit.

Pieces of duck or goose confit may be used with a variety of meats such as salt pork, garlic sausage, and a shoulder of lamb, to create a hearty cassoulet.

The cooking fat may be used over and over again, as long as you check it every so often to make sure it is not becoming too salty. If it is, discard, and begin again with fresh fat.

WILD DUCK WITH LEMON, ACCOMPANIED BY A CRÊPE OF ENGLISH SPINACH

Serves 2 people

1 x 1kg (2 lb) fresh wild duck
1 tablespoon fresh garlic shallot, sliced
1 tablespoon onion, sliced
1 tablespoon lemon peel, roughly chopped
1 tablespoon lemon peel, in fine julienne
2 tablespoons lemon juice
light brown chicken stock, to cover
salt and freshly ground black pepper
knob butter

BASIC CRÊPE BATTER
(makes approximately 16 crêpes)
100g (3½ oz) flour
large pinch salt
2 eggs
150ml (5 fl oz) milk
150ml (5 fl oz) water
2 tablespoons melted butter

FILLING FOR 2 CRÊPES
½ bunch English spinach (125g (4 oz) leaves without stems)
2 tablespoons butter
large pinch salt and freshly ground black pepper

Small 20-24cm (8-9½ in) frypan for the crêpes

The crêpes can be prepared a little in advance and reheated to serve.

Make the crêpe batter and let it rest for ½ hour before making the crêpes.

Sift the flour and salt into a bowl. Add the eggs, and then the milk and water, bit by bit. Stir the melted butter in at the end. When the mixture is smooth, strain, and let stand for another ½ hour.

Prepare the spinach filling. Chop the stems from the leaves, blanch, drain very well, and purée with the butter, and pepper and salt to taste.

To cook the crêpes, melt a small knob of butter in the frypan. When sizzling hot, swirl around to coat the bottom well. Pour off any excess. Ladle in enough crêpe batter to cover the bottom evenly when the pan is tilted. When the underside of the crêpe is well browned, lift with a spatula, turn over, and brown the other side. Stack the required number of crêpes on top of each other on a plate.

To fill the crêpes, lay them out flat on your workbench, and put the spinach mixture down the centre of each one. Roll up, and keep to one side until it is time to reheat them in the oven.

Now for the duck. First of all it will need cleaning. Make a slit from the bottom of the breastbone, straight down to the parson's nose, and pull out all the entrails. Wash the cavity very clean and pat dry. Now remove the meat from the carcass in two sections. Start at the neck and work downwards on either side of the breastbone, slicing the meat cleanly away from the bone, severing the wing off completely. Continue until you have the bird in two halves, each composed of the breast and leg, with the only bone still attached being the leg bone. Now slice the breasts from the legs, and trim away unnecessary fatty bits neatly from each.

Put the breasts skin side down on a plate, season generously with black pepper and a pinch of salt. Cover the plate with clear plastic film, and set to one side.

Melt a small knob of butter in a frypan, and when sizzling put in the sliced garlic shallot and the onion. When softened, add the legs which have been seasoned with salt and pepper. Brown on both sides. Put everything into a small ovenproof casserole dish, add the rough chopped peel and juice, and cover with the stock. Put on the lid and cook at 180°C (350°F) for 1 hour. When done, the legs will be nicely tender, but not to the point where they are falling off the bone. Remove the legs from the stock and keep warm while you finish cooking the breasts and sauce.

Strain the stock and return it to the frypan. Add the lemon peel julienne and boil until it becomes a syrupy sauce consistency (when ready the bubbles will be large). While the sauce is reducing, attend to the cooking of the breasts.

I use a heavy based ridged grid to cook them — well buttered and very hot. The breasts are placed skin side down to begin, so that the skin is seared in stripes by the sizzling hot ridges of the grid. Leave this side down to cook for 4 minutes, then turn them over and cook for a futher 1 minute only. Remove from the grid, and slice neatly on the slant. The breasts should be rosy pink inside crisped skin.

TO SERVE

Arrange the leg and the sliced breast on serving plates and spoon a little of the sauce (including some of the peel) over. Accompany with the crêpe on a separate side plate.

Breast of Goose with Pear

Serves 2 people

1 x 2½kg (5lb) goose (a nice young bird)
salt and freshly ground black pepper
1 tablespoon butter
1 pear
1 tablespoon sugar
water to cover

FOR THE SAUCE
125ml (4 fl oz) (½ cup) concentrated chicken or duck stock
(see recipe on page 24)
25ml (1 fl oz) Poire William eau-de-vie
2 teaspoons sugar

Cut the meat from the carcass of the goose in two halves. Slice down either side of the breastbone and sever the wing completely at the joint. When the two halves of breast and leg are separated from the carcass, the leg bone will be the only bone still attached.

Now slice the legs from the breasts and reserve the legs for another meal. I usually make a confit. The recipe is the same as for duck confit on page 137). Lay the breasts skin side down and dust liberally with the salt and pepper. Set aside until serving time.

Peel the pear and put into a small saucepan with the sugar. Cover with water, bring to the boil and then simmer until tender. Drain and cool. Slice in half and take out the core.

To make the sauce: Put the stock, the eau-de-vie and sugar into a pan and boil until it reduces to a syrupy sauce consistency.

TO COOK AND SERVE

Melt the butter in a small roasting pan on top of the stove. Put the breasts in skin side down and cook for 5 minutes to brown and crisp the skin very well. Cover the breasts with a sheet of aluminium foil and roast in a 200°C (400°F) oven for 15 minutes. The breasts when done should be still slightly pink. Take the breasts out of the pan and slice on the slant into thin strips.

Warm the pear halves in the sauce, then slice each half lengthwise into thin strips. Arrange the pear strips across each serving plate. Arrange the goose strips on top of the pear and ladle a little sauce over the meat.

ROASTED GUINEA FOWL WITH BACON CREAM AND LENTILS

Ingredients for 4 people

2 fresh guinea fowls, approximately 750g (1½ lb) each
(one fowl serves 2 people)
½ cup dried brown lentils
9 rashers bacon
1 cup cream
1 tablespoon concentrated brown chicken stock
2 knobs butter
1 tablespoon peanut oil
freshly ground black pepper
1 tablespoon chives, finely sliced, to garnish

Cover the lentils with cold water and soak until soft.

Prepare the fowls. This usually means simply lopping off the heads at the base of the neck, near the body. These birds generally come to our shops already cleaned. Nip the wings off at the first joint from the body and clean all skin and meat away from this little bone.

Wrap the bacon rashers around the breasts of each bird, and put a knob of butter in the abdominal cavity. Place the birds in a buttered roasting tray, and roast them sideways. Allow 20 minutes for each side. After this time, remove the bacon, and roast for a further 5 minutes on each side to brown the breasts and to complete the cooking. Slice each half of the bird away from the bone, beginning at the head and keeping close to the breastbone. The breast will separate from the leg very easily. Chop the leg in two, at the joint, where the drumstick meets the thigh.

The sauce and garnish can be prepared well ahead of time.

To make the sauce: cut away the fat and rind from the 3 remaining bacon rashers, then slice them into 2 parts, the *eye* and the *tail*. Chop the tail into small pieces and fry in some of the peanut oil for a couple of minutes. Drain well and return the bacon to the pan. Add the black pepper, cream, chicken stock, and half the chives. Boil sauce mixture for a few minutes until thick, then strain. Remember not to add any salt to the sauce as the bacon has already imparted enough of a salty flavour.

To make the garnish: slice the *eye* of the bacon into tiny cubes and fry in a little peanut oil until crisp. Boil the soaked lentils in salted water until tender. Drain, then toss in a frypan with a knob of butter.

TO SERVE

Allowing one half bird to each person, put the cut leg in the centre of each serving plate, and place the breast on top. Spoon some sauce over. At one side, put a spoonful of the lentils mixed with the crisped bacon dice and accompany with vegetables of your choice.

PHEASANT BREAST WITH THYME CREAM AND A QUENELLE OF THE LEG SERVED WITH CELERIAC PURÉE

Ingredients for 4 people

2 fresh pheasants (about 800g (26 oz) each)
bunch fresh thyme
freshly ground black pepper
butter
aluminium foil

FOR THE QUENELLES
200g (6½ oz) pheasant leg meat
1 whole egg
1 egg yolk
1 tablespoon carrot, well cooked and diced
1 tablespoon celery, well cooked and diced
75ml (2½ fl oz) cream
pinch salt and fine white pepper
2 cups light chicken stock (see recipe on page 23)

FOR THE SAUCE
1 small onion, peeled and chopped
1 clove garlic, peeled and chopped
1 tablespoon butter
1 teaspoon cracked black peppercorns
pinch salt
25ml (⅝ fl oz) lemon juice
25ml (⅝ fl oz) concentrated chicken stock
250ml (8 fl oz) cream
2 tablespoons fresh thyme leaves

FOR THE CELERIAC PURÉE
1 head celeriac
1 tablespoon of the leaves
1 large potato
50g (1¾ oz) butter
125ml (4 fl oz) cream
salt and pepper to taste

Fresh pheasants are sold with heads and insides still intact, so the first job is to clean them. Cut the neck off at the base and discard. Now, just above the tail, make a small slit towards the breastbone. The insides will pull out easily. Discard these also and wash the cavity. Cut the wing off at the first joint from the body. Trim the meat away from this little bone so that it is very clean. Cut the legs off, ready for the quenelles. Dot the breast generously with knobs of butter. Lay thyme branches on top and put a bunch inside the now cleaned abdominal cavity. Grind black pepper all over, and some salt. Place a sheet of aluminium foil on the work bench, place the bird in the centre, and make a well-sealed parcel, folding the ends together all the way along the top. You can leave the parcels like this until it is time to cook them, about 30 minutes before serving. Place the parcels in a lightly greased baking pan and cook in the oven at 200°C (400°F) for 25-30 minutes, depending on the size of the bird. When cooked it should still be a little pink on the bone.

The quenelles and sauce can both be prepared and cooked earlier on the day.

Put the chopped leg meat – minus tendons and skin – into a food processor, with the whole egg, the extra yolk, pepper and salt. Purée finely, then pass through a fine sieve or mouli. Purée the vegetables with a little drop of the cream and pass through the mouli also. Mix the purées together. Stir in the cream, a little at time, and chill the mixture thoroughly.

Prepare a deep pan of gently simmering light chicken stock. Now take an ordinary dessert spoon. Warm it in the hot stock then drag it quickly through the cold mousse mixture to form a rounded quenelle shape. Drop these into the simmering stock and poach for a minute or two on each side until firm. Remember that this mixture is very light and it may at first appear difficult to form a shape at all, but you will find that a shape will set immediately the mousse makes contact with the hot liquid. Make sure that you allow the first side time to cook firmly before turning it over to cook the other side. From this mixture you should obtain 8 quenelles – 2 per person. When they are done, remove with a slotted spoon, drain on kitchen paper, and set to one side until you wish to serve them.

To make the sauce, put your chopped onion and garlic into a saucepan with the butter and cook gently until soft. Add the peppercorns, salt and lemon juice and cook for a further minute. Now add the concentrated chicken stock and cream, and boil until thick. Strain, stir in the thyme leaves, taste and adjust the seasoning if necessary.

Peel, wash and chop the celeriac and the potato into small pieces. Melt the butter in the bottom of a saucepan and stir in the vegetables, the leaves, salt and pepper. Cook for a couple of minutes, stirring frequently. Add water to just cover the vegetables and simmer until soft (about 20 minutes). By this time the water will be almost gone. Stir in the cream. Purée in a food processor, and adjust the seasoning if necessary.

TO SERVE

Warm the quenelles gently in the sauce, turning them several times.

Slice the breasts away from the carcass. Arrange on hot serving plates with the quenelles and ladle some sauce over. Serve the celeriac purée separately.

QUAIL AND CABBAGE PIE SERVED WITH TWO SAUCES

Serves 4 people as a main course, or 6-8 people as a small first course

*4 fresh plump quails
pinch salt and freshly ground black pepper
a couple of knobs butter
250g (8 oz) puff pastry
egg wash (1 yolk mixed with 1 teaspoon water)*

*FOR THE CABBAGE
2 cups firmly packed, finely shredded cabbage
1 tablespoon water
1 tablespoon butter
pinch salt and freshly ground black pepper*

*SAUCES
1 cup beurre blanc (see recipe on page 28)
1 cup concentrated brown chicken stock (see recipe on page 23)
⅓ cup good port*

Roll out the pastry. Cut out the top first—a circle 20cm (8 in) across—score with decorative slash marks, taking care not to cut right through the pastry, and chill very well. Cut out the base using the leftover pastry. Make it a smaller circle—about 18cm (7 in) across—and chill also.

Put the quails into a small roasting pan with the knobs of butter, and dust liberally with the pepper and salt. Roast at 190°C (375°F) for 20 minutes. When cooked, the breasts will be still slightly pink. Take them out of the pan, slice away the breasts neatly and pull the meat off the legs. Cool. Discard the bones.

Put the cabbage with the butter, water and seasoning into a pan and cook briskly, stirring all the while, until nicely softened. Drain and cool.

Prepare the beurre blanc and keep warm. Boil the stock and port together until it reaches a thickened sauce consistency.

When the pastry is well chilled and the cabbage and quail meat is cooled, begin to assemble the pie. Do this on the baking tray on which it will be cooked. Pile the cabbage onto the pastry base, leaving a 2cm (¾ in) gap all around the edge. Lay the breasts, slightly overlapping on one another, all around the outer edge of cabbage. Pile the leg meat in the space in the centre. Put the lid over and press down well onto the edge of the base. Glaze with the egg wash and chill again—for at least 10 minutes—then bake at 200°C (400°F) for 35-40 minutes.

TO SERVE

Warm the sauces. Cut the hot pie into wedges and divide onto serving plates. Ladle a little of the buerre blanc on one side of the pie wedge and a little of the port sauce on the other. Serve at once.

Note: these pies can be prepared well in advance, refrigerated, and cooked when needed. They are better freshly baked than reheated.

ROASTED QUAILS WITH LIME STUFFING AND SAUCE

Ingredients for 4 quails — you can serve 1 or 2 per person. I find that 1 is usually ample.

4 plump fresh quails
1 cup concentrated quail stock, made from the bones or 1 cup concentrated brown chicken stock
(see recipe on page 23)
lime juice to taste

FOR THE STUFFING
1 small white onion, peeled and chopped
butter
1 cup fine fresh breadcrumbs
2 parsley stalks (minced)
1 teaspoon fresh thyme leaves
2 tablespoons lime zest (approximately 3 limes)
salt and pepper
1 egg

Bone out the quails leaving only the leg and wing bones attached. I do this with a small sharp knife, commencing at the back of the bird, lifting the skin at the parson's nose, and continuing close to the carcass all the way around, breaking and severing the legs at the joints. Fold back the skin, a little at a time at the breast, and cut close to the bone on either side of the breast plate. Fold back the skin and flesh, as you would turn a sock inside out. Work your way gradually up to the neck, making sure that you do not break the skin — this is one reason why it is most important to work with fresh birds, for once frozen, the skin becomes soft and easily torn.

Cut off the wing tips and make a stock with the bones.

Cook the onion in a little butter until it is soft and golden. Prepare the fine breadcrumbs and combine with the minced parsley, thyme leaves and onion. Mix everything together, including the lime zest and salt and pepper to taste, then combine with the slightly beaten egg.

Fill the cavity of each quail with this stuffing (about 2 tablespoons per bird) and secure each end neatly with strong toothpicks. I lop a bit of the neck skin off and secure the remainder underneath at the back. The legs should be crossed and pinned together neatly. Put the quails into a buttered roasting pan and brown on top of the stove. Continue the cooking by roasting in a hot 220°C (430°F) oven for about 10 minutes. When done, remove the toothpicks, and place the birds on hot serving plates.

To make the sauce, stir some lime juice into the concentrated bird stock and boil to combine. Do this according to your own taste. It should have a good limey tang. Ladle sauce generously over each quail and serve with separate vegetables of your choice.

GRILLED SPATCHCOCK WITH SAGE BUTTER, FRIED ZUCCHINI DICE AND CHERRY TOMATOES

Ingredients per person

1 × 400-500g (13-16 oz) fresh free-range spatchcock
2 tablespoons soft butter
1 tablespoon fresh sage leaves, chopped
1 small zucchini
3 cherry tomatoes
25ml (8 fl oz) concentrated brown chicken stock
squeeze lemon juice
pinch salt and freshly ground black pepper
extra knob of butter for frying

Trim the wing tips off at the first joint from the body.

Starting at the neck, slice down either side of the breast bone, so as to remove the flesh from the carcass in two halves leaving only the wing and leg bones attached.

Mix the soft butter and finely chopped sage leaves together (this can be done in a food processor) to make a herb butter.

Lay the bird portions, skin side down to start, on a flat tray, dot with one-third of the butter, season with salt and pepper, squeeze lemon over, and place under a very hot grill until golden brown (about 8 minutes). Turn the bird over and repeat the procedure, one-third of the butter, seasoning and lemon juice, and grilling until the bird is done (a further 8 minutes or thereabouts). Test the leg with the point of your knife. The juices should run clear.

Wash the zucchini and chop into a small dice. Toss with a knob of butter and a pinch of salt and pepper in a hot frypan to soften and brown slightly (this will take only a minute). Slice the cherry tomatoes in half and put them in with the zucchini for a few seconds only.

TO SERVE

Arrange the portions on hot serving plates, dot with the remaining butter and grill just long enough to melt the butter. Put little piles of zucchini dice and tomato about, and a drizzling of the hot chicken stock — just a bit here and there will do — and accompany with a crisp green salad.

Note: This is an easy and delicious way to serve spatchcock, ideal for a lunch or an informal dinner. The bird remains succulent inside crisped skin and, having most of the bones removed, it is easy to eat. Provide finger bowls so that the drumsticks and wings can be picked up and enjoyed.

Spatchcock in a Honey and Sesame Crust with Crisped Noodles

Ingredients for 4 people

4 fresh 400-500g (13-16 oz) spatchcocks
1 medium onion
1 tablespoon fresh sage leaves
2 tablespoons peanut oil
2 tablespoons sesame seeds
4 tablespoons honey

FOR THE NOODLES
1 recipe fresh pasta noodles (see recipe on page 214)
1 tablespoon butter
1 tablespoon peanut oil

Peel the onion and mince with the sage and 1 tablespoon only of the peanut oil. You can do this in a food processor or chop very finely by hand.

Put the rest of the oil in a roasting pan.

Prepare the birds by cutting away the necks at the base and lopping off the wings at the first joint away from the body. Trim the remaining little wing bone so that it is free of all skin and flesh.

Put the birds into the pan and divide the onion mixture between them. Coat their breasts and legs evenly. Spoon 1 tablespoon of honey over each portion, then sprinkle 1 tablespoon of seeds on top of the honey.

Roast in a 190°C (375°F) oven for 45 minutes. Baste the birds frequently with the pan juices so that when they are done they are richly golden and the crust is crunchy hard.

Cook the noodles in boiling salted water until just tender. Drain very well. Heat the butter and oil together in a frypan, and when foaming toss the noodles in. Fry till crisp, making sure that you keep turning them all the while so that they do not stick together in one clump.

TO SERVE

Split the spatchcocks in half down the breast bone. Put a pile of the crispy fried noodles in the centre of each serving plate and place the halved birds on top. As this is a dish to finish eating with the fingers, make sure that there are finger bowls and napkins well at hand.

Rare Roasted Breast of Squab with Jerusalem Artichokes

Ingredients per person

1 plump fresh squab
3 medium Jerusalem artichokes
pinch salt and freshly ground black pepper
100ml (3 fl oz) concentrated brown stock, made with the squab bones (see recipe on page 23)
assorted salad greens, such as witloof and butter lettuce
vinaigrette dressing of your choice to dress the leaves
(The walnut dressing used on page 68 will do nicely)

Remove the breasts from the birds by cutting cleanly along each side of the breastbone, working with a small sharp knife close to the bone all the way. Put the breasts to one side and prepare a stock with the remaining legs and chopped carcass. This stock should be completed well before the final cooking of the breasts.

Peel the artichokes. Put them in a buttered roasting pan, season with salt and pepper, and roast at 200°C (400°F). Turn them frequently, to brown all sides, until they are tender — about 20 minutes. When they are ready, put the squab breasts in alongside, skin side down first, season and roast on both sides, for about 2 minutes per side. Take care not to overcook them, as they are to be served *rare*. Remove the artichokes and breasts from the roasting pan and degrease. Swirl in the concentrated stock and boil for just a few seconds.

TO SERVE

Slice the artichokes once, lengthwise, and spread across the serving plate. Slice the breasts once, on the slant, and place on top of the artichokes. Pour a little of the strained reduced stock over, and accompany separately with the well-dressed salad greens.

GRILLED SQUAB WITH ROSEMARY AND FRESH FIGS

Ingredients for 4 people

4 plump fresh squab
4 figs
4 tablespoons honey
2 teaspoons mild chilli sauce
salt and freshly ground black pepper
a small bunch fresh rosemary (about 3 branches per bird)
3 bacon rashers
knob butter
½ cup concentrated chicken stock (see recipe on page 23)

Split the birds in half lengthwise, remove the back bones, and place in a dish. Sprinkle with the honey, chilli sauce, pepper, a pinch of salt, and the rosemary leaves (removed from the stems) and let stand for 1 hour.

Remove all the fat from the bacon and chop to small dice. Panfry in a little butter, then add the honey, stock and the juices left in the bottom of the dish, and boil for a couple of minutes. When almost sauce consistency, add the figs—sliced in three—and cook until they are soft, but not squishy.

In the meantime, grill the birds under a very hot pre-heated grill for 5 minutes per side, or use a charcoal grill or barbecue. When done, they should be rosy inside, with the juices running a little pink.

TO SERVE

Braised cabbage goes well with this dish. Spoon some of the sauce over the cabbage, put the figs on top, and then the halved birds. Don't forget to supply fingerbowls as the bones are meant to be picked up and well chewed.

FOR THE BRAISED CABBAGE
4 cups finely shredded cabbage
2 tablespoons butter
2 tablespoons water
large pinch salt and freshly ground black pepper

Put the butter and water into a pan and bring to the boil. Put the cabbage in and briskly toss for 2 minutes. Drain and keep warm.

Squab Stuffed with Cabbage and Bacon

Ingredients per person

1 plump fresh squab
1 cup chopped cabbage
½ cup chopped bacon, without fat or rind
1 medium cultivated mushroom
black pepper, freshly ground
1 tablespoon cream
a knob of butter for frying

FOR THE SAUCE
200ml (7 fl oz) concentrated brown chicken stock or 200ml
(7 fl oz) of the same stock made from the bones of the
squab (see recipe on page 23)
1 teaspoon butter

De-bone the bird. Lift the skin carefully at the breast and slice the meat away from either side of the breastbone. Continue right around the back, severing the flesh close to the carcass, lifting the skin as you go and being careful not to tear it. I work slowly and carefully, folding the flesh back from the bone as if I am folding back a sock. Leave some of the skin of the neck attached so that you have something to fold over and secure firmly at the back. Lop the wings off at the first joint away from the body. Trim neatly so that the little bone is free of all skin and flesh.

Prepare the stuffing. Fry separately and briskly all the listed ingredients, the cabbage very briefly until it is just limp, the bacon so that it is cooked but not crisp, and the mushroom to soften. Put these together in a food processor with some pepper and the cream, then purée for a few seconds only, so that everything is *fine* but not mushy. Alternatively, you can mix everything together well, then chop finely, by hand, and stir in the cream at the end.

Fill the bird with the stuffing and secure with toothpicks at each end. Cross the legs and pin neatly together and set aside until about 20 minutes before you wish to serve.

You can either prepare a stock from the wing tips and carcass of the bird or use a pre-prepared quantity of brown chicken stock. Reduce it to a thickened sauce consistency, and just before serving whisk in the teaspoon of butter.

Put the bird in a buttered roasting pan and roast in a hot 220°C (430°F) oven for 25 minutes. Baste every few minutes.

TO SERVE

Slice the bird in half. Place one side of the bird downwards and the other facing up, so as to expose the stuffing. Pour a little sauce over the side facing down and serve at once.

Roast Saddle of Hare with Pepper Sauce and Parsnip Purée & Rich Hare Stew with Damper

TWO HARE RECIPES TO PREPARE AT THE SAME TIME

For 4 people

2 fresh young hare (1 hare for every 2 people)

FOR THE SADDLE
the saddle of the hare
1 cup of the strained 24 hour marinade for the stew
1 cup concentrated veal or game stock (prepared with the hare bones, including the little front legs)
1 teaspoon cracked black peppercorns
pinch salt and freshly ground black pepper

FOR THE STEW
the hind legs of the hare
1½ litres (51 fl oz) red wine
2 large onions
2 large carrots
2 stalks celery
1 bay leaf
2 teaspoons black peppercorns
6 stalks parsley
knob butter
salt to taste
light veal stock, to cover
some extra parsley, finely chopped

FOR THE DAMPER
2 cups S.R. flour
½ teaspoon baking powder
pinch salt
25g (scant 1 oz) butter
2 tablespoons boiling water
¾ cup milk

FOR THE PARSNIP PURÉE
8 young parsnips
2 generous knobs butter
milk, to cover
salt to taste and freshly ground black pepper
¾ cup cream
2 tablespoons parsley, finely chopped

Begin by cutting the hare into its various portions. Peel and slice the legs away first, cutting cleanly through the joints attached to the body. Put the legs into a bowl, cover with 1 litre (35 fl oz) of the red wine, and *one* of each of the listed vegetables, all chopped, along with 3 of the parsley stalks, 1 teaspoon of the peppercorns, and a bay leaf. Refrigerate for 24 hours.

Trim the saddle. This should be left *on the bone*, but the surrounding bones from the ribs and neck should be neatly cut away. Now, with a very sharp knife, trim all the tissues away from the meat. You should end up with a very clean rectangular piece of bone, with neatly trimmed, membrane-free fillets of dark red meat on either side of the backbone. As we are going to make the sauce from the 24 hour marinade, cover the saddle with clear plastic wrap, and refrigerate for a day.

TO PREPARE THE SAUCE FOR THE SADDLE

Strain off 1 cup of the marinade from the legs. Boil and reduce this to 2 tablespoons. Stir in the cup of veal stock or the game stock, and the cracked peppercorns. Boil again until it reaches sauce consistency. Set aside until needed.

TO COOK THE PARSNIP PURÉE

Peel and slice the parsnips into rounds. Melt a knob of butter in a saucepan, put in the parsnips with the salt and pepper, and sauté, stirring from time to time, for 5 minutes. Cover with milk, bring to the boil, then simmer until tender (about 25 minutes). Purée with another knob of butter and the cream until very smooth. Stir in the parsley at the end.

TO COOK THE SADDLE

Pre-heat the oven to 200°C (400°F). Sprinkle with a little salt and grind fresh black pepper over the meat, put into a buttered roasting pan, and roast for 15-20 minutes, basting from time to time. It is important that the meat is served *rare* or at the most pink. To finger touch it will feel firm, but still with some give. Let the saddle rest for a couple of minutes before carving. Slice thinly along each fillet and arrange the tender strips on hot serving plates. Pour any juices and blood that escapes into the sauce, and spoon over the meat. Accompany with the parsnip purée, roasted French échalotes, and buttered green beans.

TO COOK THE STEW

Take the legs out of the marinade and pat dry. Chop the remaining vegetables, peppercorns and parsley, put into a baking dish with a knob of butter, and fry golden. Push these into a corner of the pan and put in the legs. Season with salt and pepper, then brown on both sides. Put everything into a casserole dish, and cover with the remaining ½ litre (16 fl oz) of wine and light veal stock. Put the lid on the dish and cook in a 160°C (325°F) oven for 3 hours. When done, the legs should be very tender without falling off the bone. Strain 2 cups of the cooking liquid into a pan, boil to reduce by half, and whisk a knob of butter in at the end. While the legs are cooking, make the damper.

TO MAKE THE DAMPER
Sift the flour, baking powder and salt into a bowl. Melt the butter in the boiling water, add to the milk, then mix in with the dry ingredients to form a soft dough. Pat the dough into a round flat loaf about 20cm (8 in) across. Bake in a very hot 240°C (470°F) oven for 15 minutes, then reduce the temperature to 200°C (400°F) for a further 5 minutes.

TO SERVE
Give 1 leg to each person, pour some sauce over, and sprinkle a little finely chopped parsley on top. Accompany with the freshly baked damper and boiled buttered carrots.

CREAMY TART OF RABBIT, GARLIC AND ENGLISH SPINACH

Serves 4 people

1 × 1kg (2 lb) rabbit
1 medium onion
1 medium carrot
1 stick celery
6 cloves garlic
1 teaspoon black peppercorns
1 bunch English spinach
50g (1¾ oz) butter
6 egg yolks
300ml (9 fl oz) cream
250ml (8 fl oz) concentrated rabbit stock (follow method and ingredients for brown chicken stock on page 23 substituting rabbit for chicken)
pinch salt and freshly ground black pepper
300g (9½ oz) puff pastry leftovers

1 × 23cm (1 × 9½ in) tart tin

Cut the rabbit into its various portions, the legs and the fillets (which lie either side of the backbone), and chop up the remaining carcass for the stock. You can include the fillets in this dish or save them for another purpose — any of the recipes that call for fillets only.

Prepare the stock first in the same manner as you would a brown chicken stock. It will be used first of all to braise the rabbit pieces, and finally in a reduced form as part of the tart filling.

When the stock is ready, it is time to start braising the meat. Put the butter into a frypan, and when foaming stir in the chopped onion, carrot, celery and garlic, along with the peppercorns. When the vegetables have browned, push them to one side of the pan and add the rabbit pieces. Season and brown on both sides. Cover with the stock, continue to cook with lid on at a low simmer until the meat is very tender — for about 2 hours. Remove the rabbit from the cooking liquid and, when cool enough to handle, remove the meat from the bones in small pieces and put to one side.

Blanch the spinach leaves. Drain well and pat dry.

Strain the cooking liquid and let it rest for a few minutes, then skim away any surface fat. Boil to reduce to 250ml (8 fl oz). Add the cream, season with salt and pepper, and boil again until thick.

In the meantime prepare the pastry case. Roll out the pastry to line the tart tin, allowing an overhang of pastry of about 2cm (¾ in) all the way around. This will help to stop the pastry shrinking. Spread a sheet of aluminium foil over the pastry and press down well into the corners and fold over the crimped edge. Fill with dried beans or rice and chill for 20 minutes. Bake at 190°C (375°F) for 10 minutes. Remove the foil.

Stir the rabbit meat, the spinach and the egg yolks into the stock/cream mixture, and pour into the prepared pastry case. Continue baking for 30 minutes until a lovely golden brown.

TO SERVE

Cut into wedges and serve hot with a salad of choice young greens. Serve as a first course or a light main meal.

Rabbit fillets in ham with a mustard cream sauce served with a cabbage cake

Serves 4 people

4 fresh 1kg (2 lb) rabbits
4 large thin slices ham
16 sage leaves
knob butter
freshly ground black pepper

FOR THE SAUCE
125ml (4 fl oz) concentrated rabbit stock (made with the bones)
125ml (4 fl oz) cream
2 teaspoons Dijon mustard

FOR THE CABBAGE CAKES
12 young cabbage leaves (tender green leaves only)
⅔ cup ham, cut to a fine dice
1 medium carrot
1 stalk celery
1 tablespoon shallot tops, finely sliced
½ cup cooked peas
1 tablespoon butter
black pepper

4 × 150ml (4 × 4½ fl oz) dariole moulds or ramekins

The rolls are best made the day before so that the flavour of the ham can penetrate the rabbit.

Cut away the large hind legs of the rabbit and reserve for another purpose.*

Working along either side of the backbone with a sharp knife, carefully remove the two little fillets. Trim these thoroughly of all the covering membranes. This is important if the meat is not to shrink or toughen. You should end up with two very clean pale pink fillets, about 20cm (8 in) long, thick at one end and tapering to a narrow tail.

Lay the ham slice (or overlapping smaller slices, if that is easier) on your work bench. Place the two fillets in the centre of the ham, with their tails pointing in opposite directions, so that the meat is more or less the same width all the way along. Chop the ends off the tails and put to the centre so that they are not wasted. Lay 4 sage leaves along the centre of the fillets. Grind

---

*Chop up the carcass, including the front legs, to make the stock. Prepare it as you would a brown chicken stock, see recipe on page 23. Reduce to a rich syrupy consistency and reserve 125ml (4 fl oz).

black pepper all over (remember no salt as the ham is already salty enough) and roll up tightly like a sausage. Secure with toothpicks and refrigerate until the next day.

The cabbage cakes can be prepared in advance and rewarmed in a bain-marie. Cut the ham, carrot and celery into a fine dice. Gently fry all these along with the shallot tops in the butter until they are soft. Season with the pepper. Blanch the cabbage leaves and drain very well. Lightly butter the moulds and line each with three leaves. Do this so as to leave no gaps and allowing some of the leaves to overhang at the top. Stir the cooked peas into the filling mixture, and press well into each mould. Cover the tops with the leaf ends, place the moulds in a bain-marie, and cover with a buttered sheet of aluminium foil. Bake in a moderate 180°C (350°F) oven for 20 minutes.

To cook the rabbit rolls, melt a knob of butter in a frypan, and when sizzling, put the rolls in. Rotate them every few minutes so that all the sides are evenly cooked, for about 10 minutes. When done, the rabbit should be still pink at the centre. Let the rolls rest in a warm place while you finish the sauce.

Degrease the pan very well, then deglaze with the stock. Boil rapidly and reduce to about a tablespoon before whisking in the mustard, then the cream, and boiling again, whisking all the while until it is smooth and thick.

TO SERVE

Slice the rabbit rolls across into medallions. Arrange on hot serving plates with a little sauce spooned around. Unmould a hot cabbage cake alongside. Accompany with fried potatoes, and serve any leftover sauce in a sauceboat.

AN ALTERNATIVE MUSTARD CREAM SAUCE

This sauce is made without the rabbit stock, so it can be made up at any time. It goes well with tongue, hot ham, and corned beef as well.

1 spring onion, chopped
125ml (4 fl oz) cream
2 teaspoons Dijon mustard
1 teaspoon butter
freshly ground black pepper

Fry the chopped onion in the butter until it is soft and golden. Add the ground pepper, then cream, and boil for one minute. Strain out the onion, then return the cream to the pan, and whisk in the mustard.

Rabbit fillets in cabbage with a casserole of the leg and baby beets

Ingredients for 2 people

2 fresh rabbits with the kidneys and livers intact
4 baby beetroot

FOR THE FILLETS IN CABBAGE
3 or 4 whole young green cabbage leaves
a small quantity of the rabbit liver pâté

FOR THE RABBIT PÂTÉ
the rabbit livers
1 tablespoon shallots, finely sliced
1 tablespoon mixed fresh herbs, such as parsley,
marjoram, basil, tarragon, thyme, chopped
1 teaspoon juniper berries
25g (¾ oz) butter
50ml (1½ fl oz) cream
pinch salt and freshly ground black pepper

FOR THE RABBIT STOCK
rabbit carcasses, including the front legs
1 medium carrot
2 medium onions
2 shallots, green and white parts, chopped
3 mushrooms
1 stalk celery
2 litres (70 fl oz) water

FOR THE RABBIT CASSEROLE
the large hind legs of the rabbits
1 medium carrot
1 medium onion
4 stalks parsley
3 tablespoons dry vermouth or calvados
1 litre (35 fl oz) light veal or chicken stock
25g (¾ oz) butter
salt to taste and freshly ground black pepper

FOR THE GARNISH
1 slice plain white bread
the kidneys
the pâté
1 teaspoon parsley, finely chopped

Remove the kidneys and livers from the rabbits and reserve.

Now cut the rabbit into portions. Cut off the back legs for the casserole. Carefully remove the 2 little fillets from either side of the backbone. Trim away all the covering membranes as neatly and thoroughly as you can. Put these to one side and chop the remaining carcass, including the small front legs, into pieces for the stock.

Chop up all the stock vegetables and put into a baking pan with the carcass pieces on top. Brown these very well in the oven, then put into a pot and cover with the water. Bring to the boil and simmer for 1 hour. Skim away the scum which rises to the top regularly. Strain, and boil to reduce the liquid to about 1 cup.

Next is the casserole. Fry all the chopped vegetables in the butter, then add the legs and brown on both sides. Season with salt and pepper. Deglaze the pan with the vermouth and then the stock. Put the legs into a small but deep casserole dish, cover with the stock and the fried vegetables, put the lid on the casserole, and cook in a moderate 190°C (375°F) oven for 1½ hours — until the meat is tender. Do not cook for longer than necessary or the meat can become very dry.

To make the pâté, gently sweat the shallots, herbs and berries in the butter, then add the livers and sauté briskly. Season with the salt and pepper, add the cream and boil for a few more seconds, then purée.

Now to assemble the rabbit fillets in the cabbage leaves. Boil the leaves until they are very tender (about 10 minutes), then refresh immediately in iced water so that they remain nice and green. Drain very well and slice away the hard cores so that they lie flat with the rest of the leaf. Pat the leaves dry, lay out flat, overlapping onto one another. Place 2 of the fillets, side by side on top of, and in the centre of, the leaves. As one end of the fillet is somewhat thicker than the other, have them facing in opposite directions (rather than having both thick ends together). Along the centre of the two fillets, smear a very small amount of the pâté. Place the other 2 fillets on top facing again in opposite directions. Roll the fillets tightly in the leaves like a sausage. Trim any overhanging bits of cabbage away and refrigerate until needed.

Wash 2 of the beetroot very carefully so as not to break the skin. Boil in salted water until tender. Hold them under cold running water so that you are able to hold them and peel off the skins while they are still warm. Slice into neat wedges. Chop up the other beetroot, just cover with water, and boil until the liquid is rich with juice. Reserve 1 cup of this juice.

Cut 4 croûton shapes from the bread and fry golden brown in the butter. Put to one side.

FINAL COOKING

Strain the liquid from the casserole. Combine this with the beetroot juice and boil to a thickened sauce consistency.

Put the rolled fillets in a buttered roasting pan and roast in a 200°C (400°F) oven for 5 minutes on each side. When done, the meat should be nice and pink inside. Test by prodding the roll with your finger towards the end of the allotted cooking time. It should not feel spongy, but *firm* with just a little *give*. Reheat the seasoned rabbit stock. Briefly panfry the kidneys and keep hot.

TO SERVE

Slice the roll into medallions. Allow 3 medallions per person and nap with a little of the hot rabbit stock.

Warm 1 leg per person, with the beetroot wedges, in the beetroot sauce. Serve on a separate plate with a couple of the kidneys and croûtons, onto which some of the pâté has been decoratively piped. Finish the pâté with a sprinkling of fine parsley.

Note: Well there is a lot to do, but I don't think we have wasted a thing. Have the remaining casseroled legs for lunch next day, or prepare a rabbit pâté along similar lines to the hare pâté on page 66 and serve as a snack with toast.

Gratin of Rabbit

Ingredients for the rabbit, per person
Sauce serves 6

1 saddle of rabbit per person
(reserve the legs for another dish)
freshly ground black pepper
knob of butter for frying

FOR THE SAUCE
4 egg yolks
1 tablespoon lemon juice
1 tablespoon white wine vinegar
1 teaspoon fine chives or shallot tops
6 peppercorns
a broken piece of bay leaf
¼ teaspoon each salt and ground pepper
250g (8 oz) unsalted butter
¼ cup cream

Prepare the rabbit fillets (which comprise the saddle) as described already in the previous recipe. Carefully remove the fillets from either side of the backbone and trim away every bit of the covering membranes with a small sharp knife. Now, put the well-trimmed fillets to one side until 10 minutes before you wish to serve them.

TO PREPARE THE SAUCE

Put all the listed ingredients, except the butter and cream, together in the top of a double saucepan. Whisk together, then begin cooking gently. When the liquid is warm, begin adding the butter a bit at a time. When all the butter is incorporated, strain, and stir in the cream. Keep warm until needed (back in the top of the double saucepan if you like). It is best not to make this sauce too far in advance.

TO COOK AND SERVE

Melt a knob of butter in a frypan. Grind some pepper over the fillets and panfry briskly, rolling them over and over, so that they are cooked evenly. Cook for absolutely *no more than 5 minutes*. Slice the fillets diagonally and fairly thinly in long strips. (The rabbit should be quite pink at the centre.) Arrange the strips across serving plates. Ladle some sauce over the strips and *brown quickly* (taking care that in forming a slight crust you do not overcook the rabbit) under a very hot pre-heated grill.

Accompany with crisp fried potatoes and green salad.

DESSERTS

There are two desserts which I always think of with special fondness when I think of *You and Me*.

The Fine Apple Tart was the recreation of another tart once enjoyed so very much at the restaurant *Lameloise* in Chagny in Burgundy. On that occasion, Chef Lameloise's tart, thin as a wafer, sweet with caramelised butter and sugar, crisped and browned under a hot salamander, came piping hot to the table with a little bowl of apple sorbet to accompany. Like so much that is good, it was simple, fuss-free, and absolutely delicious. I have since made so many fine tarts of so many different persuasions, that it would be impossible to recall them all — the onion and prosciutto, the crab, and the smoked salmon recorded elsewhere are but a few. Of them all it is the apple tart, as inspired by M. Lameloise, which remains a constant favourite. It is a dessert which is sure to please all tastes, and because my family prefers it, it is served with the most creamy of vanilla icecreams.

The other dessert, by chance, became a special part of the restaurant's own history.

In 1981, I was invited, along with five other chefs from both Sydney and Melbourne, to take part in creating a dinner for 200 people at the Rothbury Estate in the Hunter Valley. It fell to me to do the dessert.

As I could not be certain which ingredients would be available on the designated day, and having a great dread of planning things too far ahead, I chose to do a dessert using fruits which are usually easy to come by — the citrus fruits.

We had been working on the Citrus Quartet for some time prior to the dinner. It was an *air with variations*, if you like a musical analogy, an idea I used from time to time, sometimes with strawberries, once with chocolate, the idea of taking a theme and presenting it in a variety of ways. The Citrus Quartet as it was then, was composed of an orange tart, a lime pot, a creamy lemon mousse spooned straight onto the plate, and a little chou puff filled with grapefruit cream. In the centre, a salad of orange, garnished with the candied peels of the various fruits, brought the dessert together, and provided a refreshing contrast to the pastries and creams.

The inimitable Fiona Baxter was at that time mistress

of desserts, and it was she who worked on refining all the recipes. What I like about this concept is that you can go on and on changing a little bit here or there, according to your own fancy. Use tangerines, mandarins, tangellos and pink grapefruit if you like. Make little bavarois, crème caramels, sorbets, cakes, gratins, tiny aspics, and icecreams — the sky's the limit, but always aim for contrast of textures. The citrus trio recorded in these pages is but one example; the rest is up to you.

THE CITRUS TRIO: LEMON ICECREAM, LIME POTS O'CREME, AND AN ORANGE TART

LEMON ICECREAM
250g (8 oz) castor sugar
12 egg yolks
zest and juice of 4 juicy lemons 225ml (7 fl oz)
600ml (19 fl oz) cream

Whisk the sugar, eggs and zest together until thick, pale and creamy. Bring the cream to the boil and pour onto the egg mixture gradually, while continuing to whisky slowly.

Put the mixture back into the saucepan and cook gently, stirring continuously, until the custard thickens to coat the back of a spoon. Pour through a sieve into a bowl. Stir in the juice. Chill the mixture, then churn in your icecream maker.

LIME POTS O'CREME
Per person (per pot)

25ml (⅝ fl oz) lime juice
25g (¾ oz) castor sugar
1 egg yolk
25ml (⅝ fl oz) cream

Whisk the egg yolks gently, just to break them up. Pour in the cold cream and continue to stir until all is well combined. Stir in the juice/sugar, then spoon into the pots through a fine sieve. Remove any bubbles or scum that settles on top with a teaspoon. Put the pots in a bain-marie filled with water so that it comes two-thirds of the way up the sides of the pots. Cook uncovered in a moderate 160°C (325°F) oven until the custard is firm (about 15 minutes). Test by giving the pot a shake to see if the centre is still runny. Remember it will firm up as it cools.

THE ORANGE TART
(Based on an original recipe by Alain Chapel)

Serves 8 people

150g (5 oz) delicate sweet shortcrust (about ½ recipe on page 210)
1 whole egg
1 egg yolk (keep the white for sealing the pastry base)
1 orange, zest and juice
½ lemon, zest and juice

75g (2½ oz) icing sugar
25g (¾ oz) unsalted butter, melted

18cm (7 in) loose based flan tin

Roll out the pastry thinly to line the flan tin. Press a double layer of foil well into the base and chill thoroughly. Bake in a 180°C (350°F) oven for about 10 minutes, then remove the foil. Brush the pastry all over with the reserved egg white, return to the oven, and bake until browned, but not well done.

Make the filling. Beat the egg yolk, zest and sugar together until thick and pale. Pour in the juice and last of all the melted butter. Ladle the filling into the pastry case, making sure none is spilled or escapes underneath the base. It sometimes makes things easier to fill the tart sitting on the oven rack, so that it doesn't have to be moved.

Bake in the 180°C (350°F) oven for 20 minutes or till done. It doesn't matter if it browns slightly on top. When done, it will be wobbly firm, but not runny, and will firm up further as it cools. Just before serving, dust with icing sugar.

TO SERVE

Arrange a scoop of icecream, a little pot and a slice of tart on each plate. Garnish with a little salad of orange segments and perhaps some fine julienne of lime, lemon, and orange peel which has been covered with sugar and cooked until transparent.

PLATE OF SORBETS AND ICECREAMS

At my cooking classes I am often asked what was the most popular dessert at *You and Me*. Without a doubt, it was the plate of sorbets and icecreams. The flavours varied as the seasons went by. The vanilla and caramel icecreams were popular and permanent features. We churned these daily to make sure they were fresh and velvety smooth.

Serve a variety. They can be scooped or rolled by using a spoon dipped in hot water. Arrange around the outer edge of a chilled plate and accompany with dainty pieces of fresh and poached fruits in the centre.

BASIC SUGAR SYRUP
2 cups sugar
2 cups water

Dissolve the sugar in the water, bring to the boil, and continue boiling for 5 minutes.
Stored in the refrigerator, it will keep indefinitely.

TROPICAL SORBET
8 passionfruit
1 ripe pineapple
2 bananas
2 mangoes
2 oranges

Prepare the various fruit juices. Squeeze the oranges. Cut up the pineapple and put through a juicer. Sieve the pulp of the passionfruit. Purée the banana and mango flesh in a food processor. Combine all these, sweeten with sugar syrup to taste, and churn in your icecream machine.

GIN SORBET
4 oranges
2 lemons
½ cup sugar syrup
½ cup gin

Juice the oranges and lemons and combine with the sugar syrup and gin. Churn.

PASSIONFRUIT SORBET
the juice of 20 passionfruit (approximately 250 ml (1 cup))
250ml (1 cup) sugar syrup

Combine the two, and churn.

MANGO SORBET
4 medium-sized mangoes
100ml (5 tablespoons) sugar syrup

Peel, purée and sieve the mangoes. Stir in the sugar syrup and churn.

ROCKMELON AND GINGER SORBET
1 large rockmelon (cantaloup), puréed and sieved, to yield approximately
900ml (3½ cups) juice
100ml (5 tablespoons) sugar syrup (or to taste)
1 tablespoon sweet ginger syrup or fresh ginger juice (or to taste)

Combine the puréed, sieved rockmelon with the other syrups. Taste, adjust flavour if necessary, and churn.

PINEAPPLE SORBET
1 large pineapple
1 tablespoon mint leaves, chopped
150ml (7½ tablespoons) sugar syrup (or to taste, depending on the sweetness of the pineapple)

Slice up the pineapple and put through the juicer. One medium to large pineapple will yield about 400ml (1½ cups) of juice. Stir in the mint leaves and the sugar syrup. Leave for 1 hour, then strain out the mint. Churn.

RHUBARB ICECREAM
½ kg (1 lb) trimmed rhubarb
½ cup sugar
200ml (¾ cup) cream

First cook the rhubarb. Wash and cut into small pieces. Put into a saucepan, cover with the sugar, and cook gently until the rhubarb is very soft and much of the liquid has been evaporated. It should still be a nice bright colour. Cooking takes about 30 minutes.

Cool, then purée in a food processor, stir in the cream and churn.

ORANGE PEKOE TEA ICECREAM
1 litre (4 cups) milk
⅓ cup orange pekoe tea leaves
12 egg yolks
300g (9½ oz) castor sugar

Scald the milk and stir in the tea leaves. Leave to infuse for 20 minutes. Beat the egg yolks and sugar together until the mixture is very thick and creamy. Strain the milk onto the yolk mixture while continuing to beat. Put the mixture into a saucepan and cook gently, stirring all the while, until the custard thickens to coat the back of a spoon. Strain, cool and churn.

MULBERRY ICECREAM
250g (½ lb) mulberries, stalks removed
125g (¼ lb) castor sugar (or to taste)
250ml (1 cup) cream

Weigh the berries after the thick stalks have been removed. Purée the berries and sugar, then sieve. Warm the berry purée slightly to completely dissolve the sugar. Stir in the cream and churn.

COFFEE ICECREAM
12 egg yolks
300g (9½ oz) castor sugar
1 litre (4 cups) milk
1 tablespoon medium-fine freshly ground coffee

Beat the egg yolks and sugar together until very thick and creamy. Mix the ground coffee into the milk, and scald.

Pour the hot coffee and milk combination onto the egg mixture, while continuing to beat. Put back into the saucepan and cook gently, stirring all the while, until it thickens to coat the back of a spoon. Strain, cool and churn.

BANANA, CINNAMON AND HONEY ICECREAM
4 egg yolks
¼ cup honey
2 bananas
½ teaspoon cinnamon
1½ cups cream

Whisk the egg yolks and honey together until thick and creamy. Mash or purée the bananas with the cinnamon, and add to the yolk mixture. Combine well. Scald the cream and pour slowly onto the yolk mixture. Put everything back into the saucepan and cook gently, stirring all the while, until the mixture thickens like a crème anglaise. Cool and churn.

CARAMEL ICECREAM
1 cup sugar
½ cup water
600ml (2½ cups) cream

Put the sugar and water together in a saucepan and bring to the boil, stirring just a little to dissolve the sugar. Continue to boil without stirring until it has reached a dark caramel. Take the saucepan from the stove (if gas, simply turn off) and pour the cream in. Take care when you do this, as the caramel will spit violently. The cream will stop the caramel cooking any further. Keep stirring, this time over a gentle heat, to dissolve any solid lumps of *toffee*. When all is smooth, pour into a bowl to cool. As it cools it will thicken slightly.

At this stage you will have an excellent cream caramel sauce which goes very nicely with poached pears or stewed apples, and has a good many other uses as well. For the icecream, simply churn the sauce in your icecream machine. Because it is made with all cream, take care not to over-churn. It's better to leave it a bit on the soft side, as it will firm up a bit more in the freezer.

The other icecreams are: vanilla, page 196; treacle, page 186; lemon, page 164; and strawberry sorbet on page 180.

GRATIN OF QUINCE AND CINNAMON WITH ITS SORBET

Serves 6 people

3 large quinces, peeled, cored and sliced into 8

POACHING SYRUP
1 litre (32 fl oz) water
1 cup sugar
1 cinnamon quill
4 cloves
½ teaspoon pure vanilla
1 recipe crème anglaise (see recipe on page 215)
powdered cinnamon for dusting

individual gratin dishes

Put all the ingredients for the poaching syrup in a shallow baking pan and bring to the boil. Put in the quince slices, cover with aluminium foil, and cook in a slow 120°C (250°F) oven for 4 hours. With the long slow cooking they will turn quite red in colour.

Strain the poaching syrup away from the quince and chill. Taste the syrup and if it is too concentrated and sweet, add a little more water. Churn this syrup in an icecream maker. It will turn into a pale pink and very creamy sorbet.

When you wish to serve the dessert, put the quince slices into the bottom of the individual gratin dishes. Cover with crème anglaise, sprinkle cinnamon on top and put into a hot oven. When the custard is piping hot, put under a very hot pre-heated grill to brown the tops. This will take only a few seconds. Serve immediately with a little sorbet either in a side dish or served from a larger bowl in the centre of the table.

Cornucopia of Fruit

Serves 8 people

FOR THE PASTRY HORNS
300g (9½ oz) approximately puff pastry
egg wash (1 egg yolk beaten with 1 teaspoon water)
3 tablespoons castor sugar

FOR THE FRESH AND POACHED FRUITS
a selection of various fresh fruits in season:
1 punnet strawberries (or other berries)
2 kiwi fruit
1 small bunch grapes
1 pear
1 orange
1 mango or banana

1½ cups vanilla pastry cream (substitute Chantilly cream if you prefer — the recipe is on page 215)
raspberry coulis (the recipe is on page 216)
8 metal pastry horns

To make the horns, roll out the dough to 3mm (⅛ inch) thick on a floured surface and cut into strips 13mm (½ inch wide). Wind a strip around each of the metal pastry horn moulds, piecing the strips together if necessary, and overlapping slightly. Arrange the moulds on their sides on a dampened baking sheet, and brush with egg wash. Sprinkle with sugar, and chill them for about 30 minutes. Bake the horns in a fairly hot 200°C (400°F) oven for 8-10 minutes, or until they are golden brown. Remove them carefully from the moulds while they are still hot and let them cool on a rack. The pastry horns may be prepared up to one day ahead and kept in airtight containers.

When selecting the fruit available choose the best that is fresh with an eye to colour. The selection given here is only a suggestion.

Slice the orange into segments, free of all pith and membranes. If using Kiwi fruit, banana or mango, keep fresh and slice only at the very last minute. Peel and poach the pear until tender and slice into strips. Gently poach the grapes. As berries overcook very easily, just pour some of the hot poaching liquor over them, and leave to cool.

POACHING LIQUOR
2 cups water
1 cup sugar

Dissolve the sugar and boil for 5 minutes.

TO SERVE
Fill a pastry bag, using a decorative nozzle, with the vanilla pastry cream,

and pipe into the pastry horns. Spoon rasberry coulis onto the plates, arrange a filled pastry horn on each, and divide the fruit among them, as if spilling from each horn.

UPSIDE-DOWN APRICOT TARTS

Ingredients for 2 people

6 ripe apricots, halved (3 per person)
puff pastry leftovers
250ml (8 fl oz) water
125g (4 oz) castor sugar
50g (1¾ oz) unsalted butter
a little extra sugar for sprinkling

2 x 14cm (6 in) pie tins

Roll out your pastry very thinly and cut out 2 circles that are just a bit wider than the tops of your pie tins. Chill these while you prepare the apricots.

Put the sugar and water in a frypan and cook to a light golden caramel. Add the butter. Let this mixture bubble for a couple of minutes without stirring, then add the apricots, cooking them for 3 minutes on each side.

Put the apricots rounded side down in the bottom of the tins and cover with the caramel butter. Do not fill quite to the top.

Now drape your pastry circles over the top of each of the tins and sprinkle with some of the extra sugar. Put the pie tins on a tray to catch any of the caramel which may spill over, and bake at 190°C (375°F) until the pastry is crisp. This will take about 20 minutes.

TO SERVE

Trim off the excess pastry edges and tip upside down (so that the pastry is now underneath) onto serving plates. Serve with thick fresh cream or crème anglaise (the recipe is on page 215).

Note: These tarts are extremely versatile. They can be made smaller or larger, as you please. Plums can be substituted for the apricots, or in winter try rounds of Granny Smith apples.

Deep lemon tart

Serves 6 people

300g (9½ oz) plain shortcrust pastry (see recipe on page 210)
2 whole eggs
4 egg yolks
zest of 1 lemon
75g (2½ oz) castor sugar
100ml (3 fl oz) lemon juice
200ml (6 fl oz) cream
icing sugar for dusting

crème anglaise to accompany (see recipe on page 215)
24cm (9½ in) tart tin

Line the tart tin with the pastry, making the edge about 2cm (¾ in) higher than the edge of the tin. Fold the edge over and crimp all the way around. This will help to prevent shrinkage. Prick the pastry base very well all over, paint with some of the leftover egg white, and bake blind at 190°C (375°F). Watch closely, and from time to time, press the base of the pastry down, using a kitchen towel. This will help to stop any bubbles that might form. Cook the pastry case until it is quite well done and a nice brown colour.

In the meantime prepare the filling. Whisk the eggs, yolks and zest together very lightly. Try not to create a lot of froth and bubble. Dissolve the sugar in the juice and stir in. Finish by stirring in the cold cream. Pour the filling into the case. This job is sometimes best done in the oven itself, using a ladle, so that you are able to fill the case right up to the top without spilling any. Bake for 30 minutes at 190°C (375°F). Do not be concerned when the top browns slightly. When cooked, the filling will be *wobbly* but not *runny* in the centre. It firms up as it cools.

TO SERVE

Dust with sifted icing sugar until the top is all powdery white. Serve cut into wedges, and ladle a pool of crème anglaise alongside.

Poached Peach with Sauterne Sabayon and Strawberries

Ingredients for 6 people

Nothing can beat fresh ripe peaches in summer. When they are at their best it is a crime to do other than eat them just as they are. If, however, this is not the case, and nature needs a little improving upon, then poaching them in a syrup or sweetened wine is a starting point for many lovely desserts.

6 medium-sized slip-stone peaches
1 cup sugar
water to cover

THE SABAYON
8 egg yolks
6 tablespoons castor sugar
¼ cup sauterne

THE STRAWBERRIES
2 punnets strawberries
icing sugar to taste

Put the peaches into a saucepan and cover with water. Add the sugar, bring to the boil, and simmer gently until the peach is tender enough for the point of a sharp knife to pierce through to the stone easily. When done, hold them under cold water to peel off the skins. Place the peaches side by side on a tray, cover with the clear plastic film, and leave to stand at room temperature.

Pick over the strawberries for the best ones, and reserve about 1 punnet. Purée and sieve the remainder, and sweeten to taste. Hull and slice in half the reserved strawberries.

The sabayon should be made at the very last minute, just as you are about to serve the dessert. It will take 5-10 minutes of good hard whisking. Use a copper bowl and wire whisk over a pot of steaming water, whisk the yolks, sugar and sauterne vigorously until it swells and thickens to a consistency like mayonnaise. Be careful not to let the mixture become too hot or you will end up with scrambled eggs.

TO SERVE

Put one peach in the centre of each plate. Pour some of the sabayon over each peach. Drizzle and streak the strawberry purée through the sabayon and scatter the sliced strawberries where you will.

Note: If you are using little strawberries, there is no need to slice them.

Substitute strawberry liqueur for the sauterne if you like.

POACHED PEARS WITH ORANGE SYRUP AND CHOCOLATE MOUSSE

Ingredients for 6 people

THE PEARS
6 firm pears (choose any variety you like)
water to cover
225g (7 oz) sugar

THE ORANGE SYRUP
10 juicy oranges
225g (7 oz) sugar
1 tablespoon orange rind, cut into fine julienne strips

THE CHOCOLATE MOUSSE
200g (7 oz) dark chocolate (good quality)
2 eggs
50g (1¾ oz) unsalted butter, softened
50g (1¾ oz) icing sugar
300ml (9 fl oz) cream
½ teaspoon concentrated coffee flavouring

Peel the pears leaving the stem and any leaves (these can look very decorative). Trim the bottoms of the pears flat, so that they can sit upright easily. Put them into a large pot, cover with water, add the sugar, and bring to the boil. Continue to simmer gently until the pears are tender but not too soft, just until a sharp knife can pierce them easily. Drain and put onto a tray to cool.

Juice the oranges. Dissolve half the sugar in the juice, and boil to reduce by about half until syrupy. Skim while it reduces. Chill.

Put the julienne rind into a small saucepan and cover with the rest of the sugar. Cook gently until translucent. Set aside and cool.

Break the chocolate into very small pieces and melt in a double saucepan or in a bowl suspended over a pan of hot water. When melted, stir in the soft butter, remove from the stove, stir in the egg yolks, and then the coffee flavouring. Whip the cream until it is stiff with half the icing sugar. Whip the egg whites with the remaining half. Fold these into the chocolate mousse together, lightly and thoroughly. Refrigerate, preferably overnight, until needed.

TO SERVE

Put one pear in the centre of each serving plate, spoon over a little of the orange syrup, then with a spoon dipped in boiling water roll some of the mousse and drop alongside. Put a little of the candied rind over the pear and mousse.

Winter Fruit Pie with Mascarpone

Serves 8 people

1 recipe delicate sweet shortcrust pastry (see recipe on page 216)
egg wash (1 yolk mixed with 1 teaspoon water)
125g (4 oz) raisins
125g (4 oz) sultanas
125g (4 oz) currants
125g (4 oz) dried figs
125g (4 oz) fresh pear, peeled, cored and sliced into small pieces
75ml (2½ fl oz) fresh orange juice
25ml (1 fl oz) Grand Marnier
25g (1 oz) brown sugar (and a little extra for sprinkling on top)

THE MASCARPONE
Mascarpone is a very rich thickened cream cheese which can be bought in speciality cheese shops. It has the taste and texture of a very rich pure cream. In this dessert, King Island pure cream makes an excellent substitution if mascarpone is unavailable.

22cm (9 in) pie dish

Prepare the pastry and chill for a couple of hours.

Soak the dried figs in water for 1 hour, then slice into strips. Mix all the dried fruits, including the figs, together in a bowl and marinate in the sugar, orange juice, and Grand Marnier for another hour, stirring every so often. Towards the end, mix in the fresh pear.

Roll out the pastry for the base and line the pie dish. Drain the fruit mixture by putting everything into a sieve and pressing down hard with a spoon to press out most of the liquid. Fill the pie base. Roll out the pastry again and drape over the filled pie, cut around the top, and press the edges together firmly. Glaze the top with the egg wash and sprinkle with the extra brown sugar. Bake at 180°C (350°F) for 30 minutes until well browned.

TO SERVE
Serve warm in wedges, and pass around a bowl of the mascarpone.

NICE WAYS WITH BERRIES

Fresh berries can be used in so many different ways to prepare simple delicious desserts that I just don't know what we did in those days not so long ago when any berry other than a strawberry was almost impossible to come by. There were usually enough mulberries to keep all the neighbours and the silkworms going, but even though these familiar fruits of the back garden have a particular flavour that I like, they are devils to deal with. I find them a bit too 'stalky' to eat any other way than 'de-stalked', crushed and sugared with cream, or turned into a somewhat lurid, violet-coloured icecream (the recipe is on page 168).

When the other berries, the blueberries, the raspberries and loganberries, blackberries and strawberries, are at their peak, mix them together in a bowl, splash with a light white rum, and you have a berry daiquiri.

At *You and Me* we used to serve these berries piled on a plate, in separate little pyramid-like heaps, with a bowl of sugar, heavy cream or mascarpone, and a jug of raspberry coulis to pass around.

Put fresh berries in a pot, with just enough coulis to coat them, and warm ever so slightly so that the berries are warm but not cooked and do not disintegrate. Accompany with vanilla icecream (the recipe is on page 196).

But if you want something with just a little more to it, try any of these — my favourite berry recipes.

BLACKBERRY SHORTBREAD CRUMBLE

Serves 6 people

300g (9½ oz) blackberries
50g (1¾ oz) castor sugar

FOR THE CRUMBLE
75g (2½ oz) S.R. flour
2 tablespoons brown sugar
2 tablespoons coconut
1 tablespoon soft butter

FOR THE SHORTBREAD DOUGH
125g (4 oz) flour
50g (1¾ oz) castor sugar
pinch salt
60g (2 oz) unsalted butter
1 small egg (or the yolk of a large egg)
1 tablespoon milk

ACCOMPANIMENTS
heavy cream or crème anglaise (see recipe on page 215)

21cm (8½ in) flan tin

To prepare the base, sift the flour into a bowl with the salt and sugar. Rub in the softened butter with the fingertips, then mix in the egg and milk to make a smooth dough. Chill the pastry very well before rolling out. As it is a little difficult to work with, it makes things easier if you lay a sheet of plastic film on top of your work bench, dust the plastic with flour, and roll the pastry out on top of this with a lightly floured rolling pin. When you have the pastry rolled, lift it in one piece by means of the plastic sheet right into the flan tin, peel off the plastic and press well in. Chill for 20 minutes before baking.

Prepare the crumble in the meantime. Sift the flour into a bowl with the brown sugar and coconut. Rub in the soft butter until the mixture resembles breadcrumbs.

Spread the blackberries over the uncooked pastry base. Sprinkle the castor sugar all over them, then the crumble topping. Bake at 190°C (375°F) until the pastry is crisp and golden brown (about 30 minutes).

Serve wedges hot or cold with heavy cream or some crème anglaise.

Gratin of red berries

Ingredients per person

1 punnet of berries per person (strawberries, raspberries, blackberries and blueberries are all ideal and the more varied the selection the better)
2 egg yolks per person
1 tablespoon castor sugar per person
a little cold water or strawberry liqueur
(about ¼ cup for 4 people)

Choose a shallow heat resistant serving pan from which you are happy to serve at the table. Into the bottom of this dish put all your berries, with the strawberries halved. Alternatively, you can use individual dishes.

Using a copper bowl and a wire whisk, beat the egg yolks and sugar together over a pot of steaming water. Add the liquid and continue to beat until the mixture is very thick and creamy, rather like a mayonnaise. This will take between 5 and 10 minutes. Take care that the mixture does not become overheated or you will end up with scrambled eggs.

Pour this sauce over the berries at once, and brown under a very hot grill. This will take only a few seconds. Serve immediately.

Note: I like this dessert because it does nothing to detract from the natural beauty and flavour of the ripe fruit. It is perfect for the busy host or hostess. It is a great last minute stand-by for those unexpected dinners which have to be prepared at a moment's notice, or simply as a laid-back finale for flagging appetites when the dinner has been a bit heavy at the front end.

BAKED BLACKBERRY PUDDINGS

Ingredients for 4 people

400g (14 oz) blackberries
2 eggs, separated
75g (2½ oz) castor sugar
½ teaspoon pure vanilla
2 teaspoons dark rum
pinch salt
75g (2½ oz) flour, sifted
300ml (9 fl oz) milk
icing sugar for dusting

ACCOMPANIMENTS
Chantilly cream (see recipe on page 215)
4 shallow 16cm (6 in) ovenproof dishes, well buttered
(I use circular gratin dishes)

Divide the berries and put into the bottom of the buttered dishes.
Whisk the egg whites until they form stiffened peaks.
Whisk the yolks with the sugar until they are light and creamy. Add the vanilla, rum and the salt, then the milk. When the mixture is well combined and smooth, whisk in the flour and fold in the stiff egg whites last of all.
Pour the batter over the berries and bake at 190°C (375°F) for 25-30 minutes. When done, the centre of the sponge pudding will feel firm and springy. Dust the tops with sifted icing sugar, and serve immediately with Chantilly cream.
Note: Substitute any other berry or small dark pitted cherries.

VARIATIONS ON A STRAWBERRY: A MILLEFEUILLE WITH SORBET AND SALAD

This dessert has changed more times than I can remember. At one time it was a little tartlet with a bavarois, at another time it was an icecream with strawberry beignets, and yet another time, it was a tiny Paris-Brest with a baked custard. It can be whatever you want it to be — variations on a theme in miniature.

THE MILLEFEUILLE
puff pastry, leftovers
egg wash (2 yolks beaten with 2 teaspoons water)
3 punnets strawberries, hulled (small berries are best)
vanilla pastry cream
icing sugar for dusting

THE SORBET
3 punnets strawberries
150ml (5 fl oz) sugar syrup (see recipe on page 166)

THE SALAD
3 punnets strawberries
2 tablespoons icing sugar
1 tablespoon strawberry liqueur or a light white rum

To make the millefeuille, roll out the pastry as thinly as you can. Drape onto a baking sheet and cut the edges to form a large square. (Use these leftover bits of pastry again). Prick the pastry all over with a fork and paint with the egg wash. Bake at 200°C (400°F) until golden brown, about 20 minutes. While baking, use a kitchen cloth to keep pressing the pastry down very flat every 5 minutes or so. When done, you will end up with a sheet of pastry that is very crisp and wafer thin. With a sharp chopper, cut the pastry into rectangles about 4cm (3 in) wide × 14cm (7 in) long. You will need 18 of these, so you may have to repeat the baking operation a couple of times until you have enough. Return these to the oven to crisp further and brown — about another 10 minutes (30 minutes cooking time in all). Cool, then store in an airtight container.

To make the sorbet, wash and hull the strawberries. Purée in a food processor and pass through a sieve to remove the seeds. Stir in the sugar syrup and churn in your icecream maker.

For the salad, wash and hull the berries. Put into a bowl with the icing sugar and liqueur, refrigerate and mascerate for 2-3 hours.

TO SERVE
Spread one pastry rectangle with 2cm (1 in) of vanilla pastry cream and

cover with two rows of berries. Trim the tops of the berries flat with a sharp knife, put another pastry rectangle on top of them, more pastry cream and berries as before, and top with a final pastry which has been dusted with icing sugar.

Sit the millefeuille at one side of the serving plate, with a swirl of sorbet (rolled with a hot spoon) at another, and a pile of salad berries at another.

BAKED STRAWBERRY CUSTARDS

Ingredients for 2 people

*1 punnet strawberries
4 egg yolks
4 teaspoonfuls icing sugar
100ml (3 fl oz) cream
pinch cinnamon*

2 x 15cm (6 in) shallow oven dishes

Slice the strawberries in half and spread over the bottom of each dish.

Whisk the egg yolks, sugar and cream together lightly and strain over the berries. The mixture will not completely cover the berries. Sprinkle cinnamon on top. Bake at 180°C (375°F) for 15-20 minutes until set.

Note: This is a quick and easy dessert which can be served hot or cold, and with or without a bowl of thick cream to accompany it. Make a smaller version in little ramekins as part of a 'variations' dish.

BARBARA'S INDIVIDUAL CHRISTMAS PUDDINGS WITH RUM ANGLAISE

Makes 10 puddings

A.
225g (7 oz) brown sugar
225g (7 oz) unsalted butter
the grated rind 1 orange

B.
4 eggs, beaten

C.
225g (7 oz) raisins, chopped
50g (1¾ oz) mixed peel
225g (7 oz) sultanas
100g (3½ oz) currants
50g (1¾ oz) glacé apricots or pineapple, chopped

D.
150g (5 oz) plain flour
½ teaspoon ground ginger
1 teaspoon mixed spice
½ teaspoon cinnamon

E.
50g (1¾ oz) almonds, chopped
50g (1¾ oz) grated carrot
100g (3½ oz) soft white breadcrumbs

crème anglaise (see recipe on page 215)
rum

10 × 150ml (5 fl oz) pudding moulds

Mix all the fruit listed under C together in a large bowl. Sprinkle liberally with rum and leave to soak overnight.

Cream together the ingredients listed under A and add the beaten eggs.

Sift all the dry ingredients listed under D together.

Now add C D and E gradually and alternately to A.

Butter the moulds thoroughly and line the base of each with a circle of kitchen greaseproof or parchment paper. Spoon the mixture in and cover tightly with buttered aluminium foil. Cook in a baking pan filled with enough water to come halfway up the sides of the moulds. Bake in a moderate 180°C (350°F) oven for 1½ hours. When done, the puddings will feel firm to touch and an inserted skewer will come out hot and clean.

Fine apple tart with vanilla icecream, page 196.

Variations on a strawberry: a millefeuille with sorbet and salad, page 180.

Poached peach with sauterne sabayon and strawberries, page 173.

Individual steamed treacle and currant pudding with treacle icecream, page 186.

Baked blackberry pudding, page 179.

The citrus trio: lemon icecream, lime pot o'creme and an orange tart, page 164.

Gratin of red berries, page 178.
Vanilla bavarois served with fresh strawberries and a berry coulis, page 188.

Orange tiles, page 205; Sugared almond sticks, page 200; and Florentines, page 201.
A selection of petits-fours: (from top to bottom)
Tiny lemon and passionfruit butter tarts, page 202; Caramel almond slices, page 201; Pink iced raspberry jam tarts, page 207; Currant and rum drops, page 205; Tiny fruit tarts, page 202; Coffee éclairs, page 206; Orange butter cake squares, iced and decorated, page 204; Almond shortbreads, page 200; Berry puffs, page 207; and Tiny fruit tarts, page 202.

For the rum anglaise. Make a plain anglaise and add rum to taste. Take care not to boil the sauce when reheating. Stir continuously.

Note: every Christmas at *You and Me* we made these little puddings. The recipe was given to me by Barbara Whitehouse, an exceptional cook who was something of a superwoman in our kitchen. She was a perfectionist with tons of commonsense who could cook anything and cook it beautifully. She cared not only about the food, but also about the people she worked with, often taking home things to do after a busy day — broadbeans to pod, a batch of puff pastry to make. We must have made hundreds of her puddings, and I continue to make them every year. With a light rum or lemon custard, a bowl of heavy cream and fresh cherries on the side, I still think they are hard to beat.

STEAMED GINGER AND LEMON PUDDINGS WITH LEMON ANGLAISE

Ingredients for 8 individual puddings

2 eggs, separated
100g (3½ oz) castor sugar
2 teaspoons lemon zest
1 cup milk
175g (5½ oz) S.R. flour
1½ teaspoons cinnamon
1½ teaspoons powdered ginger
50g (1¾ oz) unsalted butter, melted
a little extra butter for greasing the moulds

FOR THE TOPPING
the peel of 1 orange and 1 lemon
¼ cup sugar
water to cover
1 tablespoon candied ginger

FOR THE ANGLAISE
(see recipe on page 215)
900ml (28 fl oz) cream
10 egg yolks
200g (6½ oz) castor sugar
1 tablespoon lemon zest (from 1 medium lemon)

8 × 150ml (5 fl oz) pudding moulds

Butter the moulds very well and line the base of each mould with a little circle of kitchen parchment paper.

Prepare the topping. Peel the orange and lemon thinly so that there is no pith. Slice into thin strips and put into a saucepan with the sugar and enough water to cover. Cook gently until the peel is very soft (about 10 minutes). Drain, and chop finely with the candied ginger. Put a heaped teaspoon of this mixture onto the paper circle in the bottom of each mould.

Now prepare the pudding mixture. Beat the yolks with the sugar and the zest until thick and white. Add the cold milk gradually. Fold in the sifted flour, cinnamon and ginger, and the melted butter, alternately. Whisk the egg whites to peaks and fold in at the end.

Fill the moulds two-thirds full with the mixture. Cover tightly with pieces of buttered aluminium foil and place in a pan with enough water to come halfway up the sides of the moulds. Bake at 190°C (375°F) for 40 minutes. Test with a skewer inserted in the centre of the pudding for a few seconds — it should come out clean and hot to touch.

The lemon anglaise is a nice variation on the plain crème anglaise. Follow the method given already in that recipe with this slight variation. Mix the lemon zest into the cream and leave to steep for 3 hours before continuing with the whisking of the eggs, sugar and so on. The zest will be strained out when the cooked custard is finally strained into a bowl.

Note: These puddings can be prepared in advance and reheated.

STEAMED CHOCOLATE AND WALNUT PUDDINGS

Makes 8 puddings

200ml (6 fl oz) milk
200g (6½ oz) dark chocolate
50g (1¾ oz) unsalted butter, softened
3 eggs, separated
150g (5 oz) stale cake crumbs
50g (1¾ oz) castor sugar
150g (5 oz) walnut pieces, chopped up small
1 teaspoon vanilla

FOR THE HOT CHOCOLATE CREAM
200g (6½ oz) dark chocolate melted with
150ml (5 fl oz) cream

8 × 150ml (5 fl oz) pudding moulds
vanilla sauce to accompany (see recipe on page 215)

Chop the chocolate into small pieces, then place in a saucepan with the milk. Bring to the boil, stirring all the while, and pour over the cake crumbs in a bowl. Mix everything together thoroughly, cover, and leave to stand for 30 minutes.

Whisk the butter and sugar together until the mixture is light. Beat in the egg yolks, then the soaked crumbs, vanilla and walnuts.

Whisk the egg whites stiff, and fold them carefully into the mixture.

Butter the moulds well. Cut out circles of kitchen parchment paper and put into the base (this will help to stop it from sticking) and pour in the mixture. Cover tightly with a piece of buttered aluminium foil and put into a baking pan. Fill with enough water to come halfway up the sides of the moulds and bake at 160°C (325°F) until done — 45-50 minutes.

татьTO SERVE

Tip the hot puddings onto serving plates and spoon over hot vanilla sauce and streamers of hot chocolate cream.

Individual Steamed Treacle and Currant Puddings with Treacle Icecream

Makes 9 puddings

2 eggs, separated
100g (3½ oz) castor sugar
250ml (8 fl oz) milk
1 teaspoon vanilla
175g (5½ oz) S.R. flour
1 tablespoon unsalted butter
9 tablespoons treacle — 1 tablespoon per pudding
9 tablespoons currants — 1 tablespoon per pudding
crème anglaise to accompany (see recipe on page 215)

FOR THE TREACLE ICECREAM
4 whole eggs
2 egg yolks
900ml (29 fl oz) cream
250ml (8 fl oz) treacle (or to taste)

9 × 150ml (5 fl oz) pudding moulds
extra butter

Cream the egg yolks and sugar together. Add the vanilla and milk, then the sifted flour and melted butter alternately. Whisk the egg whites until they are stiff and fold into the pudding mixture.

Butter the moulds thoroughly. Spoon the treacle and currants into the bottom of each mould. Fill with the pudding mixture almost to the top, and seal tightly with a piece of buttered aluminium foil. Put the puddings in a baking pan, and fill with water to come halfway up the sides of the moulds. Cook for 45 minutes in an oven at 190°C (375°F). When done, they will feel springy in the centre and an inserted skewer will come out clean.

To make the icecream, whisk the whole eggs and yolks together until they are thick and pale. Add the cream and treacle and mix well. Churn in an icecream maker.

TO SERVE

Ladle a pool of warmed crème anglaise onto hot serving plates. Tip the hot pudding out, letting the treacle run freely. Accompany with a separate bowl of the icecream.

Note: These puddings can be made well in advance and reheated in a water bath.

Honey can replace the treacle in both the pudding and the icecream.

Chocolate Roll Cake with Fresh Raspberries

Serves 8 people

THE CAKE
6 large eggs, separated
200g (7 oz) castor sugar
150g (5 oz) dark chocolate, good quality
50g (¾ oz) plain flour

GANACHE FILLING
1½ cups cream
250g (8 oz) dark chocolate
1 punnet fresh raspberries
a little cocoa powder and icing sugar for dusting
raspberry coulis (see recipe on page 216)
crème anglaise to accompany (see recipe on page 215)

baking tray 31 × 43cms (12½ × 16 in)

Preheat the oven to 190°C (375°F).
Prepare baking tray. Lightly grease and line with kitchen parchment paper.
Separate the eggs. Whisk the yolks with half the sugar until they are very thick, pale and creamy. Using an electric mixer, this will take about 5 minutes. While you are doing this, melt the chocolate. When the yolk mixture is ready, stir in the chocolate evenly. Put to one side.
Whisk the egg whites with the remaining sugar until it forms a firm (but not stiff) meringue. Drop this on top of the yolk mixture, sift the flour over, and fold everything together evenly, lightly and quickly. Pour the batter into the prepared pan and bake at 190°C (375°F) for 20 minutes.
Spread a tea towel out on the bench and cover with a sheet of parchment. When the cake is done, tip it out onto this and cover with another sheet of parchment. Roll up immediately in the paper and towel and leave to cool.

FOR THE GANACHE
Melt the chocolate in a stainless steel bowl over steaming hot water. Warm the cream to boiling point, and slowly pour into the melted chocolate, stirring all the while to combine smoothly. Chill for 1 hour, then whip carefully.
Unroll the cooled cake and spread the ganache evenly all over. Cover completely with 1 layer of fresh raspberries. Roll up and dust the top lightly with a 50/50 mixture of cocoa powder and icing sugar.

TO SERVE
Ladle a pool of crème anglaise onto each serving plate. Top with a slice of the cake, and add a decorative drizzle of the coulis.

VANILLA BAVAROIS

Ingredients for 7 individual serves

3 egg yolks
125g (4 oz) castor sugar
150ml (5 fl oz) milk
400ml (13 fl oz) cream
6g (2 level teaspoons) powdered gelatine
1 good vanilla bean

7 x 150ml (5 fl oz) dariole moulds

Whisk the egg yolks and sugar together until thick, pale and creamy.

Put the milk into a saucepan. Slice the vanilla bean lengthwise and scrape the insides into the milk so that it is well "peppered". Add the split bean as well and scald. While continuing to whisk the yolk and sugar mixture slowly, add the warmed milk gradually.

When combined, put the mixture back into the saucepan and cook gently, stirring all the while, until the custard thickens to coat the back of a spoon. Do not boil. When ready, pour the custard through a sieve and into a bowl. This will remove the beans and any lumps of egg. Cool a little.

Put 50ml (1½ fl oz) of the cream, together with the gelatine which has been *measured exactly*, into a saucepan, and stir over a gentle heat until the gelatine is dissolved. Pour through a fine sieve into the cooling custard and stir through evenly.

Leave the mixture to cool further. It will start to thicken slightly.

Whip the remaining cream, and fold evenly through the cool custard.

Refrigerate until *half set*, then stir again with a folding action, pour through a sieve for the last time and into the wetted moulds.

Set in the refrigerator overnight, or for at least 6 hours.

TO SERVE

Warm a knife in hot water, run it around the bavarios, and tip out onto serving plates.

SERVING SUGGESTIONS
WITH FRESH AND POACHED FRUITS

Almost any fruit will do. Choose whatever is fresh, available, and with an eye to colour. For instance, a fresh orange in segments free of all pith and membranes and slices of fresh banana and kiwi fruit, go nicely with gently poached seedless sultana grapes, slices of pear and hulled strawberries.

POACHING LIQUOR
2 cups water
1 cup sugar

Warm through to dissove the sugar and boil for 5 minutes. Strawberries will overcook very easily, so just pour some hot syrup over them and leave to cool.

WITH FRESH BERRIES

When available, a selection of fresh berries such as raspberries, loganberries, blackberries, and blueberries team beautifully with the creamy bavarois. In this case a jug of berry coulis would be served separately.

Note: The exact measurement of gelatine is very important. The bavarois should be creamy and just able to hold its shape. Too much gelatine and you will end up with something quite solid and rubbery.

You will see that I pour the mixture through a sieve *twice*. As far as I can see it does not harm the texture one bit, and it certainly makes sure that there are no stray lumps of any kind lurking around.

HONEY BAVAROIS WITH FRESH FIGS

Serves 6

Follow the recipe for the vanilla bavarois, omitting the vanilla beans and adding ¼ cup of your favourite honey.

Allow 1 large, or 2 small, figs per person. Some raspberry coulis (see recipe on page 216).

TO SERVE

Unmould the bavarois, arrange the sliced figs as you please, and a drizzling of raspberry coulis. Pass a jug of the remaining coulis around separately.

SURPRISE BAVAROIS
(TWO LITTLE BAVAROIS — CARAMEL AND ORANGE — WITH STRAWBERRIES UNDER A HAT)

Ingredients for 10 serves

FOR THE ORANGE BAVAROIS
3 egg yolks
125g (¼ lb) castor sugar
550ml (17½ fl oz) cream
6g (2 level teaspoons) powdered gelatine
zest 1 medium orange
10 × 100ml (10 × 3 fl oz) moulds, wetted

FOR THE CARAMEL BAVAROIS
3 egg yolks
100g (3½ oz) castor sugar
550ml (17½ fl oz) cream
6g (2 level teaspoons) powdered gelatine
10 × 100ml (10 × 3 fl oz) moulds, wetted

FOR THE CARAMEL
25g (¾ oz) castor sugar
50ml (1½ fl oz) water

FOR THE STRAWBERRIES
4 punnets of berries (little ones are best)
icing sugar to taste

FOR THE 'HATS'
1 recipe for plain tiles *(see the footnote recipe on page 205)*

To prepare the orange bavarois, combine the orange zest with 100ml (3 fl oz) of the cream, leave to steep for 3 hours, then scald.

Whisk the egg yolks and sugar together until thick and pale, then pour on the orange cream gradually, continuing to whisk as you do. When combined, put the mixture back into the saucepan and cook gently until the custard thickens to coat the back of a spoon. Do not boil. Pass the mixture through a sieve to remove the zest or any lumps of egg, then cool. Put 50ml (1½ fl oz) of the cream into a saucepan together with the gelatine, warm gently and stir until the gelatine is dissolved. Pour through a sieve into the cooling custard and mix thoroughly. Let the mixture cool further to lukewarm. It will start to thicken slightly. Whip the remaining cream and fold in evenly.

Refrigerate the mixture until it is half set, stir again with a folding action to ensure all the ingredients are evenly distributed, pour through a sieve for the last time and into the wetted moulds. Set in the refrigerator (overnight is best or for at least 6 hours).

Prepare the caramel bavarois in the same way *with the following difference*: put the water and the sugar for the caramel into a saucepan and boil to a golden caramel (it will be little more than a golden film on the bottom of the pan). Pour in 150ml (¼ pint) of cream, and stir well to combine the caramel with the cream. (To do this, you will bring the caramel cream mixture back to the boil, while continuing to stir.)

Continue now as before, whisking the egg yolks and sugar together and pouring on the hot caramel cream to make the custard. When it thickens, strain and cool and proceed as before, with the additions of gelatine and whipped cream.

Now to tackle the strawberries. Purée and sieve 2 punnets, and sweeten with the sieved icing sugar, to your own taste. Hull the remaining berries and stir into this coulis.

The 'hats' are plain, flat, circular tile biscuits.

Omit the zest and add 1 teaspoon each of rum and vanilla to the mixture. Cut out a cardboard circle about 10cm (4 in) in diameter. Spread tablespoons of mixture out thinly on a heavy flat baking tray. To do this use a fork dipped in milk and work in a circular fashion so that the circles are slightly larger than the cardboard model. It is best not to attempt more than 4 at a time. When the biscuits are done, let them cool for 10 seconds, then, doing one at a time, put the cardboard circle on top, and trace around the circle with a sharp knife. Lift the perfectly circular biscuits onto a smooth surface to cool, then store in an airtight container. Be gentle as they are brittle and extremely fragile.

TO SERVE

On each serving plate, tip out 1 orange and 1 caramel bavarois side by side. Spoon some berries and coulis around the bavarois (not too much) and sit a 'hat' on top. Now, what is under the 'hat' is hidden and something of a surprise. Don't be put off by the length of preparation of this dessert as it looks as wonderful as it tastes and all the bits and pieces can be made well in advance.

Passionfruit miroir

Serves 8 people

FOR THE BAVAROIS CENTRE
3 egg yolks
125g (¼ lb) castor sugar
150ml (5 fl oz) milk
350ml (10½ fl oz) cream
150ml (4½ fl oz) passionfruit juice (approximately 16 juicy passionfruit)
10g (3½ level teaspoons) powdered gelatine

FOR THE SIMPLE PIPED SPONGE BASE
2 eggs, separated
40g (1 oz) S.R. flour
50g (1½ oz) castor sugar
1 teaspoon vanilla

FOR THE JELLY TOP
100ml (3 fl oz) passionfruit juice
3g (1 level teaspoon) powdered gelatine

1 × 20cm (8 in) cake ring

Begin with the sponge base. You can make a genoise (see recipe on page 216) in the cake ring used in this recipe. Split the cake into three and use one of the circles as the base for this dessert. (You can freeze the others for another occasion.) Alternately, you can make up the following simple piped sponge base.

Beat the egg yolks until they are thick and pale with 25g (¾ oz) of the sugar. Add the vanilla towards the end and mix in well. In a clean bowl, whisk the egg whites with the remaining 25g (¾ oz) of sugar until it makes a stiff peak. Put the stiffened egg whites on top of the yolk mixture, sift the flour on top, and fold everything together, lightly and thoroughly, all at once.

Put the cake ring on a very flat tray and line with non-stick kitchen parchment paper. Pipe the cake batter into the base in a circular manner, and bake at 190°C (375°F) for 10-15 minutes. When done the centre of the cake will feel springy and the sides will shrink away from the ring a little. Lift the cake ring away and cool the cake on a wire rack. Clean, and put the wetted ring back onto a large flat plate or tray. When the cake is cool, put it back into the base of the ring.

Now for the bavarois. Prepare the passionfruit juice by scooping out the pulp and passing it through a sieve to remove all the seeds. Set to one side.

Whisk the egg yolks and sugar together until the mixture becomes pale, thick and creamy. Scald the milk and pour slowly onto the yolk mixture, whisking all the while. When thoroughly combined, transfer the mixture back into the saucepan and cook the custard gently, stirring all the while, until it thickens to coat the back of a spoon. Do not boil. Pour the custard immediately through a sieve into a bowl and stir in 100ml (3 fl oz) of the passionfruit juice.

Warm the remaining 50ml (1½ fl oz) of juice and into this dissolve the carefully measured gelatine. Pour through a fine sieve into the custard and stir in well. Place the bowl of custard into the refrigerator or over a bowl of ice to commence chilling, stirring with a whisk every so often, so that it sets evenly.

Whisk the cream until stiff and fold into the chilled, slightly thickened custard. Continue to chill, stirring as before, until *half set*, then pour once more through a sieve into the cake ring, on top of the sponge base. Smooth the top and refrigerate for a good 8 hours or overnight.

When the bavarois is quite firm, warm the remaining 100ml (3 fl oz) passionfruit juice and into this dissolve the 3g (1 level teaspoon) of gelatine. Set in a dish over ice (or pop into the refrigerator) and stir frequently until the consistency is like jam (see note below). Using a knife dipped in hot water, spread the jelly evenly across the top of the bavarois. Leave to finish firming in the refrigerator before serving.

TO SERVE

Run a hot knife around the inside of the cake ring and lift off. Serve in wedges with a crème anglaise (see recipe on page 215), a halved passionfruit, or some fresh raspberries.

Note: you can also set the jelly firm in the refrigerator, and reverse the process by warming gently to the spreading consistency.

SNOW EGGS

Ingredients for 6 people

FOR THE EGGS
¾ cup egg whites
1 cup castor sugar
pinch salt
1 teaspoon vanilla essence
water for poaching
¼ cup sugar

FOR THE SPUN TOFFEE
2 cups sugar
1 cup water
pinch cream of tartar

rich vanilla sauce to accompany (see recipe on page 215)

Fill a baking pan approximately 6cm (2½ in) deep three-quarters full of water. Add the vanilla and the ¼ cup of sugar, bring to the boil, then adjust to a very low simmer.

In the meantime, whisk the egg whites until soft peaks start to form. Add the salt, then the castor sugar a bit at a time. Continue whisking until all the sugar is dissolved and the mixture is very stiff and shiny.

Shape the eggs with 2 tablespoons or 2 large kitchen spoons, dipped in the simmering water. When you have made a nice smooth egg shape (I usually make them quite large, a bit like medium-sized Easter eggs) drop the mixture gently into the water and poach for about 1½ minutes on each side. When done, it will feel firm and resistant to touch.

Put the eggs on a tray lined with paper towelling to drain, and keep in a cool dry place (not the refrigerator) until needed.

Make the rich vanilla sauce and cool.

The first stage in making the spun toffee can be done in advance (in fact it's a good idea to do so if you want to save time later on). Put the sugar, cream of tartar and water together in a saucepan. Gently dissolve the sugar, then bring to a rapid boil. Do not stir or it will turn *sugary*. When the syrup is a light golden caramel approximately 160°C (325°F) remove the saucepan from the stove, and allow the toffee to cool. It can be left in the pan indefinitely until needed, and simply reheated when required.

To make the spun toffee, re-warm the prepared toffee gently. When it is once more hot and liquid, remove from the stove. If it is too hot, you will need to wait a minute for it to cool and thicken a little. Dip the prongs of a fork, or the chopped off prongs of an old balloon whisk, into the slightly thickened syrup, and lift it high into the air. As it falls it cools rapidly, and fine strands of toffee fall from the prongs like fine hair. Alternatively, you can shake the fork backwards and forwards very quickly as the toffee is falling. Repeat the process over and over again until you have enough fine toffee to mount in airy balls atop the eggs.

TO SERVE

Put a puddle of rich vanilla sauce onto each serving plate. Put one large or two smaller sized eggs on top and mount finely spun toffee over all.

Note: It is not a good idea to make this dessert if the weather is very humid. The eggs themselves will become quite sticky and spinning the toffee is much more difficult.

CRÈME BRÛLÉE

Ingredients for 6 serves*

FOR THE CUSTARD
600ml (19 fl oz) cream
12 egg yolks
150g (5 oz) castor sugar
1 vanilla bean

extra sugar for the toffee glaze
9cm (3½ in) souffle moulds
1 blow torch
1 water spray
or a brûlée iron

*This recipe will make 7 serves, an odd number, so you will have one in reserve to practise on if you like.

Split the vanilla bean lengthwise and scape the insides into the cream. Throw in the scraped pod and scald. Put the egg yolks and sugar together in a bowl and whisk until they are very thick, pale, and creamy. Pour the hot cream onto the mixture while continuing to whisk at a slow speed. When combined, return the mixture to the saucepan and cook gently, stirring all the while, until it thickens to coat the back of your spoon.

Strain, then fill the moulds right to the top. Chill very well, preferably overnight.

When the custard is very cold, sprinkle a layer of sugar over the top. To caramelise the sugar, use the brûlée iron heated over a gas flame or with a lighted blow torch on a low flame in one hand and a water sprinkler in the other, proceed. Heat the sugar all over so that it melts to a toffee. If it begins to burn, spray instantly with the water. When all the sugar is melted and golden, sprinkle another layer over and repeat the procedure. Chill very well before serving.

Note: You can make the toffee glaze by holding the custards very close to the flame of a pre-heated and very hot grill. You will need to wrap your hand in a cloth to protect yourself from injury, and use a water spray to prevent the toffee burning. I have found my blowtorch so useful for browning meringue Italienne, unmoulding aspics and the like, that quite apart from the ease with which it performs this very special task, I wouldn't be without it.

FINE APPLE TART WITH VANILLA ICECREAM

Ingredients for 6 people

FOR THE TARTS
4 or 5 large Granny Smith apples
castor sugar
unsalted butter
puff pastry leftovers

FOR THE ICE-CREAM
800ml (25 fl oz) cream
8 egg yolks
125g (4 oz) castor sugar
2 good vanilla beans
1 teaspoon pure vanilla (optional)

THE TARTS

Roll out the pastry as thinly as you can and drape it over a baking tray. Using a bread and butter plate to trace around, cut out a circle. Prick this very well all over with a fork. Repeat this until you have 6 perfect well-pricked and *very thin* pastry circles on your trays (you might need a couple of these). If you don't wish to bake them straight away, pile them like crepes onto a plate, each one separated from the other by plastic film. Chill to firm and make handling easier.

You can make the tarts up several hours ahead of serving time if you wish, just leaving them on the baking trays and simply reheating them when needed, Peel, core, and slice the apples very thinly crossways. Arrange the apple slices in overlapping circles on top of the pastry, finishing in the centre of each tart. Sprinkle liberally with the sugar, dot just as liberally with butter, and bake in a moderate 190°C (375°F) oven until the sugar caramelises, the apples are golden, and the pastry crisp. If the apples are lacking a little colour, put the tarts under a very hot grill for a few seconds right at the end.

THE VANILLA ICECREAM

Combine the milk and cream together in a saucepan. Split the vanilla beans lengthwise and scrape all the powdery black insides into the cream, throw the scraped pods in as well — and the extra dash of pure vanilla if you like — and leave to stand for 1-2 hours.

Whisk the egg yolks and the sugar together until pale and thick. Scald the cream mixture and pour gradually onto the yolks and sugar, whisking all the while.

Pour all this back into the saucepan and cook gently, while stirring, until the custard thickens. It will not thicken very much, because there are not a lot of yolks, so take great care not to boil and curdle the custard. When lots of tiny bubbles appear on the surface and it swells a little, it is time to stop cooking. Pour through a sieve to remove the vanilla beans and set aside to cool before churning.

Note: don't throw the used vanilla beans away. They can be washed and put into your sugar jar to perfume the sugar, or they can be added to your next icecream *in addition to* fresh beans.

Pure vanilla is very thick and syrupy, its perfume is rich and strong, and it is very expensive. Don't mistake it for the thin, cheap liquid which is sometimes called pure vanilla in the health food stores.

OLD FASHIONED BAKED APPLES

Ingredients per person

*2 medium Granny Smith Apples
a couple of knobs unsalted butter
honey
pinch cinnamon*

Peel and core 1 apple per person and place in a baking dish. Grate the other apple and pack into the hollowed out centre. Put a knob of butter on top of the apple and a few extra pieces around in the pan. Spoon honey liberally all over. Add a pinch of cinnamon, cover with aluminium foil and bake at 190°C (375°F) for 1 hour. When done, the apple should be soft all the way through, while maintaining a nice shape. If overcooked, they will collapse. During the baking, baste frequently with the pan juices to ensure they become a caramel colour.

Serve hot with a drizzling of the caramelised honey and butter, and accompany with a bowl of thick cream.

PETITS-FOURS

Back in the good old days, my Auntie Nellie took the minutes for the Christian Women's Temperance Union (I don't think she would have approved of my liquor licence) and her recipes were written in an old exercise book which was used at one time by that excellent body. I am always intrigued by some of the titles of the recipes contained in that book: Economical Pudding, Depression Pudding, Foundation Cake and, one which I always find amusing, A Very Nice Cake. Amongst the mock creams, mock sponges, and mock turkey, I discovered a good recipe for orange butter cake, and I use it as the base for some prettily iced petits-fours.

Another Auntie, this time Aunt Bessie, took out first prize, year after year, at the Sydney Royal Easter Show for what would have been the most straightforward raspberry jam ever invented, and I use it in the petits-fours tartlets. (I think part of Aunt's success was in growing her own berries.)

While going back in time, I must mention that the recipe for chou pastry, used in the little coffee éclairs, came originally from an 'antique' manual known as *The Goulburn Cookbook*. I have added a few more eggs to my recipe.

After 5 years of cooking and serving main courses for 50 people each day, I decided I needed either a psychiatrist or rest and recuperation on desserts and petits-fours for a while. I chose the latter. Whether it was indicative of my pottiness I don't know, but the petits-fours tray grew and grew, until it became a major part of each morning's production. We made all the traditional French favourites—the madeleines and palmiers, tuiles, cats tongues, tiny meringues and macaroons, handmade chocolate truffles and candied peels. We even made a few dubious Australian varieties, like peanut butter crisps and gingernuts.

One day I knew it was all worthwhile. We had been making Dutch biscuits for some time, using the recipe from L. J. Hannerman's *Patissière*. These shortbread-like biscuits, of plain vanilla and chocolate colouring, set in a chequerboard pattern, were something of a technical wonder, and prone to all sorts of vaguaries of misbehaviour. On this day the waiter came rushing back to the kitchen with the words, 'The lady on table x says that these biscuits are truly magical!'

Well, whether the magic was in her own mind or in the biscuits, there is something a little elfin and fairy-like about a plate of pretty petits-fours. It is not necessary in the home to go to the extraordinary lengths of a time-consuming, decorated trayful. But 1 or 2, freshly baked, are worth a thousand words, when dinner is over and everything is coming to an end.

ALMOND SHORTBREADS

*2 tablespoons ground toasted almonds (use flaked almonds
and reserve some for decoration)
150g (5 oz) unsalted butter
3 tablespoons icing sugar
½ teaspoon pure vanilla essence
⅔ cup plain flour
⅓ cup cornflour*

Put the blanched flaked almonds onto a baking tray in a moderate oven until brown. Grind in a food processor.

Have the butter at room temperature. Beat with the icing sugar until creamy, then add the vanilla and sifted flours and finally the ground almonds, until the mixture is smooth.

Put the mixture into a piping bag with a decorative nozzle, and pipe little shapes onto a greased and floured baking sheet. Decorate with a blanched almond flake. Chill for 30 minutes before baking at 200°C (400°F) for about 10 minutes.

SUGARED ALMOND STICKS

*puff pastry leftovers
flaked almonds
castor sugar
egg yolk*

The quantities will depend on how many you wish to make, and this usually depends on how much leftover pastry you have. In fact, along with the palmiers, I began making these sticks as a way to use up such leftovers.

Roll out the pastry *very thinly* and drape onto a baking tray. Trim the sides to form a square (and use these bits another time). Prick the pastry very well all over and paint with egg yolk. Sprinkle the sugar liberally all over, and then flaked almonds. Bake at 200°C (400°F).

After 15 minutes, when about half-way cooked, use a large knife (better still a Chinese chopper) to slice up the pastry into fingers of any width and length you like. Very long ones can look quite dramatic on the petits-fours tray. The idea is to do this before the pastry becomes brittle and easily broken. Continue the cooking until the pastry is crisp and brown (about 30 minutes from start to finish). Cool on a wire rack. All the almonds that fall off can be stored and used again.

Caramel almond slice

250g (8 oz) flaked almonds
250g (8 oz) shortcrust pastry
2 tablespoons glucose
125g (4 oz) castor sugar
75ml (2½ fl oz) cream
125g (4 oz) unsalted butter

32 × 20cm (12¾ × 8 in) slice tin

Pre-heat the oven to 190°C (375°F).
Put the almonds on a tray and toast golden brown. Roll out the pastry to line the bottom of the slice tin. Prick well then bake golden for about 15 minutes.
Cover the pastry with the toasted almonds.
Put the glucose and the sugar together in a saucepan and cook to a golden caramel. Add the cream and butter and boil for a couple of minutes. Strain over the almonds and put back into the oven for a further 5 minutes.
Cool and cut into squares.

Florentines

Ingredients for 4 dozen

50g (1¾ oz) unsalted butter
50ml (1½ fl oz) cream
60ml (2 fl oz) honey
25g (¾ oz) flour
125g (4 oz) red glacé cherries (1 packet)
150g (5 oz) blanched almonds, roughly chopped
75g (2½ oz) mixed citrus peel
dark chocolate

Put the butter, cream and honey together in a saucepan. Bring to the boil. Stir in the flour, nuts and fruits, then take off the stove.
Line a baking tray with kitchen parchment paper. Put teaspoonfuls at intervals across the paper and press out into neatly shaped circles using the palm of the hand and fingers to shape. They should be quite thin, almost lacy. Bake at 180°C (350°F) for 12 minutes, till well browned. Do not undercook these biscuits or they won't stay crisp. Cool on a flat surface like stainless steel or marble.
Melt the chocolate in a double saucepan, or in a bowl resting over a pan of hot water. When the biscuits are cold, ice on the flat side with the chocolate. Draw wavy lines through the chocolate using a fork, and leave to set in a cool, dry place. Store in an airtight container, but do not refrigerate.
Note: these biscuits are also very nice without the chocolate icing.

Tiny lemon and passionfruit butter tarts

delicate sweet shortcrust pastry (see recipe on page 210)

FOR THE LEMON BUTTER
150ml (5 fl oz) lemon juice (2 juicy lemons)
75g (2½ oz) unsalted butter
125g (4 oz) castor sugar
1 whole egg
3 egg yolks

FOR THE PASSIONFRUIT BUTTER
the pulp of 10 passionfruit
100g (3½ oz) castor sugar
75g (2½ oz) unsalted butter
1 whole egg
3 egg yolks

Prepare the little pastry cases the same way as for the fruit tarts.

To make the lemon butter, put all the ingredients together in a saucepan and stir patiently over a gentle heat until it thickens. Pour through a sieve to catch any bits of cooked egg, and store in the refrigerator until needed. It keeps very well.

To make the passionfruit butter, put the passionfruit pulp, including the seeds, and all the other listed ingredients into a saucepan and cook gently, stirring continuously until it thickens. Push through a sieve to remove the seeds, and use the same way as the lemon butter.

TO DECORATE THE TARTS

Dust a little icing sugar over the pastry cases. Fit a decorative nozzle to your piping bag, and pipe a little of the butter into each pastry case.

Tiny fruit tarts

delicate sweet shortcrust pastry (see recipe on page 210)
vanilla pastry cream or crème anglaise
fruits of your choice for decoration, strawberries,
raspberries, kiwi, orange segments, thin plum slices

petits-fours size tart tins

Roll out the pastry thinly, line the petits-fours tart tins (any shape you like), prick the base with a fork, and bake blind until well browned. Remove from the tins immediately and cool. Store in an airtight container. You can even freeze a batch, and use just as many as you wish at any one time. They thaw out very quickly, and popping them back in the oven for just a few minutes will have them as fresh as if just baked. Do not decorate too far in advance or they will go soft and the delicate pastry will fall to pieces very easily.

To decorate: put a drop of custard inside each shell and cover completely with slices of fruit or whole berries. I used to once brush them with a little jam glaze, but not any more. Decorate at the last minute, leave the fruit fresh, and they will not only look colourful with their own true colours, but also be inviting and good to eat. My petits-fours tray is not complete without these little tarts.

TINY FRUIT MINCE PIES

delicate sweet shortcrust pastry (see recipe on page 210)
egg wash (made with an egg yolk mixed with
1 teaspoon water)

FOR THE FRUIT MINCE
200g (6½ oz) sultanas
50g (1¾ oz) mixed peel
50g (1¾ oz) currants
50g (1¾ oz) glacé apricots
1 slice glacé pineapple
50g (1¾ oz) brown sugar
50ml (1½ fl oz) brandy

icing sugar for dusting
petits-fours tart tins

To make the mince, put all the fruits and sugar together in a food processor and purée roughly, pouring the brandy over everything at the end. (Alternatively, chop everything up very well by hand, mix together in a bowl and stir in the brandy and sugar.) Store in an airtight sealed jar for several days before using. It gets better as it ages, and will keep indefinitely.

Roll out the pastry and line the petits-fours tins. Keep one tin spare to use as a cutter for the lids. Put a teaspoon of mince inside, press a lid firmly on top, making sure it is well sealed at the edges. Glaze with egg wash, and pierce a little hole in the centre to let the steam out.

Bake until golden brown at 190°C (375°F) for about 30 minutes. Remove from the tart tins immediately and leave to cool.

TO SERVE

Dust the lids with a little icing sugar.

Orange Butter Cake Squares, Iced and Decorated

FOR THE CAKE
200g (7 oz) castor sugar
125g (4 oz) unsalted butter, softened
2 eggs, well beaten
rind of 1 orange, finely grated
125ml (4 fl oz) strained orange juice
150g (5 oz) S.R. flour

FOR THE ICING
600g (19 oz) pure icing sugar
1 tablespoon unsalted butter
2 tablespoons strained orange juice
4 tablespoons boiling water

rectangular cake tin 28 x 19cm (11 x 4½ in)
yellow food colouring
paper cases for presentation

Lightly grease the tin and line the base with kitchen parchment paper.

Beat the butter and sugar together until the mixture is very light and creamy. Add the beaten eggs, a little at a time, then add the orange rind. Lastly, add the sifted flour and orange juice alternately, mixing a little at a time.

Pour the mixture into a prepared tin and bake at 180°C (350°F) for 25-30 minutes. (The cake will shrink away from the sides when done.) Tip it out to cool on a wire rack.

Put the sifted icing sugar into a bowl with the butter and orange juice. Pour the boiling water over the butter and stir to combine everything smoothly. The icing should be a firm but workable consistency. If you find it is too stiff, just add a little more juice or water.

Cut the cake into squares, approximately 3 x 3cm (1½ x 1½ in). Working with a knife dipped into hot water, cover each cake square smoothly with the icing, using only a little icing at a time, and making sure that the knife is always wiped clean before it touches the cake. When the icing is completed, leave the cakes in a cool place to set firmly.

To decorate, colour some of the leftover icing with some yellow food colouring. Add only a little food colouring at a time, to achieve a soft colour. Using an icing kit with a fine nozzle, or a paper piping bag snipped at the point to make only the tiniest opening, decorate the cake squares with swirls and squiggles, or as you please.

ORANGE TILES

75g (2½ oz) flour
75g (2½ oz) icing sugar
pinch salt
2 egg whites (lightly beaten)
grated zest 2 oranges
125g (4 oz) unsalted butter, melted
25ml (⅝ fl oz) cream

Grease a heavy flat baking tray very well.

Sift the flour, icing sugar and salt together into a bowl, then stir in the egg whites, zest and finally the melted butter and cream.

Put tablespoons of mixture well apart on the tray and spread thinly in a circular manner using a fork dipped in milk. At this stage you can sprinkle on some extra zest if you want an extra orangey flavour.

Bake at 180°C (350°F) until nicely browned. Rest for a moment to allow the tiles to cool and set slightly (but not too long or they will stick). Then lift them carefully with a spatula, and place along curved baguette baking tubes, or drape them over bottles or rolling pins. When they cool and harden they will maintain this curved shape.

Store very carefully in an airtight container in a cool dry place. Avoid contact with humidity.

Note: for almond tiles, omit the zest and stir 1 teaspoon vanilla, 1 teaspoon rum, and 2 tablespoons flaked almonds into the mixture.

For the plain flat circles that I have called *'hats'* in the dessert Surprise Bavarois, omit the zest and simply add the rum and vanilla.

CURRANT AND RUM DROPS

100g (3½ oz) castor sugar
2 eggs
100g (3½ oz) unsalted butter
100g (3½ oz) flour
100g (3½ oz) currants
rum to taste

Beat the sugar and the eggs together until smooth. Add the softened butter, then the flour and the currants. Add the rum at the end. Pipe teaspoons of mixture onto a greased tray and bake at 180°C (350°F) for 10-15 minutes. When done, the outer edges will be quite brown and the centres pale but firm. Cool, then put into an airtight container. These little biscuits do not keep very well, but they can be revived by putting back into the oven for a minute or two and cooling all over again. It is generally best to bake and eat them on the same day.

COFFEE ECLAIRS

chou pastry

FOR THE ICING
200g (6½ oz) icing sugar
2 teaspoons soft unsalted butter
2 teaspoons milk
1 teaspoon coffee liqueur or essence
decorative chocolate 'coffee beans'

FOR THE FILLING
Vanilla pastry cream (if you have some leftover; if not make a small batch of Chantilly cream following the recipe on page 215)
coffee liqueur or essence to flavour

Pipe 5cm (2 in) long éclairs onto a lightly greased, floured tray and bake at 200°C (400°F) for 15 minutes, or until the éclairs are firm and browned. Pierce the sides with a knife to let the steam out, turn the oven down very low, and leave them for another 10 or 15 minutes to dry out.

Prepare the icing. Sift the icing sugar into a bowl and work in the butter, milk and coffee flavouring until the mixture is smooth and glossy. For the filling, add the coffee flavouring to Chantilly cream or a small quantity of pastry cream, to taste.

Split the cooled éclairs in half lengthwise and fill with the flavoured cream. Ice the tops and decorate with a little chocolate 'coffee bean'.

TO SERVE
Put the finished éclairs inside little individual paper cases.

Note: the cooked, undecorated éclairs freeze very well. When needed, they can be thawed at room temperature for just a few moments, popped back in the oven to crisp, cooled and decorated as before. At *You and Me* we always kept a container of little éclairs in the freezer. It saved a lot of time baking each day, and was a wonderful emergency stand-by petit-four on extra busy days.

Pink iced raspberry jam tarts

delicate sweet shortcrust pastry (see recipe on page 210)

FOR THE JAM
500g (1 lb) raspberries
500g (1 lb) sugar

FOR THE ICING
200g (6½ oz) icing sugar
2 teaspoons soft unsalted butter
1 teaspoon milk
a tiny droplet of red food colouring — just enough to colour the icing a pretty pale pink

Prepare the little tart cases in the same way as for the fruit tarts on page 202.

To make the raspberry jam, mash the raspberries very well (a bottle is good for doing this), then bring to the boil and cook for 5 minutes. Add the sugar and cook for another 5 minutes. Set aside to cool.

Sift the icing sugar into a bowl and work in the butter, milk, and colouring until you have a smooth pretty pink icing.

Put a teaspoon of jam inside each tart case. Smooth the jam level with the pastry edges, and ice.

These tarts can be left with just the plain iced tops, or they can be decorated with a slightly deeper shade of pink icing, forced through a very fine piping nozzle. I usually make a little paper piping bag, snip the point to make a very small hole, and pipe the icing in swirls and squiggles over the tart.

Berry puffs

chou pastry (see recipe on page 212)
vanilla pastry cream (see recipe on page 217)
fresh berries, such as raspberries, little strawberries or blackberries

Pipe a couple of teaspoonfuls of mixture into rounded heaps onto a lightly greased, floured baking tray. Cook the same way as the éclairs described on page 206. When cooled, split open and fill with a little vanilla pastry cream. Pop a fresh, sweet berry under each lid. Dust the top with sifted icing sugar and present in a frilly paper case.

Note: a nice dessert idea is to make these puffs slightly larger and put 2 or 3 berries inside each one. Serve in a pool of crème anglaise with raspberry coulis streaked decoratively and a little pile of fresh berries to one side.

Chocolate and Walnut Squares

75g (2½ oz) dark chocolate
75g (2½ oz) unsalted butter
150g (5 oz) castor sugar
3 eggs, separated
50ml (1½ fl oz) milk
150g (5 oz) broken walnuts
100g (3½ oz) S.R. flour

FOR THE ICING
50g (1¾ oz) dark chocolate
1 teaspoon unsalted butter
halved walnuts

32 × 20cm (12¾ × 8 in) slice tin

Pre-heat the oven to 190°C (375°F).
Lightly grease the tin and line the base with kitchen parchment paper.
Melt the chocolate in a double saucepan or in a bowl held over a pan of hot water.
Cream the butter and sugar, stir in the melted chocolate, egg yolks, milk and the broken walnuts.
Fold in the flour. Beat the egg whites stiff and fold in. Pour the batter into the prepared tin and bake for 20 minutes or until done. Turn out and cool.
Melt the extra chocolate and stir in the butter. Ice the cooled cake thinly with the chocolate and put halved walnuts at equidistant intervals all over. Leave to set in a cooled place, but not the refrigerator. When it is time to serve, slice into squares. There should be a walnut in the centre of each square. Do not slice too far in advance or the cake will dry on the edges.

Pastry, pasta and sweet sauces

It is not easy making puff pastry in a hot kitchen in the middle of a Sydney summer. On one such day close to Christmas, with trousers rolled to the knee, barefooted and standing in a bucket of iced water for relief, and with a cool damp napkin tied around my forehead, I plied the soft buttery dough on my cooled marble slab, with speed and a freezer close by for the resting. There will be those who will no doubt ask, well, why not do it first thing in the day when it's cooler? This *was* first thing in the day, for what turned out to be a real scorcher. Miracles can be achieved, and this was just such a one.

Making good puff is always a challenge. I know of no greater satisfaction than to peep into the oven at just the right moment and see the feathery light golden layers pushing upwards — 5, 6, 7, even 8 times the original pastry height. Airy pastry to melt in the mouth and disappear in a trice, and after so much effort.

In the restaurant, having made the *feuilletées* for the appetisers and various first courses, the leftover scraps were always rolled into balls, covered with plastic film, and refrigerated or frozen. Numerous recipes were sought, or sprang into being, as a means of using up these bits of non-rising puff. We made palmiers and cornets, millefeuilles and sacristans — both savoury and sweet — and little filled turnovers. The most popular of all were the various fine tarts. These were rolled out, piled on top of one another like crepes with interleafing plastic film to prevent them from sticking together, and frozen ready for use. In the end these tarts became so popular, that we ended up making puff just to have plenty of scraps.

There is no easy way that I know to achieve perfection in the art of puff other than by practising. This was the way I taught myself — by trial and error, and after countless moments of despair, *success*. No two cooks go about their puff in quite the same way, but the principle remains the same and, generally speaking, so do the ingredients: butter, flour, iced water and a little salt. Apart from this, all you need is a little elbow grease, a cool breeze, and the resolution *never* to reach into the supermarket freezer again!

Plain Shortcrust Pastry

275g (9 oz) flour
pinch salt
125g (4 oz) unsalted butter
1 egg
50ml (1½ fl oz) cold water

BY MACHINE

Sift the flour and salt into the bowl of a food processor. Put in the butter in small pieces and combine with an on/off movement until the mixture resembles breadcrumbs.

Add the egg and water, a little at a time, until the mixture becomes a smooth ball. Chill for ½ hour before rolling.

BY HAND

Sift the flour with the salt in a heap on your workbench. Cut the butter into small pieces and work into the flour until the mixture resembles breadcrumbs.

Work in the egg and water, bit by bit, until the mixture is nice and smooth. Chill for ½ hour before rolling.

Note: this pastry is a delight to work with. You should have no problems at all handling and rolling, and it is a lovely flaky, short pastry to eat too.

Delicate Sweet Shortcrust Pastry

75g (2½ oz) unsalted butter
125g (4 oz) flour
50g (1¾ oz) icing sugar
2 egg yolks
¼ teaspoon pure vanilla
pinch salt

BY MACHINE

Put the sifted flour, sugar and salt into your food processor. Cut the butter into small pieces, then combine with the dry ingredients using an on/off movement. Add the egg yolks and vanilla at the end. Wrap in plastic wrap and chill thoroughly.

BY HAND

Sift the flour, sugar and salt into a bowl. Rub the softened butter in with the fingertips until it resembles breadcrumbs. Mix the egg yolk and vanilla in and knead briefly to make smooth. Wrap in plastic wrap and chill.

PUFF PASTRY

500g (1 lb) plain flour
500g (1 lb) salted butter
1½ cups iced water
pinch salt

Let the butter sit at room temperature for a while to soften slightly. It should be neither *too soft* or *too hard*.

Sift the flour into a bowl and add the water, little by little, until you have worked it to a pliable dough (it will feel a bit like your ear lobe). Rest in the refrigerator for 20 minutes before continuing.

Roll the dough out into a rectangular shape, approximately 60 × 20cm (24 × 8 in). Slice the blocks of butter in two lengthwise. Place the four rectangles of butter, long edge to long edge, in the lower half of the rolled out dough, leaving an edge of dough all the way around. Fold the top half of the dough over, and press the edges firmly together all the way around to enclose the butter in a parcel.

Give the 'parcel' a few whacks with the rolling pin to start to flatten it, then roll the pastry out away from you, flattening the butter inside as you do.

Now fold the rolled out pastry into three. Do this just as you would fold a business letter, with one edge inside. Make sure that the edges are neatly aligned, and press down the outer edges firmly.

Turn the pastry package so that the *pressed edge* is at your right, and the *folded edge* is at your left (and you could open it up as you would a book).

Roll it out again, and fold as before, turn, press the edges together, roll out, fold, press edges and turn. Mark the dough with two thumbprints, wrap in aluminium foil, and rest in the refrigerator for 20 minutes before continuing.

Repeat this folding procedure 4 more times.

Rest for 20 minutes before using.

Note: When rolling out the dough, sprinkle a little extra flour on the board and the rolling pin so that things don't stick. Brush off excess flour with a pastry brush. If little breaks in the dough should occur, patch and brush with a little flour. The length of the resting time will depend a bit on the weather — if it is very hot it will certainly need longer.

CHOU PASTRY

50g (1 ¾ oz) unsalted butter
135g (4 ½ oz) flour
6 eggs
250ml (8 fl oz) cold water
pinch salt

Put the cold water and butter together in a saucepan and bring to the boil. Remove from the stove and stir the flour and salt in all at once, stirring briskly all the while.

Return to the stove and cook gently while continuing to stir, until the mixture dries and leaves the sides of the pan.

Remove from the stove once again and add the eggs one at a time, making sure that each egg is well incorporated before adding the next. The mixture will become smooth and shiny.

Pipe required shapes onto a lightly greased and floured baking tray and bake for 15 minutes at 200°C (400°F). When the pastry is puffed and golden brown, make a tiny slit in the side of each 'puff' to let the steam out and to dry the insides. Continue baking at a very low temperature (in a just warm oven) for another 15 minutes.

Soft and easy brioche loaf

500g (1 lb) flour
20g (¾ oz) fresh yeast (or 30g (1 oz) frozen yeast)
4 tablespoons warm water
60g (2 oz) castor sugar
6 eggs
300g (9½ oz) unsalted butter, softened
a little egg wash (1 yolk mixed with a teaspoon water)

Mix the yeast with the warm water until pasty.

Sift the flour into a mixing bowl. Add the sugar and stir in the yeast mixture. Now add the eggs, one at a time. This is most easily done in an electric mixer using a dough hook. Add the butter, bit by bit, as you continue to mix, and the dough begins to form an elastic ball. At a slow speed, it will take about 10-15 minutes for the desired elasticity to be reached.

Put the dough into a well greased loaf pan, or little individual brioche tins, and set in a warm place to rise. This will take between 1 and 2 hours. To begin with, the dough should half fill the tin. When risen it will have doubled in bulk.

When ready, brush the top with egg wash and bake in a hot 240°C (475°F) oven for 10 minutes, turning it right down to 180°C (350°F) for a further 30 minutes. Test with a skewer. When inserted right through the centre of the loaf for a few seconds, it should come out clean and hot to touch. If the skewer is quite cold, then the inside is not yet cooked. You may need to cover the loaf with aluminium foil during the final stages of the cooking to prevent the top burning. When done, turn out on a wire rack to cool.

Note: This brioche is *quick* in that it is allowed to rise once only (unlike traditional recipes which call for the dough to be knocked back and allowed to rise for a second time).

Its texture is very light and soft, which does not make it better, but certainly makes it very useful for a variety of dishes.

Basic Pasta

Enough for 4 people as a small course or as a side accompaniment to a main dish

210g (6½ oz) flour
2 eggs
¼ teaspoon salt

BY MACHINE

Sift the flour and salt into a food processor. Break in the eggs and combine with an on/off motion until the mixture resembles breadcrumbs. Tip the mixture out onto the work bench — preferably *not marble* — and knead for several minutes until the dough feels smooth and pliable.

BY HAND

Sift the flour and salt in a heap onto the work bench. Make a well in the centre and break the eggs in. Mix the eggs, bit by bit, into the flour until everything is well combined, then knead.

Whether you roll out the dough by hand or use a pasta rolling machine is entirely up to you. I use a small Imperia noodle making machine and find it makes the work very easy indeed. Cut the dough into 2 pieces, and working 1 at a time, commence at the widest margin and knead the dough through 2 or 3 times. Gradually adjust and narrow the rolling margin, and when the sheet of pasta has been rolled to the finest point, cut the sheet in half. This makes the handling a lot easier. Now pass the sheets through the cutting section, and spread the noodles out on a tray or hang on wire coathangers until needed. It may be necessary to loosen them a little with your hands lightly dusted with flour.

Cook in boiling salted water until done. This will take only a couple of minutes. Drain and serve immediately.

Crème fraîche

600ml (19 fl oz) pouring cream
100ml (3 fl oz) cultured buttermilk

Mix the two together, preferably in a stainless steel bowl, over a gentle heat. Stir continuously until it is just warm to touch (about blood temperature).

Cover the bowl with aluminium foil and leave in a warm place (e.g. an oven with a pilot light on) for 8-10 hours, or overnight, for the mixture to thicken. It will keep very well in the refrigerator for a couple of weeks.

Crème Anglaise

900ml (28 fl oz) cream
10 egg yolks
200g (6½ oz) castor sugar

Whisk the egg yolks and sugar together until they are very thick, pale and creamy.

Scald the cream, then pour it in a slow, steady stream into the yolk/sugar mixture, while continuing to whisk slowly. When combined, put the mixture back into the saucepan and cook very gently, stirring all the while, until the custard thickens to coat the back of your spoon. Take care not to let it boil. When cooked, pour through a sieve into a bowl and leave to cool.

Note: For a *rich vanilla sauce*, the method of preparation is exactly the same, with the addition of 2 good vanilla beans.

Split the beans lengthwise, scraping their powdery black centres into the cream 1 hour before proceeding with the recipe. Add the scraped pods as well to the cream to develop a full vanilla flavour. The beans will be removed when you strain the custard at the end.

Chantilly cream

300ml (9½ oz) cold cream
3 tablespoons icing sugar

Combine the cream and sugar together in a bowl and whip until stiff peaks form.

GENOISE

6 whole eggs
175g (5½ oz) castor sugar
150g (5 oz) plain flour
75g (2½ oz) unsalted butter, melted
1 teaspoon pure vanilla

20cm (8 in) cake ring

Pre-heat the oven to 180°C (350°F). Prepare the cake ring by lightly greasing and dusting with flour. Place it on a flat baking tray lined with kitchen parchment paper.

Break the eggs into a bowl and add the sugar. Suspend the bowl over a pan of simmering water, and whisk the eggs and sugar together until the mixture becomes thick, pale and warm to touch, and falls in ribbons from the whisk.

Now take the bowl away from the heat and continue whisking until the mixture becomes quite cold. This will take about 12 minutes by machine and about 20 minutes by hand. The mixture will have trebled in bulk. Add the melted butter, the vanilla, and mix well. Sift the flour on top, a little at a time, and fold in gently and thoroughly.

Pour the batter into the prepared cake ring and bake for 35-40 minutes. When done the cake will feel springy at the centre and will shrink a little from the sides of the ring. Having taken it from the oven, let it sit for a moment in the ring before turning out onto a wire rack to cool.

Note: This sponge can be split into 2 or 3 parts and used as the base for charlottes, miroirs or mousse cakes.

RASPBERRY COULIS

1kg (2 lb) fresh or frozen raspberries
1 cup sugar (or to taste)

Put the *frozen berries* into a saucepan with the sugar and cook until all is bubbling for just a minute. Do not overcook or the lovely bright colour will darken. Sieve.

For *fresh berries*, wash and purée with the sugar in a food processor. Sieve out the seeds, taste, and if not sweet enough add a little more sugar.

A jug of coulis stored in the refrigerator will keep very well for several weeks. It has a multitude of uses, including being churned into sorbet when you need a quick dessert.

Vanilla pastry cream

1 vanilla bean or 1 teaspoon pure vanilla extract
500ml (16 fl oz) milk
6 egg yolks
125g (4 oz) castor sugar
25g plain flour
600ml (19 fl oz) whipped sweetened cream (see note below)

Scrape the split vanilla bean into the milk. Add the scraped pods as well and scald.

Whisk the yolks and sugar together until they are very thick and creamy. Mix the flour with a little of the hot milk and stir into the yolk mixture. Pour on the rest of the hot milk, return to the stove in a saucepan, and cook gently, stirring all the while, until the custard thickens.

Strain into a bowl, cover with a sheet of buttered greaseproof paper and cool.

When you wish to use the pastry cream, fold in lightly an equal quantity of the whipped sweetened cream.

FOR THE WHIPPED SWEETENED CREAM
600ml (19 fl oz) cream
100g (3½ oz) pure icing sugar, sifted

Whip the cream and sugar together until stiff peaks form.

BIBLIOGRAPHY

Paul Bocuse, *Paul Bocuse's French Cooking*, Random House NY 1977.
Alain Chapel, *La Cuisine c'est beaucoup plus que des recettes*, Robert Laffont Paris 1980.
Julia Child, *From Julia Child's Kitchen*, Alfred A. Kopf Inc USA 1975.
Elizabeth David, *French Country Cooking*, Penguin Books Ltd UK 1974.
Elizabeth David, *French Provincial Cooking*, Penguin Books Ltd UK 1972.
Elizabeth David, *Summer Cooking*, Penguin Books Ltd UK 1976.
Fredy Girardet, *La Cuisine Spontanée*, Robert Laffont Paris 1982.
Jane Grigson, *English Food*, Penguin Books Ltd UK 1983.
Jane Grigson, *Good Things*, Penguin Books Ltd UK 1981
Jane Grigson, *The Mushroom Feast*, Penguin Books Ltd UK 1978.
Paul et Jean-Pierre Haeberlin, *Les Recettes de L'Auberge de L'Ill*, Flammarion France 1982.
Lizzie Heritage, *Cassell's New Universal Cookery Book*, Cassell & Co London 1894.
Di Houligue, *The French Kitchen*, Methuen Australia 1983.
Prosper Montagné, *New Larousse Gastronomique*, Hamlyn UK 1977.
Alain et Eventhia Senderens, *La Cuisine Réussie*, J. C. Lattès Paris 1981.
Penny Smith, *Feast in Season*, Methuen Haynes Australia 1984.
Time-Life International, *The Good Cook Series: Fish and Shellfish*, and other titles, Nederlands 1981.
Anne Willan and Jane Grigson, *The Observer French Cookery School*, Macdonald UK 1980.

INDEX

Note. Some of the recipes listed in this index are accompaniments for other dishes. In such cases the ingredients may be given on one page and the directions a page or so later. Thus for Saffron cream the references 109, 110 mean that the ingredients are listed on page 109 and the directions given on page 110. Trout soufflé 104-5 means that the directions follow immediately after the list of ingredients.

almond shortbreads 200
almond slice, caramel 201
almond sticks, sugared 200
amuse-gueule 29
apple: fine tart, with vanilla icecream 196-7, old fashioned baked 179
apricot tarts, upside-down 171

bacon cream 141
bain-marie described 20
baking, blind, described 20
Balmain bugs, octopus and prawns with little vegetables and a watercress and pine nut mayonnaise 110-11
banana, cinnamon and honey icecream 168
bar cod, poached cubes of, with mustard butter and chives 98
Barbara's individual Christmas puddings with rum anglaise 182-3
basil butter sauce 100
basil cream 73
bavarois: caramel 190-1, honey 189, orange 190-1, surprise 190-1, vanilla 188-9
Baxter, Fiona 162-3
beef: fillet, with port and échalotes 115, prime rib of, with carrot and onion marmalade and a purée of cauliflower and dill 114
beets, baby, in sauce 158, 159
berries: baked blackberry puddings 179, baked strawberry custard 181, berry puffs 207, blackberry shortbread crumble 177, gratin of red 178, mulberry icecream 168, raspberry coulis 216, raspberry jam tarts 207, strawberry baked custard 181, strawberry millefueille 180-1, strawberry salad 180, strawberry sorbet 180, berry puffs 207, beurre blanc sauce 28, mustard 51, 52; 98 blackberry puddings, baked 179, blackberry shortbread crumble 177
blanching described 20
blanquette of baby lamb shoulder 123
blind baking described 20
brains. *See* lambs brains
brioche loaf, soft and easy 213
butter, unsalted, reason for using 19

cabbage: braised 150, cake 156, 157, red, confit of 102
calves liver with fresh black currants 129
capsicum: and tomato sauce 88, red, sauce 75, roasted 62, 63, to peel and de-seed 19-20
caramel almond slice 201
caramel icecream 168-9
carrot and onion marmalade 114
cauliflower and dill purée 114

celeriac purée 142-3
cèpes and chanterelles, barbecued 70
champagne sauce 99
Chantilly cream 215
chervil and lemon dressing 58
chicken: breast, pan fried, with vegetable purée 136, breast, with sorrel and a gratin of the leg 135-6, liver pâté, as topping 34-5, livers and mushrooms in ravioli 73, mousse, with a tartlet of wild mushrooms 84-5, stock, brown or white 23
Child, Julia 45
chive and lemon dressing 59
chocolate and walnut puddings with lemon anglaise 185
chocolate and walnut squares 208
chocolate cream, hot 185
chocolate mousse 174
chocolate roll cake with fresh raspberries 187
chou pastry 212
Christmas puddings: Barbara's individual, with rum anglaise 182-3
chutney, tomato 93
citrus trio 164-5
coating described 20
coffee éclairs 206
coffee icecream 168
confit of duck 137-8
confit of red cabbage 102
Corne Claude 100-1
coulis raspberry 217
crab: bisque. *See* lobster bisque sauce 77, tarts with crab sauce 77, to kill and cook 56, 77, *See also* mud crabs
crème anglaise 215
crème brûlée 195
crème fraîche 215
croutons 87, tomato and anchovy 31
cucumber and mustard sauce, 62, 63
currant and rum drops 205
curried lamb in filo pastry 36-7

damper 152, 154
deglazing described 20
duck: confit of 137-8, liver and currant custard 86, wild, with lemon, accompanied by a crêpe of English spinach 138-9

échalotes described 19
eggplant 59, creamy fried 120, 121
eggs: omelette, mud crab 76, poached, and asparagus salad 64-5, poached, with tomato butter and caviar 88-9, scrambled, with grilled brioche and school prawns 89-90
equipment for the kitchen 18

fig jam for quail terrine 92
fine apple tart with vanilla icecream 196-7
fine crab tarts, individual, with crab sauce 77
fine onion and prosciutto tart 32
fine tarts of smoked salmon, dill cream and caviar 30
fish and shellfish: Balmain bugs, octopus and prawns 110-11, bar cod with mustard butter and chives 98, fish fillets with champagne sauce and julienne vegetables 99, John Dory with braised leeks and turnips 103, John Dory with broadbeans, etc. 102-3, John Dory with fresh tomato sauce 101, pig fish, steamed whole, with basil butter sauce 100-1, scallop mousseline, Simon's 109-10, soup 42-3, trout with fresh herbs and vegetables 106, trout soufflé 104-5, whiting fillet with a mousse and sauce of prawns 96-7. *See also* crab; lobster; mud crabs; mussels; yabbies, fish fillets with champagne sauce and julienne vegetables 99
fish soup 42-3
florentines 201
forcemeat for quail terrine 91-2
fruit, cornucopia of 170-1
fruit mince pies, tiny 203
fruit pie, winter with mascarpone 175
fruit tarts, tiny 202-3
Fusilier, Marc 39

game stock 25
ganache filling 187
garlic mayonnaise 43
gelatine, powdered and leaf 19
genoise 216
gin sorbet 166
ginger and lemon puddings, steamed, with lemon anglaise 184-5
girolles, fricassé of 70
glazing described 20
    veal 22
goats cheese and sweetbreads, grilled (salad) 68-9
goose: breast with pear 140, confit. *See* duck confit, livers with sweetbreads, etc. 132-3
gratin of quince and cinnamon with its sorbet 169
gratin of rabbit 161
gratin of red berries 178
gratin of yabbies 81
guinea fowl, roasted, with bacon cream and lentils 141

Haeberlin, Paul and Jean-Pierre 104
ham hocks, smoked, with mustard vinaigrette 126
ham rolls 35
Hannerman, L. J. 198
hare: roast saddle of, with pepper sauce, etc. 152-3, saddle, with hare pâté, etc. 66-8, stew, rich, with damper 152-4
hazelnut dressing 67-68
hazelnut loaf 66, 67-8
herb and vegetable sauce 118
herb butter 106
Heritage, Lizzie 53
hollandaise sauce 28
honey bavarois with fresh figs 189
hors d'oeuvres 29-38: creamy onion tart 33, curried lamb in filo pastry 36-7, deep fried whitebait 38, fine onion and prosciutto tart 32, fine tarts of smoked salmon, dill cream and caviar 30, ham rolls 35, miniature club sandwiches 37, puff pastry turnovers 32-3, tomato and anchovy croutons 31, toppings for fresh or toasted rounds of baguette or ficelle loaves 34-5

icecreams: banana, cinnamon and honey 168, caramel 168, coffee 168, lemon 164, mulberry 168, orange pekoe tea 167, rhubarb 167, treacle 186, vanilla 196-7

jam, fig 92
Jarvis, Joan 5-8
Jarvis, Mark 11, 13, 39
Jerusalem artichokes 149, soup 50
John Dory: with braised leeks and turnips 103, with broadbeans, etc. 102-3, with fresh tomato sauce 101
julienne vegetables 99

kidneys, *See* lamb kidneys
King Tiger prawns wrapped in leek, pan fried 83

lamb: barbecued cubes of, with rosemary and vegetables 124, brains, pan fried, with zucchini fritter 127, curried, in filo pastry 36-7, kidneys, with brioche and bone marrow 128, leg of suckling, baked in a parcel with garlic and tarragon 120-2, loin of, stuffed with carrot and celery batons with a herb and vegetable sauce 118-19, medallions of, with kidney and rosemary 122, shoulder, baby, blanquette of 123, stock 24, tongues, and roasted capsicums and cucumber and mustard (salad) 62-3
Lameloise, Chef 162
lemon and coriander dressing 56
lemon and passionfruit butter tarts, tiny 202
lemon icecream 164
lemon tart, deep 172
lime pots o' creme 164
lime sauce 79, 80
lime stuffing 146
liver. *See* calves liver
lobster: and morels in puff pastry 78, and pear salad 55, bisque, Mark's saffron 39, 44-5, cream 55, in ravioli 73, medallions of, with little vegetables in lime sauce 79-80, mousse. *See* prawn mousse, sauce 45, *See also* prawn sauce, tail, medallions of, with creamy sorrel and potatoes 108-9, tail, with basil and crushed tomatoes 107, to kill, cook and clean 44-5

mango sorbet 167
Mark's saffron lobster bisque 39, 44-5
mayonnaise: garlic 43, oil to use in 27n, plain 27, saffron 27, truffle 27, watercress and pine nut 111
mince pies, tiny fruit 203
mousse: chicken, with a tartlet of wild mushrooms 84-5, chocolate 174
mud crab: and mango salad 57, omelette 76, with lemon and coriander dressing 56-7. *See also* crab
mulberry icecream 168
mushrooms: creamy, basil and bacon topping 34, field, stewed 70-1, medley of creamed 87, sautéed 70, soup, rich 46, soup, with muscat 47, wild, tartlet of 84-5
mussels: grilled, with topping 70, soup 49-50, soup, with vegetables 48
mustard butter 51, 52; 98
mustard cream sauce (1) 156, 157; (2) 157

mustard sauce 133
mustard vinaigrette 126

napping described 20

octopus, barbecued 70
oil to use in mayonnaise 27n
omelette, mud crab 76
onion tart creamy 33, fine onion and prosciutto 32
onions, pickling, described 19
orange butter cake squares, iced and decorated 204
orange pekoe tea icecream 167
orange tart 164-5
orange tiles 205
organisation in preparation 17
ox tongue, pickled, with mustard sauce 133
oxtail consommé, accompanied by a little oxtail pie with a mustard beurre blanc 51-2

pancakes 88, 89
parsnip purée 152, 153
passionfruit miroir 192-3
passionfruit sorbet 166
pasta: basic 214, noodles with smoked salmon and basil cream 73, ravioli filled with chicken livers and mushroom 73, ravioli filled with lobster 73, ravioli of quail, rosemary and garlic 72-3
pastry: chou 212, delicate sweet shortcrust 210, plain shortcrust 210, puff 211, shortbread 177
pastry cream, vanilla 217
peach, poached with sauterne sabayon 173
pears, poached, with orange syrup and chocolate mousse 174
petits-fours: almond shortbreads 200, almond tiles 205, berry puffs 207, caramel almond slice 201, chocolate and walnut squares 208, coffee éclairs 206, currant and rum drops 205, florentines 201, fruit mince pies, tiny 203, fruit tarts, tiny 202-3, lemon and passionfruit butter tarts, tiny 202, orange butter cake squares 204, orange tiles 205, pink iced raspberry jam tarts 207, plain tiles 190, 191; 205, sugared almond sticks 200
pheasant: breast with thyme cream, etc. 142-3, quenelles of 142, 143
pickled ox tongue with mustard sauce 133
pickled vegetables 66, 67
pies: oxtail 51, 52, tiny fruit mince 203, winter fruit, with mascarpone 175
pig, roast suckling, with tarragon 125
pig fish, steamed whole, with basil butter sauce 100-1
pigeon and lentil soup 41
pineapple sorbet 167
pink iced raspberry jam tarts 207
plum tarts. See apricot tarts, upside-down
pork. See pig, roast suckling
potatoes; creamy 108, gratin of 116, layered cake 120, 121, rosette of 74
prawns; King Tiger, pan fried, wrapped in leek 83, mousse 96, 97, sauce 96
puddings, steamed: Barbara's individual Christmas 182-3, chocolate and walnut 185, ginger and lemon, with lemon anglaise 184-5, treacle and currant, with treacle icecream 186
puff pastry: to make 211, turnovers, with blue cheese 33, turnovers, with smoked salmon 32-3

quail: and cabbage pie, served with two sauces 144-5, roasted, with lime stuffing and sauce 146, stock 72, terrine with accompaniments 91-2, to de-bone 92, with rosemary and garlic in ravioli 72-3
quenelles of pheasant 142, 143
quince and cinnamon, gratin of, with its sorbet 169

rabbit: casserole 158-60, fillets in cabbage 158-60, fillets in ham, with a mushroom cream sauce, etc. 156-7, gratin of 161, pâté 158, 159, stock 158, 159, tart, creamy, with garlic and English spinach 154-5
raspberry coulis 216
raspberry jam tarts, pink iced 207
ravioli. See pasta red cabbage, confit of 102
red capsicum sauce 75
red mullet fillets with artichoke and eggplant (warm salad) 59-60
rhubarb icecream 167
rockmelon and ginger sorbet 167
rosemary and garlic sauce 72
rum anglaise 182, 183

sabayon 173
saffron cream 109, 110
saffron mayonnaise 27
sage butter 147
salad dressings: chervil and lemon 58, chive and lemon 59, cucumber and mustard sauce 62, 63, hazelnut 67, 68, lemon and coriander 56, plain 55, sweet currant and green peppercorn 61, sweet grain mustard 65, sweet orange 57, virgin olive oil 64, walnut 68, 69. See also mayonnaise; vinaigrette
salads: Balmain bugs, octopus and prawns, etc. 110-11, fresh tuna with braised vegetables 58, grilled goats cheese and sweetbreads 68, hare salad with hare pâté, pickled vegetables and hazelnut toast 66-8, lambs' tongues and roasted capsicums with cucumber and mustard 62-3, lobster and pear 55, mud crab and mango 57, mud crab with lemon and coriander dressing 56-7, poached egg and asparagus 64-5, spring vegetables with sweet currant and green peppercorn dressing 61-2, strawberry 180, warm, of baby red mullet fillets with artichoke and eggplant 59-60, warm winter vegetable 65
salmon, smoked, basil cream with fresh pasta noodles 73
sandwiches, miniature club 37
sauce making 21
sauces: bacon cream 141, basil butter 100, basil cream 73, beurre blanc 28, beurre blanc mustard 51, 52; 98, capsicum and tomato 88, champagne 99, crab 77, creamy, for eggplant 120, 121, for rabbit 161, for scrambled eggs and prawns 89, 90, for squab 151, for trout soufflé 104, 105, herb and vegetable 118-19, hollandaise 28, lime 79, 80, mustard 133, mustard cream (1) 157, 158; (2) 158, red capsicum 75, red wine 102, rosemary and garlic 72, saffron cream 109, 110, thyme cream 142, 143, tomato 101, truffle cream 116. See also mayonnaise; salad dressings; sauce making
scallop mousseline, Simon's, with shellfish in a saffron cream 109-10
Senderen, Alain 113
shallots described 19
shortbread pastry 177
shortbreads, almond 200

shortcrust: delicate sweet 210, plain 210
Simon's scallop mousseline with shellfish in a saffron cream 109-10
smoked ham hocks with mustard vinaigrette 126
    smoked salmon and basil cream with fresh pasta noodles 73
snakébeans vinaigrette for quail terrine 93
snow eggs 194-5
sorbets: gin 166, mango 166, passionfruit 166, pineapple 167, quince 169, rockmelon and ginger 167, strawberry 180, tropical 166. *See also* icecreams
sorrel, creamy 108
soufflé trout 104-5
soups: fish 42-3, Jerusalem artichoke 50, Mark's saffron lobster bisque 39, 44-5, mushroom and muscat 47, mussel 49-50, mussel and vegetable 48, oxtail consommé 51-2, pigeon and lentil 41, rich mushroom 46
spatchcock: grilled, with sage butter, etc. 147, in a honey and sesame crust with crisped noodles 148
squab: grilled, with rosemary and fresh figs 150, rare roasted breast of, with Jerusalem artichokes 149, stuffed with cabbage and bacon 151
squid, stuffed 70
stock: chicken, brown or white 23, clarification of 26, concentrated 30, duck 24, fish 25, game 24, lamb 24, making 21, other 24, lobster 44-5, quail 72, veal 22, vegetable 24
strawberries: baked custard 181, millefeuille 180-1, salad 180, sorbet 180
sugared almond sticks 200
sweet currant and green peppercorn dressing 61
sweet grain mustard dressing 65
sweet orange dressing 57
sweetbreads: and goose livers, etc. 132-3, veal with English spinach, etc. 130

tarts (savoury): creamy onion 33, fine crab 77, fine onion and prosciutto 32, fine, of smoked salmon, dill cream and caviar 30, mushroom 84-5. *See also* pies
tarts (sweet): deep lemon 172, fine apple 196-7, pink iced raspberry jam 207, orange 164, tiny fruit 202-3, tiny lemon and passionfruit 202, upside-down apricot 171. *See also* pies
tiles: almond 205, orange 205, plain 190, 191; 205
tomatoes: and anchovy croutons 31, cheese and bacon topping, grilled 35, chutney for quail terrine 93, sauce 101, to peel and de-seed 19-20
toppings: chicken liver pâté 34-5, creamy mushroom, basil and bacon 34, grilled tomato, cheese and bacon 35
treacle and currant individual steamed puddings with treacle icecream 186
treacle icecream 186
tripe, glazed, with fennel 131
tropical sorbet 166
trout boned and stuffed with fresh herbs and vegetables 106, soufflé 104-5
truffle cream 116
truffle mayonnaise 27
tuna: fresh, with braised vegetables (salad) 58, pan fried cubes of, with the cream of red capsicums 75-6, rare roasted, with a rosette of potatoes and English mustard 74, turnovers, puff pastry with smoked salmon 32-3, with blue cheese 33

upside-down apricot tarts 171

vanilla bavarois 188-9
vanilla icecream 196-7
vanilla pastry cream 217
veal: fillet, in a crust of herbs and juniper berries 117, rack of, with truffle cream and a gratin of potatoes 116-17, stock 22, sweetbreads, pan fried, with English spinach, etc. 130
vegetables: artichokes 59, beets, baby, in sauce 158, 159, cabbage, braised 150, cabbage cake 156, 157, cabbage, red, confit of 102, capsicums, roasted 62, 63, cauliflower and dill purée 142-3, celeriac purée 142-3, eggplant 59, eggplant, creamy fried, 120, 121, Jerusalem artichokes 149, julienne 99, leeks, braised 103, parsnip purée 152, 153, pickled 66, 67, sorrel, creamy 108, spinach, English, crêpe of 138-9, spring (salad) 61-2, turnips, braised 103, winter (warm salad) 65, zucchini fritters 127. *See also* mushrooms; potatoes
vinaigrette: mustard 126, snakebeans 93. *See also* salad dressings
virgin olive oil dressing 64

walnut dressing 68, 69
watercress and pine nut mayonnaise 111
whitebait, deep fried 38
Whitehouse, Barbara 183
whiting fillet with a mousse and sauce of prawns 96-7
wild duck with lemon, accompanied by a crêpe of English spinach 138
winter fruit pie with mascarpone 175

yabbies: bisque. *See* lobster bisque, gratin of 81, mousse, *See* prawn mousse, sauce. *See* prawn sauce, to kill and cook 82, with curry butter and wild rice 83

zucchini fritters 127